Also available at all good book stores

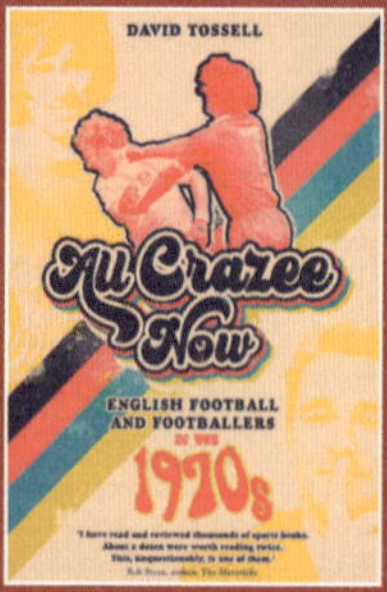

9781785317576

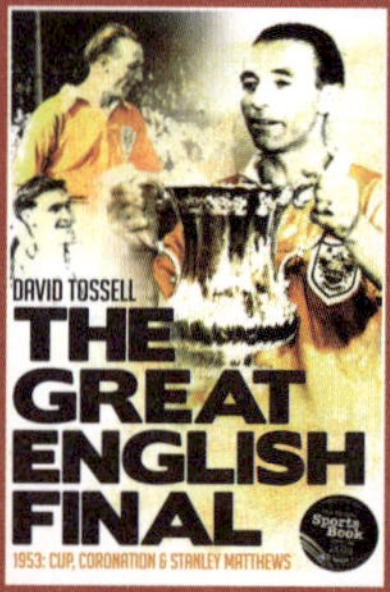

9781909178441

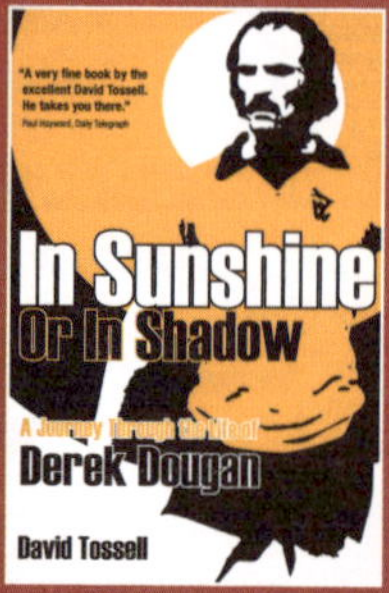

9781785314056

9781785313981

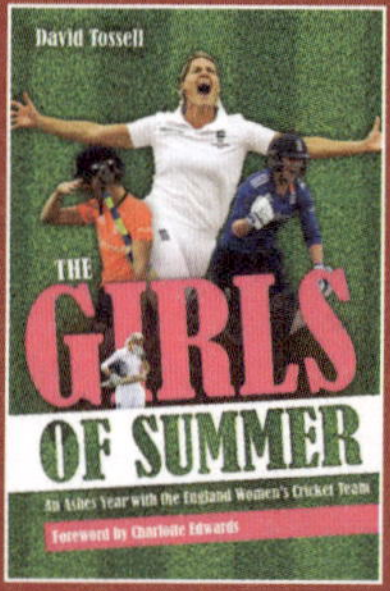

9781785311352

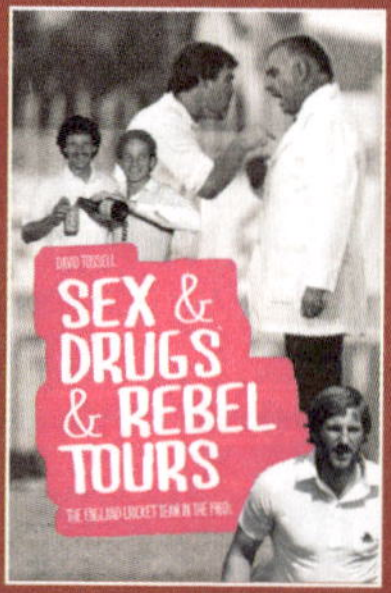

9781785310119

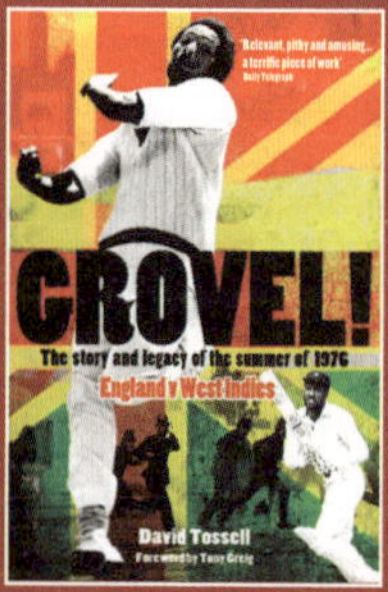

9781908051929

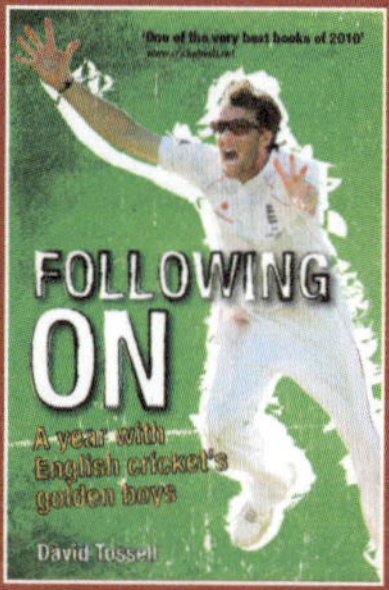

9781848187047

Hero in the Shadows

David Tossell

Hero in the Shadows

The Story of DON HOWE

English Football's Greatest Coach

pitch

First published by Pitch Publishing, 2022

Pitch Publishing
A2 Yeoman Gate
Yeoman Way
Worthing
Sussex
BN13 3QZ
www.pitchpublishing.co.uk
info@pitchpublishing.co.uk

A CIP catalogue record is available for this book from the British Library.

ISBN 978 1 80150 087 6

Typesetting and origination by Pitch Publishing

Printed and bound in India by Replika Press Pvt. Ltd.

CONTENTS

INTRODUCTION

THE CASE FOR THE DEFENCE

Few can have had so much influence in English football for so long and yet be as unheralded as Don Howe.

***FourFourTwo*, December 2015**

TWO PHOTOGRAPHS, taken nine years apart, depict happiness and achievement. They also speak of loyalty, respect and fraternity, professional and personal. One has been taken at the end of the 1979 FA Cup Final, the other at the same great Wembley occasion in 1988.

In the first, a tracksuited Don Howe is having his arm raised towards the fans by the Arsenal manager, Terry Neill, in the manner of a boxing referee presenting the winner to the crowd. 'After beating Manchester United we were coming down towards the old tunnel and all the Arsenal fans were at that end,' Neill recalls. 'It wasn't premeditated, it was just instinctive. I just grabbed Don's arm and held it up in the air. That moment sums up our relationship. He was the brother I never had. That moment wasn't about me, it wasn't about Don, it was about all of us at the club together; it was about unity. That is one of my most treasured pictures of Don.'

The second photograph was taken after one of Wembley's biggest upsets: the victory of a Howe-coached Wimbledon team over one of the finest of all Liverpool's championship-winning sides. Howe is being embraced by a shirt-sleeved, toothily grinning Wimbledon boss Bobby Gould, who has sent the picture to my phone moments after our initial conversation about this book; '1988 and jolly good company,' is the accompanying message. 'From the start of our relationship in 1968, he was like an older brother,' Gould explains. 'That is what he was to me.'

There is a contrasting image captured at Wembley in 1971, after Arsenal have beaten Liverpool to complete the Double of FA Cup and Football League title. In that shot, the handshake between Gunners manager Bertie Mee and Howe is indicative of a strictly business partnership – the former Army man Mee might have used the term 'proper'. It is that of boss and employee. The more emotive picture from that day captures full-back Bob McNab leaping into the arms of a partly obscured Howe. Yet even that picture has, historically, failed to illustrate fully the importance the players attached to their coach's contribution in taking Arsenal from also-rans to unimagined achievement. It has been wrongly captioned by its copyright holders as being Mee in the photo and is identified as such whenever it gets pulled out for use.

The point is this. Take a close look at certain English teams over a period of time and Howe is at the heart of their achievements, the constant alchemist at the shoulder of the men in charge. On occasions there were moments in the sun, but mostly his work was conducted away from the spotlight. As one Arsenal-related website, *Daily Cannon*, referred to him on his death in 2015, he was the 'hero in the shadows'.

It was a similar tale with the national team. Between England losing their title as world champions in Mexico in 1970 and reaching the semi-finals in Russia in 2018, every one of the national team's achievements worth speaking of came with Don Howe as coach. The common denominator in photographs of a proud Ron Greenwood watching his unbeaten team exit the 1982 World Cup finals, or Bobby Robson staring disbelievingly into the night sky in Turin in 1990, or Terry Venables consoling Gareth Southgate after another semi-final penalty shoot-out heartbreak at Wembley six years later is the figure of Howe at the manager's side. 'We should not forget the contribution of

Don Howe,' a knowing Robson said after he watched England's Euro 96 campaign. 'It is impossible to overestimate the contribution that he will have made.'

Howe could be said to be the last specialist England team coach. Since he left the role after serving a third boss, the trend has become for the man in charge to lean on someone who has been with him earlier in his career – in the manner of Glenn Hoddle and John Gorman; Kevin Keegan and Derek Fazackerley; Sven-Goran Eriksson and Tord Grip; Sam Allardyce and Sammy Lee, and so on. Howe's friend Roy Hodgson, who had Ray Lewington at his side with England and in many of his club appointments, says, 'You need someone you can trust and someone who can do the job as well as you can. Someone who can analyse situations and come up with the right ideas about formations and how the team should be playing. You want someone who's got every bit as much quality as you have got yourself because you are dealing with the best players in the country. Don's work ethic, his seriousness, his approach to the game and his desire to make certain that the team had all the information they need to try and win the game and become a better team were very important qualities. On top of that, when you are with people a lot of the time – especially in national team set-ups where you are virtually living in each other's pockets for several weeks – you need someone you like and whose company you enjoy. Don was great company.'

It is hard to argue a case for another English coach with a more impressive résumé than Howe's: semi-finals in the World Cup and European Championship; an unbeaten campaign in another World Cup and quarter-finalist in another; a League and Cup Double; two more FA Cups and a European trophy. Not to mention 24 England caps and trips as a player to two World Cup finals.

And there is a legacy of tributes, often from those least likely to possess any great fondness for authority figures. 'I am not a lover of coaches,' says Alan Hudson, one of the great mavericks of English football, 'but Don was a bit special.' Another renowned Arsenal individualist, Paul Merson, said, after hearing of Howe's death in 2015,

'He was so far ahead of his time it was scary. You talk about the [Arsène] Wengers and people like that; he was the best coach in the world of football – not just in England – but in the world of football. He was a phenomenal, phenomenal coach.'

One website, the *All Sports Books* blog run by Brendan Crowley, has even identified what it calls Howe's Law; 'the apparently unbreakable rule that any autobiography by a footballer who played in Britain in the last 40 years has to, at some point, mention how good the late Don Howe was as a coach.'

Yet football is never straightforward and Howe's life in the sport throws up contradictions and questions. Why, for example, was he unable to convert the magic he brought to the position of coach into comparable success when given the job of manager, as he was at West Bromwich Albion, Arsenal, Queens Park Rangers and Coventry City? Is it, as former Arsenal and England full-back Viv Anderson contends, 'Don was a fantastic coach but I don't think he was the best manager. It is a different breed. You are either one or the other and Don, in my view, was always better as a coach.'

Or was it more a case of circumstance, as Hodgson argues. 'To say Don couldn't manage was nonsense. No disrespect to Bertie Mee, but he was basically managing Arsenal. Bertie was looking after the people upstairs and Don was doing all the work with the team. Don might not have put his hand up to deal with the press and the directors rather than being on the field coaching, but that is not to say he couldn't do it.'

That's a subject to be revisited in later pages. But there is another issue that deserves to be addressed up front, one highlighted by former Wimbledon player Terry Gibson, who remembers, 'There were those jokes about how Don liked the team photo because it was the one time everybody was back behind the ball.'

Howe, it is universally accepted, was a master in organising a defence. Yet with that came the reputation – expressed in quips such as the above – that he was a 'defensive coach', one who lacked imagination or was downright 'boring', as one former England player would write. Even Trevor Brooking, too much of a gentleman to express it in the same terms as Terry Fenwick, said that whereas his two managers at West Ham, Greenwood and John Lyall, had both wanted players to express themselves, 'Don's priority was to stop the opposition from playing.'

Accusations of negativity and one-dimensionalism dogged Howe for decades and wearied him. When we spoke in 2001 about Arsenal's Double team for my book, *Seventy-One Guns*, he argued, 'If people wanted to join in the criticism then I looked at it as them not having the knowledge to know what was going on. It is a shame for them. People don't know what they mean when they talk about defending or defensive football. I know I am good at defending but that doesn't mean I am defensive. People were very inquisitive about what we were doing. It was a busy time at the training ground at London Colney, we had a lot of people coming from abroad to look at how we were doing things. We were quite open about it; we never closed our doors.'

Rob Howe, the third of Don's four sons, recalls, 'My mum used to take criticism personally, but my dad understood it went with the territory. The only time he got really angry was when John Sadler wrote about "Mad Howe Disease" in *The Sun*, criticising my dad for being negative. Dad said, "He has never seen me work, he doesn't know me, yet he is allowed to make these statements." He spoke to somebody at the paper about it. Even my oldest brother, Steve, used to take the mickey out of him for being defensive because we used to read this stuff as well, but he said that he worked with centre-forwards, not just with the defence, and he just tried to make players better. My dad had a very good tactical awareness and he could do a lot in stopping the opposition and that is what people alluded to when they said he was defensive-minded.'

George Graham, who followed Howe as Arsenal manager and achieved success with many of the same methods, believes, 'Don has been very badly portrayed in England. Everyone associated Don with defence but that is untrue. He was not only a good defensive coach, he was a good offensive coach. He got a reputation that I think was unfair. He made sure he got things right at the back first. I got the same reputation as a manager.'

You might expect that comment from a disciple such as Graham. Maybe less so from two of the most individually gifted players to grace the Football League from the mid-1970s onwards. 'I don't know where criticism of him being defensive came from,' says Liam Brady, the former Arsenal and Republic of Ireland midfielder. 'He always wanted creativity in the team. That is why Charlie George was always first pick when Don was at Arsenal first time round. I think people confuse being organised with being defensive. He worked very hard on stopping goals from set pieces, but he also worked very hard at scoring goals from them. I wouldn't label him as defensive at all.'

Glenn Hoddle, who enraptured crowds in the other half of north London and played under Howe in the England team, remembers his approach being that good discipline earned you the right to play attractively. 'He was very organised, but he liked good football,' he remembers. 'His forte was to defend well and go from there. A solid framework allowed the talented players to flourish.'

An out-and-out goalscorer such as Malcolm Macdonald would never have had much time for a coach with no interest in forward play, but he argues, 'Don wasn't a defensive coach at all. He was simply a brilliant organiser of defence. We had a back line that would go forward, and he was terrific with the midfield players and organising them as well. He was very honest with regards to the front players. He would never tell a centre-forward how to do his job because he knew that the centre-forward knew more about it than he would ever know. Instead, Don would get me to work with Frank Stapleton and pass on everything I could. He would organise training sessions around us and within that he wanted me to be talking all the while to Frank. I was happy to do it.'

At the 1982 World Cup, England were unbeaten in five matches and the only goal they conceded was in a 3-1 win against France. But their failure to break a goalless deadlock in the key games against West Germany and Spain in the second phase of the competition not only saw them eliminated but invited opprobrium for the perceived dull edge to their forward play. It left Greenwood having to dispel the notion that Howe had been a negative presence. 'It was said that Don's influence gave England's game a defensive bias, but that is being very unfair to him,' he argued. 'He loves to see a football team going forward and his whole attitude to the game is balanced and progressive … not once did we take the field with defence in mind.'

Tony Woodcock lived through the criticism of Howe's methods during the World Cup and later at Highbury, having signed for Arsenal on the eve of the tournament. 'All good teams are built from a solid defence,' argues the former Nottingham Forest striker. 'All that stuff about "Boring Arsenal" was a bit unfair. You don't want to be scoring five goals every game and having six scored against you. Brian Clough would love to win games 5-0, keep a clean sheet and play brilliantly, but you can't always do that. After Arsenal won the 1971 Double people said they were a little bit dour, but Don never saw it that way. It was certainly never his thinking to just shut up shop and hang in there and hope someone is going to score. The people I played for – Clough, Hennes Weisweiler, Rinus Michels, Udo Lattek – they all wanted to keep a clean sheet because it might be a day when you have to rely on your flair players. No one I know ever said, "Let's just attack willy-nilly and play attractive football and get beaten." If you want to win anything then you don't go letting goals in.'

The idea that Howe had a closed mind to flair and creativity was nonsense. It was he who invited Wiel Coerver, the Dutch coach who developed the 'Coerver Method' – based on analysis of the game's great dribblers and designed to find ways of adding more individualism into a team game – to the national training centre at Lilleshall, where he spent six months in the early 1980s working with boys from the FA's School of Excellence.

Nevertheless, ex-Arsenal man Stewart Robson concedes that Howe's forceful personality might have inhibited some players, even if he didn't ever send them out to play a defensive style of football. 'I really enjoyed working with him, but he made you fearful of making mistakes, which doesn't always mean that you are going to express yourself or be the best player you can possibly be. If we were doing a passing drill and the ball was coming to you he would shout, "Relax! Relax! Relax! Relax!", which is a contradiction in terms. He had that kind of mannerism which could be stifling for some players and could put them on edge. Once you were a senior player you saw through that a little bit and it didn't worry you quite so much.

'People ask if he was a defensive coach, but he wasn't. He did as much attacking work as defensive work. It was more about the way he got things across. I remember playing in midfield with Paul Davis and him trying to take too many touches and losing possession. Don would be out banging on the side of the dugout, telling him not to take liberties. In the end, you do the simple or safest thing. He didn't realise that was how it was coming across.'

It was during his period in charge of West Brom, which immediately followed the Double achievement at Arsenal, that the perceived negativity of Howe's approach converged with the challenges he faced in the role of manager. The result was that the club where he learnt the professional game now has mixed memories of him. 'Albion were unrecognisable from the free-flowing attacking side they had been since the mid-1960s. Howe turned an attacking team into a defensive one,' is the way Albion historian Gavin McOwan records his reign at The Hawthorns. 'The whole team became defensively minded and aggressive, and the forwards had to come back and help the defenders.' One of those defenders, full-back Gordon Nisbet, argues that 'Don didn't discourage attack and he encouraged me to go forward', but even he admits, 'He did like to work on the back four. He worked hard to organise us. He liked us to go forward from the back.' That approach – along with the disappointment of relegation, the failure to rebound quickly back to the First Division, and the immediate success of his replacement, Johnny Giles – is the way Howe's four-year stint at Albion has come to be characterised.

It was when Howe was back in the role of a club coach that the honours continued to mount; four major finals in a three-year spell at

Arsenal and then, having endured a challenging two years as manager at Highbury, the most unlikely of triumphs with Wimbledon.

In speaking to players who were coached by Howe, the qualities most frequently cited are his ability to make training sessions interesting and his unquenchable thirst for knowledge of the game. 'He was enthusiastic and he wanted to learn,' says Woodcock, who signed for Arsenal from FC Cologne. 'He loved talking about the game and wanted any new information about it that he could get. I remember training at the indoor hall at Highbury and he set up a one-on-one drill, which is sometimes difficult for the striker if there is nothing else happening. He said, "Get past the player and put it in the back of the net," and put me against Kenny Sansom, who was sharp, quick and powerful. First time, I tried unsuccessfully to go past; second time I have just gone to one side and, boom, had a shot. I said, "Don, I have been taught in Germany not to risk losing the ball on stuff like that. All I have to do is go to one side of him and dispatch quickly. Why take the risk of losing the ball?" You could see his brain going and he said, "I see what you are saying." He would take things on board. He understood that the most difficult save for a goalkeeper is if the defender has tried to block and it has gone through his legs. He was trying to learn all the time. He would ask me about Michels or Clough. "What do they do? How are they in training?" Don was a defender and the game is always evolving. Why wouldn't you get players and ask them what they think?'

The great Liverpool manager, Bob Paisley, would make a point of inviting visiting coaches to join him and his staff for a post-match drink in Anfield's famous Boot Room. Yet he remembered Howe as the only member of the opposition to take the opportunity to ask meaningful questions about Liverpool's methods, something which earned deep respect from Paisley and the likes of Joe Fagan and Ronnie Moran. Meanwhile, Paul Bracewell remembered Howe spending time with him and other members of Everton's trophy-winning team during England trips in the mid-1980s in search of clues.

Graeme Le Saux, who played under Howe at Chelsea in the 1992/93 season, experienced the manner in which Howe remained a relevant part of Terry Venables's England set-up almost four decades after he had first played for the national team. 'I was excited by working with him because he was a teacher and a student at the same time,' he says. 'If, like Don, you are inquisitive as a coach it means you've got an open mind to challenge your own views. The game does evolve, but that desire to keep learning means you do not have a sell-by date.'

And Hoddle contends, 'Don would enjoy this generation of football; that I can see. We are very similar now to how the Italians used to play many, many years ago. You either press high or you drop in behind and make it difficult to penetrate. And Don could get that organised.'

There is a story told by Stewart Robson that suggests that sometimes Howe wanted to learn simply as a personal challenge, not necessarily to impact on what happened on Saturday. 'He came back one day from England when I was at Coventry and said France had played two-touch the whole time. "Stop the ball and pass it. That is what we're going to do all week." We did that for a week and then on Saturday at the team meeting I said, "Do you want us to play two-touch?" And he said, "Of course I don't." He'd just wanted to prove to himself that the two-touch worked in a training session, but it didn't have any relevance to what we were doing in the game.'

For all the importance of a willingness to learn, it goes without saying that a coach needs to be able to teach. Hodgson, who was invited to watch Arsenal training sessions when he returned to England while managing in Sweden, says, 'I was very impressed by Don's coaching manner and I'm sure I have taken a lot from that because that is what you do as a coach. It is a question of putting things across effectively and how you work with the group and how you encourage and inspire them. Don was always very good; he was very inspirational, very lively.'

Former England centre-forward Macdonald went through his career with a reputation as an individual with a streak of selfishness. That might have been an important part of the goalscorer's DNA, but it did not always suggest a propensity to respond to tutorials. Yet he remains one of Howe's greatest admirers.

'He was a very amenable and pleasant guy to be in the company of. As a football coach, Don's moods could change, but there was always an underlying common sense about him. He never lost the plot or anything like that, even though he could be the most charming of men or quite fierce. But the outstanding thing about him was his ability to show somebody how to get the very best out of themselves. Don's slant was that he was going to assist, advise and cajole the player that was in front of him and help the player to get the best out of himself.

'Everything he did in that respect was quiet. He had this wonderful way and I will go as far as to say he was the best coach I have ever experienced. At the same time, he was probably the best life coach. You have to have patience, and a lot of the time in the game of football you don't have patience. And you have to work not only for yourself and improve yourself, but it is imperative that you also help those around you to improve. And if you can help them to improve, you can improve yourself. A footballer can be very insular. He goes out on the training ground just looking to improve himself, but Don made it a far wider ethic. And when you are helping others to improve, that team spirit grows so much stronger.

'I felt I had an insight into him. He would say something and I understood what his meaning was. I love the way it worked. I love the way he dealt with people. He didn't have an automatic reaction to anybody. He would look at who it was in front of him and then assess how he was going to deal with that person and that personality and character. The whole thing was so deeply thought through. He was a joy and I learnt so much from him. He was unique in the way that he went about it. I have never met anybody quite like him.'

Howe might have drilled organisation and uniformity into his defences but, having played much of his own career in the era of pounding up and down the training field to no great end, he not only understood the value of physical fitness, he also realised the importance of keeping routines varied for groups of young men not noted for great attention spans. 'Don would be up there as one of the best coaches I have ever worked with,' says Anderson, 'because his coaching sessions were very varied; they weren't boring or methodical. They would always get the best out of you by doing it the right way and, for me, that is his legacy. I enjoyed working with him.'

And another Arsenal defender, Colin Hill, remembers Howe teaching young players how to play their roles without ever making them feel they were being lectured. 'Don packed a lot into his sessions. He wouldn't necessarily take you out and work you individually. He would come and talk to you in a group, but he would maybe put on a session without telling you it was mainly for you. I was involved in some individual stuff intended for the forwards sometimes. For example, his big thing was about how hard they had to work in short spells, so he put on intense shooting sessions.'

Whether it was England's World Cup squad toiling for hours in the intense heat of Mexico, or Wimbledon on the field until dusk on the eve of the FA Cup Final, stories abound of the intensity with which Howe worked his players. His own view, expressed in his *Handbook of Soccer* in 1988, was that 'professionals soon lose respect for coaches who do not keep good discipline in training'. He argued, 'If players cheat in training or are allowed to get away with lax habits, they will cheat in matches and not work as hard as they should. That is a recipe for disaster. It is the way to lose matches.'

That intensity could make him an imposing character to some, but those who got to know him quickly recognised another side of his character. 'He had a very dour image, but that was the professional side of him,' Rob Howe says. 'I remember hearing my mum laughing in their bedroom because he would tell her the jokes that the players had told at training.

'Mum and Dad were one of four couples who used to go out every Saturday night and my mum used to say the whole night was just laughter. Everybody thinks of Harry Redknapp loving a laugh and a joke and my dad reminded me of him when he was at home. And was never negative about anything – he always saw the positive side of things.'

But at the heart of Howe's lust for life was football. 'He was a great dad and husband, but football was my dad's first love and we were second to that,' says son Rob without a trace of bitterness. 'That is the way it was. I only know my dad as a football man.'

Terry Gibson explains, 'By the time I had been working with him for a few days he had completely changed my opinion of him as a person. He loved his football and he was great company. Even if he wasn't coaching you, if you wanted to talk about football he loved it. He loved talking about teams, about players. He was a football person and now, when I talk to other players who worked with Don, they all say the same. The image that the media and other people had of him was that he was this dour character, but he wasn't. He was a quality professional, great company and as honest as the day was long. When Don said something, you didn't argue, you didn't question it, you just did what he asked you to do. I had so much respect for him and I was privileged to work for him during a period of my career.'

'He always had something to say about football,' says Woodcock. 'I have seen him sit down and have conversations with players that would almost turn into arguments about the game. Alan Sunderland used to wind him up a bit because he could hold his own.'

Woodcock might remember that Howe 'always had a cheeky smile on his face', but discussions about the business of football were not to be taken lightly, as illustrated by Hodgson. 'I was at the Arsenal training ground one Monday during the winter break in Sweden and I was going to Queens Park Rangers in the afternoon. Don said he would drive me. Also in the car was a young apprentice; obviously one of the players Arsenal thought highly of at that time. He was keen to talk to both of us and one of the questions was, "Who was the best player you have worked with?" I can't remember what I said, but I quickly came up with an answer. While Don was thinking, the traffic lights we were waiting at changed two or three times before he came up with an answer. I thought that was typical of his seriousness and not wishing to give an answer that was unworthy.'

That story will strike a chord with so many whose football experience was touched by – sometimes even shaped by – Don Howe and the lifetime he spent in the sport. A lifetime that began in one of the great hubs of the English game in the presence of one of its finest teams.

1

GUNNER AT THE ALBION

The Black Country is where it all started, where I was taught what life is. I have always thought that Black Country people are very down to earth. They haven't got an easy life, they haven't got lots and lots of money. They have to work for a living and that comes across from everybody. If you are going to have something from your life you are going to have to work for it.

Don Howe, speaking in 2005

DONALD HOWE could barely contain his excitement as he made the two-mile journey from his Wolverhampton family home to Molineux on the last day of August 1946. Born on 12 October 1935, and therefore not even four years old when the Second World War began, he had no memory of League football. But, having fallen in love with the sport through the type of street matches that not even the imminent threat of air raids could deter, he was just as eager for its return after a seven-year hiatus as any of the almost one million who attended matches around the country that day.

While the FA Cup had managed to stage a 1945/46 tournament, the change from regional competition to the reinstatement of the Football

League had taken a year of planning. 'Tomorrow afternoon is football's D-day,' the *Birmingham Gazette* had said that Friday, predicting 'the greatest season of soccer since that fateful first Saturday in September 1939'. The next day the *Gazette* announced, 'The stage is all set. Dress rehearsals are over and this afternoon – zero hour is 3pm – players and spectators will welcome the raising of the curtain.' None more so than the ten-year-old Don, attending his first match.

The cricketers of the Marylebone Cricket Club (MCC) shared that day's headlines as they set sail for an Ashes tour of Australia that would see them not return home until the football season was close to its conclusion eight months later. Yet Wally Hammond and his men merited barely a thought as Howe found his place in the children's enclosure at Wolverhampton Wanderers' ground and waited in the heavy rain for Arsenal and the home team to take the field. By the time he departed a couple of hours later he had discovered a new hero. 'Every time the ball came to me then, because I was playing a lot of football in the playground, I was Jesse Pye,' Howe would recall of the man who scored a hat-trick in a 6-1 Wolves victory. 'That is how it affected me.'

After 950,000 attended the day's 43 League matches – a total that would have been even closer to seven figures had one match not been rained off – the *Sunday People* reported, 'The cash customers were creating all-time receipt records, turnstiles were nicely oiled and clicking the sweet music of soaring returns, jam packed stands and terraces were gay with their winter make-up.' The trends of the first day continued, with grateful crowds returning in droves and Wolves continuing to win most of their matches. Only a defeat at home to Liverpool on the last day of the season saw them surrender the title to the Merseyside club by a single point.

The performances of his local team burned deep into young Don's identity. 'Everywhere I go people say, "You are from Birmingham,"' he would explain decades later in a Black Country accent that he never lost. 'I say, "No, I am from Wolverhampton," which is important to me because it was a football town. It was not just a football town it was a world football town. They used to win the League, they had great players.'

Over the next three seasons, Wolves continued to challenge for the title – beaten on goal average by Portsmouth in 1949/50 – and would win the 1949 FA Cup. Their reputation made them popular opponents for European teams, serving to fire Howe's football imagination and ambition. 'All those things, if you are going to be a footballer, that is the way to be a footballer,' he recalled. And being a footballer was his purpose, he had decided – although it would not be his beloved Wolves who allowed him to fulfil his destiny.

Attending St Peter's Collegiate School, in the west of his hometown, Howe became known as a right-back of promise and considerable skill. Full-backs of the post-war era, when the WM formation was still in vogue, were frequently condemned to play the role of no-man-shall-pass stopper. Yet Howe saw more to the role than that. 'I was brought up on a belief that brains will always beat brawn, at least in the long run. After I had seen [Tottenham Hotspur and England's] Alf Ramsey play once, I knew that the ball-playing type of defender was suited to me. I wanted to be a defender in the so-called classic mould, where the ball is always used to the best advantage, where defending is a game of wits rather than strength.'

His father Richard – who Don called his 'fiercest critic' – had been an enthusiastic player for his works team in the Birmingham Combination, while older brother Dick played as a part-time professional for Banbury Spencer in the Birmingham League. 'Dad always said his brother, who was ten years older than him, could have been an even better player than him,' says son Rob. 'He was unfortunate that the war came along.'

Don was clearly bound for higher achievement and was given an insight into the professional game while playing for Wolverhampton Schools. 'If you were in the schools team you went to Molineux on a Wednesday afternoon,' he recalled proudly. 'The coaches at Wolves took you training. It was lovely.'

But it was a rival club that made the important first move. While playing one Saturday morning at Wolverhampton racecourse, Howe was approached by a representative of West Bromwich Albion. 'A scout came over and said, "Can I talk to you?" I said, "Well my dad is over there. Go and have a chat with him." And he did. He fixed an appointment for me and my dad to go across from Wolverhampton to West Bromwich on the number 90 bus.' After a promising trial match, they met manager Jack Smith. 'He sold the club to us,' Howe remembered. 'And he said, "We would like your lad to come and join us as a groundstaff boy, which means he will be doing that job for a couple of years and then if he is improving we would sign him as a professional at the age of 17."'

Howe senior was reticent about his son becoming a full-time footballer so soon. 'You've got to get a trade, son,' he said, securing Don a job as an apprentice draughtsman at his own workplace, the Boulton Paul aircraft factory in Wolverhampton. But then, as Howe would explain, 'He let me have my way and I went to West Brom.'

There was still time for Wolves to make a late play for him, carrying out an interview at Molineux, but Howe and his father were aware of the depth of young talent at the club and opted for Albion. 'I suppose the reason for my decision was that I felt there would be more opportunities at The Hawthorns,' Howe would admit. 'Perhaps I was a little bit of a coward. The competition for places was pretty fierce at Wolves in those days.' It would be an exaggeration to say that he was an overnight success. Like so many youthful recruits, Howe took time to find his feet and to feel that he was making progress. 'Dad even asked me if I wanted to leave football and learn a trade,' he explained. 'But I decided to stick with it.'

West Bromwich Albion had begun the 1950s as a top-flight team once more, promoted in 1948/49 as runners-up in the Second Division. An average Hawthorns crowd of 38,819 – a club-record figure – watched their first season back, a late surge in form lifting them to 14th place. That revival had been partly down to the form of the man signed by manager Jack Smith from Port Vale for £20,000, winger Ronnie Allen.

Smith might not have been much of a tactician and his Albion team were considered rather dour, but he had the foresight to switch Allen to centre-forward early in the 1951/52 season. Not only did Allen go on to finish the season with 35 goals, but the move created a whole new identity for the team. After Smith was sacked in April 1952 – a development described publicly as a resignation – former Blackburn Rovers and Newcastle United centre-half Jesse Carver was appointed manager. Carver introduced The Hawthorns to some of the ideas he had been able to develop while coaching for the Dutch Football Association and Italian clubs Lazio and Juventus, where he had won the Serie A title.

As bizarre as it sounds – and as much as it was anathema to forward thinkers like Howe – this was an age when clubs typically discouraged players from spending too much time training with the ball. Promoting the theory that they wanted them to be hungry for it on match days, managers and trainers instead concentrated on physical fitness. Carver had other ideas, throwing his new players plenty of footballs and allowing them to train in their boots rather than the plimsolls that had been more suitable for endless running up and down.

Howe signed as a professional in November 1952, shortly after his 17th birthday, by which time the local press had already become aware of him. 'The success of this game was the 16-year-old full-back Don Howe, who will be seen again in Albion colours,' said Birmingham's *Sports Argus* of a Midweek League match against Stoke City a few months earlier. Reporting his promotion to professional ranks, the paper noted that 'he has developed well this season and played for the Birmingham County FA junior team'.

'In my early days we used to have eight teams,' Howe recalled, 'and you used to have to work your way through the levels to get to the top. It wasn't easy. We'd play Saturday morning, then come back to watch the games Saturday afternoon. We had jobs to do as well, but we could watch them play, be in the dressing rooms, and it was amazing how much that helped your education.'

The learning opportunities increased after Torino tempted Carver to return to Italy in February 1953. To replace him, Albion appointed Vic Buckingham, a former Tottenham defender who had begun his managerial career outside the Football League. He had led the combined Oxford and Cambridge Universities team, Pegasus, to victory in the FA

Amateur Cup in 1951 before taking charge at Bradford Park Avenue in the Third Division North.

His first act at Albion was to allow the players to carry on the training methods practised by Carver as they progressed to a fourth-place finish. And he continued to encourage Allen to develop into the style of freelancing centre-forward that Hungary would introduce to a nationwide audience when Nándor Hidegkuti roamed the Wembley pitch to help his team to a 6-3 win over England in November 1953. That result tore down England's self-satisfaction about its status in world football and opened the eyes of disciples everywhere, from the likes of professional hopefuls like Howe to more established players such as Malcolm Allison, who was frustrated by the lack of modern thought he found at his club, West Ham United. It was Hidegkuti who defined the Hungarians' eye-opening style. Dropping into deep positions, he left England's Harry Johnston wondering whether he should trail the crimson No.9 jersey into positions that would typically have given English centre-halves a nosebleed, or stay put with no one to mark. Hidegkuti helped himself to a hat-trick and created space for the great Ferenc Puskas to score two.

Allison, like many at Wembley, had initially been unimpressed when he saw the Hungarians' overweight No.10. But once Puskas began volleying 25-yard passes to team-mates as he warmed up, Allison turned to his West Ham team-mate Jimmy Andrews and said, 'Tell you what, Jim. These aren't bad.' By the end of the afternoon he was describing Hungary as having 'arrived from another planet'. According to *The Times*, England 'found themselves strangers in a strange world, a world of flitting red spirits, for such did the Hungarians seem as they moved at devastating pace with super skill and powerful finish in their cherry bright shirts'.

Also in the crowd was Ron Greenwood, who would precede Howe as Arsenal coach by a decade and later employ him as his right-hand man with England, and Bobby Robson, the successor to Greenwood. 'In the back of my mind there had always been a vision of the way I felt the game should be played,' said Greenwood. 'My ideas on the game were firm. But proof – undeniable public proof – was needed that football had more to offer than the average League club's performance on a Saturday afternoon. When the proof came it was as if someone had removed scales from my eyes. All my basic ideas on the game suddenly came together. Hungary's victory was written up like a national disaster but for me it was a new start.' Greenwood spoke for many when he praised the way they interrupted their short-passing game with a direct approach when needed; their ability to move the ball on the ground; their pace, use of the ball and understanding; and their disregard for shirt numbers and formalised positions.

Robson was at Wembley with his Fulham team-mates, saying that it 'had a profound effect' on him. 'It was not long afterwards that I began attending the FA coaching courses at Paddington Street with Ron Greenwood, Jackie Goodwin, Jimmy Hill and others. The English complacency had been well and truly shattered. We were no longer the masters. It's changed a lot of us in our thinking and approach to the game.'

The Hungarians' performance was rightly hailed as revolutionary. Yet to any Albion fans among the audience who watched the game live on the BBC in the afternoon or caught the rerun in the evening, there would have been a certain air of familiarity, shadows of the play of their own No.9, Allen. 'Whenever possible I would position myself so that no matter which of our players had the ball I would be nearby to receive it,' he said, although it could have been Hidegkuti speaking. He described himself as 'roving practically all over the field and only being in the centre-forward position when attacks approach our opponents' penalty area. I was a "free" man practically all the time because their centre-half stayed in the middle.'

It meant that Howe found himself in the kind of free-thinking club environment that allowed him to pursue his ambition of being a ball-playing defender; someone who could create thoughtfully in the style of Ramsey rather than simply booting the ball – and opponents – as hard and high as possible, in the manner of some full-backs of the era.

Acknowledging that Albion's style of play 'definitely came from Hungary', Howe recalled, '[Ronnie] was a good passer of the ball. We had these two old inside-forwards, Johnny Nicholls and Reg Ryan, and when the game started Ronnie was up there as centre-forward. Ronnie used to come back and get a lot of the ball; Johnny would make runs and Reg would make runs; and Ronnie would also be feeding the wingers.'

* * *

Before Howe played a first-team game for West Brom, he held in his hand a letter that announced, 'You are now a Gunner.' Rather than being a message from the future, welcoming him to Arsenal, it was the introduction he received as a new member of the Royal Artillery in the spring of 1954. Like the rest of the country's male population, his career would have to be placed on hiatus for two years while he fulfilled his national service commitment.

In that regard, Howe was luckier than many. Posted to Park Hall Camp, in Oswestry, Shropshire, he was only 60-odd miles from West Bromwich, meaning he could return home to play in games and continue his development with the club when his army schedule allowed.

The base was well used to having Albion players in its ranks, thanks to an unofficial reciprocal arrangement with the club. 'The chairman, Major [H. Wilson] Keys, was involved in organising the national service for the players,' explains Howe's future team-mate, Graham Williams, 'so a few of us went there. I became a PT instructor and I hardly ever wore uniform.'

Howe would recall, 'I kept playing football. They were brilliant at Oswestry. They let me come home virtually every Saturday and play for West Brom and the lack of being in the club didn't seem to hold me up in terms of improvement.'

And, as the new recruits' introduction letter emphasised, 'There will be plenty of opportunities for playing football and other sports while you are here.' After Howe's death in 2015, *The Guardian* even printed a letter by former army colleague Mike Broadbent, who said, 'I am ridiculously proud of having played football with Don Howe, albeit with a tennis ball at the Royal Artillery training camp in Oswestry, when he was an 18-year-old.'

According to Williams, 'Albion used to send a car on Friday night and drive me to West Bromwich. After the game on Saturday I would go back on the milk train on Sunday. Then I would go away and play for the regiment during the week.' It was the same for Howe, whose games for the regiment and the Western Command select team, where future West Brom and England colleague Derek Kevan was a team-mate, occupied much of his time and, he believed, helped develop his game. 'You've got to do your own training, but in match play most of the others are amateurs and this involves harder work in chasing the ball,' he said midway through a two-year military stint that brought him into opposition with the likes of young Manchester United forward Bobby Charlton and Sheffield Wednesday's Albert Quixall, who would become a British record transfer when joining United for £45,000 in 1958.

Howe's status as budding professional footballer earned him duties as a sports storeman, which meant handling kit for games and ensuring it was laundered afterwards. Broadbent also recalled, 'Officers made sure he was available for training in return for in-demand tickets for the popular mid-1950s floodlit matches.'

Howe's military call-up had come as his club were locked in a battle for the Championship with neighbours Wolves. Albion began the season with a nine-game unbeaten run, which concluded with a 7-3 victory at Newcastle United, although they gave up their early lead in the table to sit second at Christmas. As well as fighting for the title, they launched an FA Cup run that put them in position to challenge for English football's first Double of the 20th century.

Having reached Wembley by ending Third Division North Port Vale's run in the semi-finals, they lost goalkeeper Norman Heath to a career-ending injury in a defeat at Sunderland and went down 1-0 against Wolves. Typically of the era, the virtual title decider – which attracted 49,994 to The Hawthorns – was played while Albion's Allen and Nicholls and Wolves duo Billy Wright and Jimmy Mullen were playing for England against Scotland at Hampden Park. Albion ended up winning only one of their last seven matches to finish as runners-up, four points behind their rivals.

In contrast to West Brom, their opponents at Wembley, Preston North End, had been turning in impressive performances after reaching the final, prompting wing-half Tommy Docherty to recall, 'Nobody in the country at that time was playing football of the quality of Preston.' Meanwhile, the public's desire to see Tom Finney picking up a winner's medal – as Blackpool's Stanley Matthews had a year earlier – made Preston the neutrals' choice. Yet Docherty felt the club made a mistake by spending the week 'stewing' in a hotel in Weybridge, while Albion prepared as usual at home. 'As the monotony increased, the tension built up in every one of us,' Docherty remembered. 'I think we all knew the atmosphere was wrong.'

Howe was among those who would be watching on television, albeit in the NAAFI at Oswestry. 'Me and the other soldiers doing their training there were allowed to watch the final on television, so I saw the game in the army camp,' he said. 'I think it was about 12 weeks, the training to make you into a soldier. After that 12 weeks they would think, "He has done his training, he is going to be a footballer, we will give him Saturdays off." [But] you couldn't get that while you were in the first 12 weeks, and the FA Cup Final was in those weeks.'

Howe and his fellow squaddies saw Allen's 21st-minute goal quickly cancelled out, with Preston going on to take the lead after 52 minutes. Nine minutes later, Docherty was ruled to have taken down Ray Barlow in the penalty area and Allen scored from the spot to make it 2-2. It was Albion who snatched the trophy two minutes from time when outside-right Frank Griffin ran after a lofted through ball to score the winning goal.

For a brief period the West Midlands could argue to be at the centre of European football. Wolves had already embarked on a series of prestigious floodlight friendlies against some of the Continent's leading teams; a schedule that would be highlighted by victory in December

1954 against the brilliant Hungarian army club, Honved. Albion had already left their mark on those opponents when, early in the new season, they led them 3-1 during a four-team tournament in Belgium before going down 5-3. Puskas was moved to declare, 'The Hungarians are the best footballers in the world, but the England of West Bromwich is not far behind us.'

Offers to play all over the world came Albion's way, including a Russian tour in 1957 and a North American trip two years later. 'We were always invited to go abroad to sell football,' says left-back Graham Williams, who joined the club in 1954. 'Vic was brilliant at mixing with people and talking to them about the game. It was why he was able to go on to Ajax in Amsterdam and help develop Total Football, and why so many of his players went on to coach in the England set-up. We were an academy of players with a lot of knowledge under Vic.'

Yet, with Buckingham missing for much of the 1954/55 season after being injured in a car crash on the way back from a testimonial game in Hereford, Albion could only manage 17th place. Fate, in the form of bad weather, prevented Howe making a first-team debut before the season ended. 'It seems a moral certainty that this lad will command a regular place in the Albion defence in due course,' Charles Matheson wrote in the *Sports Argus*, and within days Howe was named to play for the senior team in a friendly against Leeds United.

Home on leave from military duties, he performed well enough to be chosen for a League debut at home to Chelsea four days later. When that game was frozen off, he was selected to face Tottenham Hotspur at The Hawthorns another three days hence. Again, bad weather intervened and by the time Albion returned to the field Howe was back in uniform and Stuart Williams was fit to play in his place.

But when the next campaign began it was clear that new blood was needed if Albion were to recapture the momentum of two seasons previously. In the second game, against Everton on 24 August, two significant changes were made. Centre-forward Kevan, who had played under Buckingham as a teenager at Bradford Park Avenue and been his first signing at The Hawthorns, stepped in for the injured Allen and scored both goals in a 2-0 win. At right-back, Howe, a couple of months short of his 20th birthday, finally made his League debut and 'calmly asserted himself', according to the *Birmingham Gazette*. Despite his previous near misses, Howe would recall his selection, in place of the injured Stuart Williams, as 'a big surprise to me and a big surprise to everyone else'. He added, 'It went okay because we won – it always does if you win. I think I took it in my stride. I didn't let nerves get the better of me and I did what I had to do.'

He might not have been expecting to play his first Albion game right then, but Howe was already aware that Buckingham would be a positive force for his career. The new manager had been part of the formative years of Arthur Rowe's famous 'push and run' Tottenham team, which went on to win the title in 1950/51 with Ramsey at right-back. 'Vic was great for me because I was a footballing full-back,' Howe explained. 'I loved the ball, I liked to go forward. The word "overlapping" was not used in those days, but that is what I did. I used to overlap the winger and get the crosses in. Vic encouraged me to do that; to attack from the full-back position. With Jimmy Armfield, and a lad named [John] Angus at Burnley, we were the start of the overlapping full-backs.' Until then, Howe added, 'You never went forward. It was looked on as madness. But TV came in and we saw continental full-backs going down the line and crossing the ball and it opened people's eyes.'

Graham Williams, who would spend several years across from Howe at left-back and go on to represent Wales, says, 'He was the first attacking wing-back. He used to have a guy playing in front of him called Ken Foggo and he would end up playing full-back because Don went past him and ended up being the attacker putting in the crosses.'

Howe recalled Buckingham as someone who 'loved flair', adding, 'He loved the players to express themselves and he was a bit that way himself. He was a debonair man. He would come in the dressing room with a lovely suit on and he'd have his handkerchief hanging out of his top pocket.'

And he enjoyed the sound of his voice. 'The average time of a Vic Buckingham team talk was about an hour,' said Bobby Robson, soon to join Albion. 'His record was two hours. No one dared fall asleep or let his attention wander. Vic was very strict and commanded the respect of his players.' Even if, on occasions, he confused them.

Howe continued, 'Every now and again when he was giving us a team talk he would break into French. No one understood him.' Remembering him slipping in phrases like '*comme ci, comme ça*,' he added, 'We would look at him and think, "What's he saying?" Can you imagine these Midlands boys talking French? He loved flair and imagination and I loved that because it suited the way I played. If I had to be just an ordinary full-back, clomping the opponents' outside-left, I wouldn't have been the player that eventually I became.'

The combined influence of Ramsey, Hungary and Buckingham shaped not only the way Howe played football, but also the manner in which he studied the game. Commuting from Wolverhampton early in his Albion career gave him the opportunity to get to know Johnny Nicholls and goalkeeper Norman Heath, who travelled from Wednesfield on the same bus. 'That was an education,' Howe recalled in 2002. 'It started once we'd finished training. We'd get the bus into West Brom, stop and have a cup of coffee, and then get the bus home. In this little coffee shop, there'd be six or seven of us, Joe Kennedy, Derek Kevan, lots of the lads, and it was a great talking shop, which players miss these days, I think, because they get in the car and go their separate ways. We went upstairs on the bus and talked football.'

The discussions continued in later years once Howe had moved closer to the Spring Road training ground and was no longer catching buses. Williams explains, 'We would meet in the morning and have coffee and a custard tart before training. We would go into a café bar and we would talk about football and tactics and individual players. He was absolutely brilliant at analysing players and opposition – different class. He was always going to end up a coach. He was so bright. On Friday morning we would be sitting there saying, "Right, this is what this winger does and we should be attacking this area and we should be doing this and should be doing that." As a defender he would always be aware that they were trying to get into a certain area in order to do damage. And he would have been looking at that during the week or talking to other people in football who had played against our opponents. I learnt so much from listening to him and talking to him. The only time he wouldn't speak to me was when England and Wales were playing each other.'

By the end of Howe's first season in Albion's senior team, midfielder Robson had arrived on a £25,000 transfer from Fulham. 'Over the next two years Robson, Howe and Kevan helped revitalise the team,' is the citation in Gavin McOwan's *The Essential History of West Bromwich Albion*. Significantly, the signing began a footballing relationship that would last for almost four decades and a personal bond that extended even further.

'We quickly became friends as we shared the same intense dedicated approach to the game, always wanting to discuss its finer points,' Robson explained. 'Playing in front of [Don] helped us to develop mutual understanding on the field and we progressed together into the international team and both decided to go into coaching at the same time, attending the same courses.'

Howe remembered, 'Bobby lived just up the road in Handsworth. He had three boys, I had got four boys, so we had things to talk about. "How were the kids last night, did they keep you awake?" I could always get on with Bob; he has got a nice steady personality. He keeps his head at all times, he doesn't get carried away. That is why he was good in the England team. He didn't let the press rile him, he didn't let the press put him off, he didn't let any criticism get too deep inside. He could handle it.'

A great respect developed in Howe for a man who would end up making his England debut a month after him in 1957, having moved from inside-forward to half-back at Albion. 'Bobby took over the mantle of the playmaker. He could win the ball back, could pass the ball, but he really wanted to get forward. Down the right side at West Brom, as the game went on, I was going, Bobby was going, and we left it to the others to look after the back door. I suppose in some ways it was a bit risky but when it came off it was wonderful. The two of us could make goals.'

Howe remembered the latter years of the 1950s as 'good times' when Albion 'played some great football'. He said, 'We were part of a new side with Maurice Setters, Derek Kevan, Alec Jackson, building again after the 1954 team. Ronnie Allen was still there of course, and Ray Barlow, who was a very big influence on my career. They both passed things down, which was the way it was at the good clubs then.'

Playing just over half the League games in 1955/56, Howe took only six months after his first-team debut to win selection for the England Under-23 team. He had been preparing to play for his Royal Artillery unit at Oswestry when a call came through from The Hawthorns telling him he was stepping in for an injured Armfield in that night's game against Scotland at Hillsborough. Albion coach Freddie Cox went to collect him, only for his car to break down. Howe eventually got to the ground an hour before kick-off. The drama ended there as England, including five new caps, proceeded to a comfortable 3-1 win with a team skippered by Johnny Haynes and including the brightest of Manchester United's young stars, Duncan Edwards, born a year after Howe a few miles down the road from Wolverhampton in Dudley.

Packing away his army uniform permanently on the final day of February 1956, Howe was able to sign as a full-time Albion professional – a turn of events welcomed by *Sports Argus* columnist Matheson, who said, 'He plays his football as if he enjoys almost every minute of it and means to go on enjoying it. He has confidence in his own ability, plus ideal build and the qualities of pace and perception. In short, he looks a natural.'

According to future colleague Fred Street, Howe appreciated his fortune in being good at something that distinguished him from many of those he had been with at school or in the army. 'Don told me that as a young full-back at West Brom he earned first-team money, £18 a week with a £2 bonus, while the mates he left school with were earning £3 or £4. Add all the perks and he was quids in – even in those days.'

Once Howe became a fixture in the West Brom side in the 1956/57 season, it took only a couple of months before discussion began about his suitability to take over from Birmingham City's Jeff Hall as England's right-back. Prompted by a good performance for an FA XI against the RAF and selection ahead of Armfield for another Under-23 game against France at Ashton Gate, the *Sports Argus* argued, 'Howe is not so sharp in the tackle as Hall, but he has been in better form recently.' According to *The Times*, the brightest part of the Under-23s' 0-0 draw were the floodlights at Bristol City's ground, but at least Howe's proximity to achieving a senior cap was endorsed when he was named as a reserve for Walter Winterbottom's full team when they took on Yugoslavia the following month at Wembley.

February 1957 brought a first selection for the England B team in a 4-1 defeat of Scotland in front of almost 40,000 at St Andrew's.[1] Within the next few weeks he played again for the Under-23s and was named by Walter Winterbottom to represent the Football League against the Scottish League at Ibrox.[2] Despite being 'steadily groomed for stardom' – according to the *Daily Mirror* – an unconvincing performance in the League side's 3-2 defeat meant Howe remained at home when the England Under-23 team went on a summer tour to Bulgaria, Romania and Czechoslovakia, the No.2 shirt being worn instead by Armfield.

The season ended in disappointment at club level when Howe was denied his burning ambition to play in the FA Cup Final by local rivals Aston Villa. His failure to clear the ball late in the semi-final at Molineux, booting the head of Villa centre-forward Bill Myerscough instead, helped the opposition level the game at a 2-2 draw. The teams moved on to a replay at St Andrew's, where Allen went off after 20 minutes following a tackle by Jimmy Dugdale, a team-mate until a year earlier. Albion went down 1-0 and Howe remembered, 'They scored a

---

1 It was the last B international played by England until facing West Germany in 1978.

2 The Football League team – selection for which was limited to English players – was used by England managers to give potential full internationals the chance to team up with current England men in games against representatives of the leagues in Scotland and Ireland. The team continued to operate until 1976.

goal and it didn't matter what we did. We played well. It just wouldn't go in the net for us.' Howe would make it to Wembley soon enough, though, wearing the white of England rather than Albion's stripes.

2

THE WAY AHEAD AND THE WAY OUT

As a defender, the best coach you can have is the guy who's playing next to you and Don was absolutely brilliant.

West Bromwich Albion team-mate Stan Jones

WEST BROM lost only one of their first 21 games of the 1957/58 season – a campaign in which Derek Kevan, Ronnie Allen and Bobby Robson combined for 78 goals. In September, they beat Manchester City 9-2, with Don Howe scoring his first two goals for the club, one of them from the penalty spot. A month later, almost 53,000 were at The Hawthorns to see them beat Manchester United 4-3, the last time Albion would face the 'Busby Babes' before the team that had twice been champions suffered the devastating losses of the Munich air disaster the following February.

Attempting take-off after a refuelling stop on their way back from a European Cup quarter-final in Belgrade, United's plane crashed on its third attempt, with seven players and 15 others killed. After a two-week struggle in a German hospital, another player, Duncan Edwards, lost his life – and Howe was one of eight footballers asked to carry his coffin into the funeral at St Francis' Church in Dudley, while an estimated 5,000 mourners stood outside to pay their respects.

When United visited The Hawthorns in the sixth round of the FA Cup in early March, it was with a team cobbled together from a mixture of traumatised survivors, youngsters and hastily signed recruits. Having drawn 2-2 at home, Albion fell victim to the tide of emotion that accompanied all games at Old Trafford for the remainder of that season and were beaten 1-0 in the replay. 'Mass hysteria seemed to have overtaken the city of Manchester,' Bobby Robson observed. Albion beat United 4-0 in the League three days later, but another poor finish to the season – two wins in the final nine matches – saw them slip to fourth place behind eventual champions Wolves.

West Brom's challenge for honours had helped embed Howe more deeply in the international set-up. A month into the season, Tom Duckworth, quickly becoming Howe's biggest fan, had written in the *Sports Argus* that his was the 'most impressive form' of any player in the season. Comparing him with Alf Ramsey, he argued that he could 'place the ball with equal accuracy but is yards faster than the Spurs man used to be and is quicker on the turn'. He also quoted Jesse Pennington, the former England full-back whose 25 caps were the most of any Albion player, saying that he'd watched Howe play for only 15 minutes before deciding, 'That boy will play for England.'

After another game for the Football League against the Irish League and a return to the Under-23 team against Bulgaria at Stamford Bridge – where young Chelsea forward Jimmy Greaves scored twice on debut – Winterbottom and the England selectors decided that Howe had served enough of an international apprenticeship. Howe would say later that he'd sensed that a full cap was on its way and on 19 October 1957 he ended Hall's run of 17 games as England right-back and stepped out as part of this line-up to face Wales at Cardiff's Ninian Park: Eddie Hopkinson (Bolton Wanderers), Howe, Roger Byrne (Manchester United), Ronnie Clayton (Blackburn Rovers), Billy Wright (Wolves), Duncan Edwards (Manchester United), Bryan Douglas (Blackburn Rovers), Derek Kevan (West Brom), Tommy Taylor (Manchester United), Johnny Haynes (Fulham), Tom Finney (Preston North End). After a tentative start, Howe coped well with the challenge of facing Swansea Town winger Cliff Jones, who would be transferred to Tottenham three months later.

A 4-0 win took England's unbeaten sequence to 16 games and represented the first of Howe's 23 consecutive England appearances – part of a significant contingent of Midlands players. 'Albion had outstanding players when you compared them with other clubs and football was controlled by the Midlands clubs then, especially Albion and Wolves, though Villa won the Cup as well and Birmingham did OK,' Howe explained. 'That meant the likes of myself and Bobby [Robson] were in the limelight and won caps. I came through the Under-23 set-up, started with Duncan Edwards, Ronnie Clayton, and we moved up to get full caps. When we went to London to play and I got on the train to go down there, I was with Billy Wright, Ron Flowers, Bill Slater, so again there was a lot of mixing and talking, changing ideas of how you did things back home. I became big friends with Billy Wright – great player – Jimmy Mullen and Ron Flowers too.

'It was a great thrill to play for England, among these wonderful players who you'd heard about on the radio or in the press. Before my first game I went down for lunch and looked round the table and Stanley Matthews was here. Gee whizz, unbelievable. Then Tom Finney walked in. Well, you can imagine. They were Gods to me.'

Howe had been grateful to Wright for making him feel welcome and introducing him to his new team-mates. In return, Wright recalled, 'I was impressed by the debut performance of young West Bromwich Albion defender Don Howe at right-back and noticed how disciplined he was both on and off the pitch. It was a background knowledge I was happy to have when I later made him one of my major signings for Arsenal.'

In his second game, Howe achieved the ambition of performing at Wembley, against Northern Ireland. 'We stayed at Hendon Hall, went to Wembley, and it probably was more stimulating than players find it today,' said Howe in 2002, 'because we were all a bit more naïve then; life was more innocent perhaps. It was all something new and exciting. They were things you never thought could happen. I never dreamed as a kid that I'd play for England and then suddenly it happens; something from your wildest dreams. There were times standing at Wembley when they played the national anthems, I'd be shivering like mad, I couldn't keep still, and you couldn't control it until the game was underway. It was thrilling and frightening. It took a few times at Wembley before the nerves went.'

Howe's first experience of the national stadium was unhappy, as well as nerve-racking, with England's good run coming to a surprising end in a 3-2 defeat. *The Times* reserved much of its criticism for Howe's Albion colleague, Kevan, playing his third game for his country. The Emile Heskey of his era in terms of perceived shortcomings at international level, Kevan was reported to have been 'underlining the truth that he is no more than a straightforward runner and harrier, with little balance, slow reflexes and the minimum of footwork'.

The result dented the optimism that had been growing about England's chances in the following summer's World Cup finals in Sweden, although a 4-0 win over France, in which Robson scored two debut goals, reignited those hopes. Howe's thoughts, however, were closer to home. Earlier in the day he had received a phone call from his brother Dick telling him that their mother, Fanny, had died. 'He asked what he should do,' his brother explained. 'Speaking for my father as well, I told him Mother would have wanted him to go out and play his best for England.'

Another 4-0 win followed in Scotland in April, but it needed only a stumbling performance against Portugal to change the mood once more. 'Bang go dreams of World Cup' announced the *Daily Mirror* following a 2-1 home win. After two more friendlies, a 5-0 defeat in Yugoslavia and a draw in the Soviet Union, Howe was duly named in his country's 20-strong party to go to their third World Cup finals. Robbed of Manchester United stars Edwards, Byrne and Taylor – all of whom would likely have commanded places in the first-choice team – there was some surprise that populist figures Nat Lofthouse and Stanley Matthews were omitted. Lofthouse had just scored twice for Bolton Wanderers in the FA Cup Final, although Matthews was now 43 and no longer a squad member. Of those selected, there was particular concern that Fulham's Johnny Haynes and Blackburn Rovers duo Bryan Douglas and Ronnie Clayton were coming off a long and exhausting Second Division promotion battle.

There was more concern expressed about the hotel Howe and his team-mates were to be stationed in, the Park Avenue Hotel in Gothenburg – rather than one of the more remote and rural locations chosen by rival teams. Wright argued that the players were likely to be 'bored' and 'preoccupied with their own problems' in a more secluded setting, which proved to be exactly the criticism levelled at the team four years later when they spent weeks 2,000 feet up the mountains in Chile in an isolated complex kept by a mining company for its workers. Manager Walter Winterbottom was learning what a succession of England managers would discover: that every piece of planning and preparation would be scrutinised when results went against them.

The early action did little to ease fears about England's chances. Having been trailing 2-0, England were still a goal down against the Soviet Union when awarded a late penalty. As Finney stood pondering his options, he saw Howe, penalty taker at West Brom, approaching him with a purposeful stride. 'I thought Don was about to take the responsibility off my shoulders and had he offered, I would have said, "Yes, please." But he had only come to hand me the ball.' Finney scored to secure a point but was now out of the tournament injured. In his account of events, Brian Glanville recorded, 'There was no one now to compensate for the staleness of Haynes, Douglas and Robson, the banal crudeness of the huge centre-forward Derek Kevan, the patent inadequacy of [Finney's] successor Alan A'Court – and Walter Winterbottom's astonishing reluctance to make changes.' Although Kevan had scored England's first goal, Robson recalled, 'He was built like a tank and turned like one. I valued him at the time because he gave Albion qualities that were needed. But it was essential that he played in the right unit.'

There was much questioning of why Winterbottom refused to play Bobby Charlton, who felt that his appetite for the game had returned after the trauma of Munich. He spent most of his time in Sweden in the company of Howe, who 'encouraged me to believe that I would see some action before the tournament was over. But the call didn't come.'

England's second game saw them achieve a 0-0 draw against eventual winners Brazil, although neither star winger Garrincha nor the 17-year-old phenomenon, Pelé, played in the game. Howe had been part of a successful defensive plan, suggested by Bill Nicholson in his role as coach under Winterbottom after he'd watched Brazil play Austria. Seeing that left-winger Mario Zagallo operated from a deep position, wing-half Eddie Clamp was deputed to keep tabs on him, with Winterbottom telling Howe, 'Zagallo will play deep and I don't want you to go that deep. I want you to tuck in with Billy Wright in the centre and leave Zagallo to someone else.'

Howe recalled, 'Walter was really chuffed, putting his arms round the players. He was as proud of that as any result he'd ever had.' However, Robson was honest enough to admit, 'The Brazilians had failed to score against England's defensive system in our second match, but I doubt whether that would have been the case had Pelé and Garrincha been playing.'

Another draw followed, Haynes and Kevan twice pulling England level against Austria in Boras. It meant England ended Group 4 with an unbeaten record, but they had not led in any match. A play-off was required to determine second place in the group behind Brazil, with England going down 1-0 to the Soviets.

For Howe, it had been an educational few weeks, as Finney observed in conversation with author Dave Bowler. 'Bobby Robson and Don were always deep thinkers about the game. If you've any idea you learn from the best, and at the World Cup they studied what was happening in the games; like the rest of us they wanted to become better players.'

Still only 22 when he returned home from Sweden, Howe had every reason to believe there would be more World Cup finals matches in his future, especially when he reeled off another 12 consecutive England games by the end of 1959. It was not until the sixth of those matches, away to World Cup winners Brazil, that he experienced defeat again.

'I thought I was beyond big nerve trouble when I played for England against Brazil in the giant Maracanã Stadium,' he recalled. 'I was fully equipped to soak up the rich South African atmosphere. But, oh dear, what a difference when it came to the real thing. I took one look at the crowd of 180,000 and wondered what I had let myself in for. Then the fans began to set off firecrackers and by then it was a toss-up which was jumping most – me or the bangers when we had to line up for the national anthems. Wild waves of emotion, excitement and, yes, fear swept over us.'

England lost 2-0 in the first game of a tour that was said to mark the start of Winterbottom's planning for the 1962 finals in Chile. Significantly for Howe, Armfield was given a first cap – at left-back – and retained that place when the team went to Peru, where Jimmy Greaves scored a debut goal in a 4-1 defeat. After a further loss in Mexico, an 8-1 win over the USA in Los Angeles did little to gloss over the disappointments of the trip.

On his return, Howe gave an interview to Doug Gardner for the November edition of *World Sport*. Noting Howe's tan and a greater confidence than when he'd previously met him two years earlier, Gardner was keen to explore his subject's mental approach to the game. 'You have a tougher time in the League,' Howe explained when asked about the pressure of international football. 'Opponents who have not been capped tend to play harder against internationals to create an impression. It's a big chance for wingers to show what they can do against me.'

Howe expressed some frustration that much of his job went unnoticed by the crowds; something that could also apply to those who were critical of his methods as a coach in future years. 'They are very easily pleased by the obvious,' he ventured. 'My major job as a full-back is to make an opposing winger play the way I want him to – which usually means forcing him to keep the ball on his blind side or preventing him from using his strong points. If I'm successful it should mean that more often than not he has to get rid of the ball because he can't use it. But a pass or a hastily forced shot from a winger never yet got a defender any applause. I'm much more likely to be cheered for an obvious crash-tackle than for a careful bit of positioning.'

Howe had three more internationals to play, finishing with a 2-1 Wembley win against Northern Ireland. When England began the new decade against Scotland, Armfield was at right-back and an evolving team featured only four players who had reached double figures in caps. Howe would look back at his England career with satisfaction rather than any sense of regret. 'Amazing things happened to me,' he said more than four decades later. 'Billy Wright got his 100th cap at Wembley and at the end Ronnie Clayton came across and said, "Don, let's carry him off." So we put him on our shoulders and carried him off the pitch. I look at the photo of it now and I think, "How did that happen?" I was just an ordinary kid from Wolverhampton and suddenly I'm walking off at Wembley with the greatest player I'd ever thought about on my shoulders. That sense of wonder has gone these days I think, and I've got a feeling it's because everyone has everything. There's no awe, they've done it all, there's a matter of factness about it – so many big games, internationals, Champions League and all these things.'

* * *

West Brom's World Cup trio returned home to help their club to finishes of fifth and fourth in the next two seasons, a consistency that cemented what author Gavin McOwan referred to as a 'reputation as a centre of footballing excellence'. Robson, who said he 'was enjoying playing for one of the best footballing sides in the country', recalled, 'It was a good time to be a player. Teams used to attack each other and there weren't 18 players in a confined space.' Yet in the middle of those two campaigns, in the summer of 1959, the architect of Albion's renown departed. At the end of a tour of Canada and the USA, Vic Buckingham accepted the job of coaching Ajax Amsterdam.

Robson recalled that Buckingham had been cited in a divorce case, which didn't sit well with the 'honourable, straight-laced Victorian gentlemen' on the board of directors. Meanwhile, Howe had suspected that the manager he admired so much might be contemplating departure. 'He was a great man for being in the dressing room with the players and telling stories,' he explained. 'People used to sit by him and we loved him. All of a sudden he didn't appear in the dressing room. I am not saying he became a stranger … but that togetherness didn't seem the same.'

Coincidence or not, Howe struggled for a large part of former assistant manager Gordon Clark's first season in charge. Not only did he lose his England place, but when given the captaincy for a brief period in place of the injured Barlow he felt that it accelerated his loss of form. 'The responsibility has affected Don Howe, a most conscientious player,' said Clark, 'and we feel that by handing it on somewhere else we are helping him.' The job was offered instead to Robson.

But Howe had more important things than tossing the coin to worry about. 'I was perhaps the unhappiest man wearing a pair of boots in the Midlands,' he recalled a couple of years later. 'I was playing badly, I had lost my place in the England team – rightly – and was lucky not to be dropped from the Albion first team. I was full of doubts about my ability, my future.' In modern times, there would be a support system in place; sports psychologists able to help Howe recapture his focus and get to the root of his insecurity. Instead, he either had to battle his way through, or think about an alternative career. He did both.

'It was the blackest moment of my life,' he recorded. 'I was made, through the circumstances of that time, to look right through the rosy clouds that hang around a professional footballer and look a bit further than the next match. It is very easy for a player who has done reasonably well to jog along full of blissful contentment, living from day to day on the admittedly comfortable life of a soccer star. So it was with me … I was left with the realisation that outside of football I knew nothing. That, plus the obvious truth that you can't eat off your press cuttings, made me pull up my socks and go out into the commercial world to find out how to make a living when football comes to an end.' He ended up accepting a part-time role as a car salesman. 'It lasted five months,' he explained. 'I finally gave this up because it became increasingly clear that the best time to sell cars is in leisure hours and this clashed with my football commitments.'

Howe went as far as asking Albion to leave him out of a summer tour to Spain – which was subsequently cancelled – arguing that 'over the past four years I have been playing football almost continually and I thought I might be playing too much'. Having just arrived back from Spain and Hungary as an unused member of the England squad, he said he would rather spend the time working on his house and garden.

He was by now married to Pauline, whom he had met at a local dance – although they discovered they had attended the same school, where she had been two years his senior. Family was on its way too, with son Steven born in 1960, followed by David in 1962, Robert in 1964 and Richard in 1967.

Events in English football in the 1960/61 season threatened to give Howe and his fellow professionals plenty of time to attend to home improvements and paternal duties. Determined to free its members from the shackles of the Football League's £20-a-week maximum wage, the Professional Footballers' Association conducted a vote on the principle of strike action in the early days of 1961. The highest salary level was one that only those at the top of the game were able to earn and was a mere £3 more than the national weekly average.

Howe believed that sentiment for a work stoppage was much stronger in the Midlands than in London and said there was 'little hope of averting a strike' after a round of regional meetings in the middle of January. 'We shall now be forming an employment committee of four or five senior professionals, whose role it will be to keep in touch with the local labour exchange,' he explained. In the end, the Football League bowed to union pressure and the restriction was lifted, although Howe was identified during that summer as one of 14 Albion players dissatisfied by what was being offered by the club as it counted the cost of the new world it inhabited. When Robson signed for £25 per week, plus £5 appearance money – the rate that appeared to have been agreed among the Midlands clubs – others followed, but Howe and a handful of team-mates held firm for a little longer. When he signed a few weeks later, the press speculated that he had been offered the same terms as Robson, but club secretary Alan Everiss said, 'The player is happy and satisfied but the terms must remain a matter of private business.'

On the field, even though he managed to keep Albion in the upper reaches of the table in his first season, Clark was gone by October 1961 after a tenth-place finish in his second term and a poor start to 1961/62. 'Gordon was a down-to-earth man; called a spade a spade,' said Howe. 'I don't think he really wanted the job long-term; just to take over for a few months. He was OK. We did similar training to what we did with Vic, and then quite suddenly he left. It was a big wrench in the club because Gordon was popular as well.'

Former Scotland international midfielder Archie Macaulay, who had led Third Division Norwich City to the FA Cup semi-finals two years earlier, took the job for what turned out to be an unremarkable year and a half. According to Graham Williams, 'He was a nice guy. He didn't like trouble. The team sheet would go up at 12 o'clock on a Friday, but he would have already left at 11.30 to avoid confronting disappointed players.'

Macaulay's affinity with the FA Cup meant that he became especially excited when the sudden-death games came around, insisting that Albion followed a method he claimed had been the key to Norwich's unexpected run. Howe recalled, 'We go into the meeting room and there is a long table. On the tables he has got bottles of Bristol Cream sherry, trays of eggs and calf foot's jelly, which I had never heard of before. He said, "This will give you some pep." You got in the queue and he'd pour you a glass of sherry, and then he had someone breaking the eggs and dropping them into the sherry. You got a spoon and whisked it up or, if you wanted, down it goes. One or two said, "This is not bad." Then the teaspoon of calf's foot jelly. It was like raw Marmite. At the end of it he said, "Right, early to bed. Every night you really should be getting to bed between nine and ten o'clock this week." We were just young players so went along with him and did what we were told.' Albion went out of the Cup in the fifth and fourth rounds in Macaulay's two campaigns.

Macaulay's reign was notable for reasons other than team performance. It saw the departure of England men Robson and Kevan, the former returning to Fulham in the summer of 1962 and the latter sold to Chelsea for £50,000 after scoring a hat-trick against champions Ipswich Town in his final Albion game the following March.

It was under Macaulay's management that Albion were featured in a short documentary film entitled *The Saturday Men*, although by the time of its cinematic release, more than a year after shooting, he was no longer at the club. The abolition of the maximum wage, which most famously led to England's Johnny Haynes earning £100 per week at Fulham, had begun the process of England's footballers moving out of the same terraced houses inhabited by the fans who cheered them. Celebrity lifestyle was still a long way off, but an increased fascination in seeing these men away from the field led to the cameras following Albion's players in training and back to their homes, in their smart suits and in their new cars. While Robson was shown organising his team to sign autographs before going off to spend the afternoon playing golf, one of Howe's chief contributions was to joke that a footballer's life mostly involved getting changed in and out of his clothes and to be filmed at his typical 1960s suburban house. 'I would not call it a happy film,' was Howe's review. 'The point is, however, that it is an honest job. It does not show us, the players, in a glamourised light with sickening fixed grins on our faces, but as normal human beings who have problems just the same as anybody else.' Which may have been overestimating the *cinéma vérité* element of the piece somewhat – at least to modern eyes used to Netflix and Amazon crews in the dressing room.

Had it been shot a year or so later, the film could have shown Howe working in a part-time job selling small machine tools. 'It does not interfere with my soccer life at all,' he said of his sideline. 'If anything, the job has made me more self-assured. Being a well-known player, doors are opened a little more readily for me and I am getting that experience which will be of great benefit to me when the exciting larger-than-life atmosphere of big time football is replaced by reality.'

Howe's comments are interesting, given that he was already nurturing an ambition to remain in the game after his playing days. Stan Jones, a centre-half who had joined Albion from Walsall in May 1960, had quickly become aware of his new team-mate's knowledge of the game. 'I am a great admirer of Don because of the help he gave me on the pitch,' he explains. 'He never stopped talking to me during the game and if I had any queries he would sort them out with me afterwards. Football is a game of instinct and if you don't do the right things at the right time, like a snap of your fingers, it is a waste of time. Don knew that and made sure you did the right things.'

Under coach Wilf Dixon, the training shots featured in *The Saturday Men* consisted largely of players hoofing balls as far as they could and chasing after them. Recalling the amount of running involved in training, Jones says, 'We were always out on the track by about two or three minutes past ten. From the training ground you could see a great big clock tower and you could guarantee that it was almost 11 o'clock when we came off from running.'

With English football clearly still in need of some modernising, Howe sensed it could be a calling for him. When selected for England's squad for the 1962 World Cup finals, his realistic ambition was to learn all he could in Chile rather than to oust Armfield from the team. Having not played an international for two and a half years, he had not been expecting to make the trip and when a neighbour approached his car giving thumbs-up signs, he had no clue that it was a result of the squad announcement the neighbour heard on the radio. 'It promises to be a great experience,' he said before departure. 'I should be able to learn much from those crack South American sides and as I hope to stay in the game when I have finished playing it should be invaluable.'

By the time England returned – having gone out to eventual winners Brazil after squeezing into the quarter-finals with only one win in three group matches – it was clear that Howe's expectations had not been met. He described himself as 'frustrated by the trend of soccer as I saw it in South America with its accent on preventing the other side from scoring'.

That view was echoed by journalist Donald Saunders in his book chronicling the tournament. 'It became clear after only two days, during which eight matches were completed, that most teams were so anxious to avoid an early return home that they had forgotten football was only a game and the World Cup its greatest shop window,' he wrote. 'From all four centres came reports of violence, ill temper, serious injury, and precious little of the artistic football to be expected from the world's leading professionals.'

Things reached a head in the infamous 'Battle of Santiago', where Chile and Italy clashed in a game that saw David Coleman introduce the BBC highlights with the warning, 'What you are about to see is the most stupid, appalling, disgusting and disgraceful exhibition of football, possibly in the history of the game.' Punches, kicks, blood, broken bones and police intervention were the main features of the game. English referee Ken Aston sent off two Italians, but events escalated beyond his control and merited a much harsher level of justice.

Given the reputation Howe would earn once he began to achieve success as a coach, it looks strange to see him saying of the tournament, 'It made me wonder where the game is heading as an entertainment as I watched all those defensively minded sides forgetting that the art of soccer is getting the ball in the net.' He did not excuse England from blame, concluding, 'We had a defensive system rooted at the base of things, and there were obviously times when we seem more concerned with keeping goals out than in scoring them.' Critics of the 1970/71 Arsenal Double-winning team might find such comments a bit rich.

Howe was to have one final experience as an England squad member when he received a late call in February 1963 to join the team in France for Alf Ramsey's first game as manager. Summoned from a practice match at Stourbridge and rushed to London to catch a flight to Paris, he arrived at the team hotel in time to be told that Armfield, now the England captain, would be fit enough to play. Ramsey lost his opening game 5-2, and Howe would have to wait almost two decades to make another meaningful contribution to his country's cause.

* * *

Back in England, Howe was appointed as West Brom's club captain, despite his unhappy previous experience. But as his ten-year anniversary as an Albion professional approached, he turned down the offer of the testimonial match to which players with that length of service were entitled. Instead, he opted to take a second benefit payment of £1,000 – due every five years – because, he said, he didn't want to put in months of hard work preparing a testimonial, only to lose a large part of his takings to the government. 'I see no point in working for four months for the tax people,' he said. 'I shall never understand why a cricketer's benefit is not subject to tax and yet a footballer's testimonial could be treated as being part of our emolument.' He argued that testimonials and benefit payments should not be considered part of a player's contract because the wording said players 'may be entitled' to them. 'There is no compulsion on the club to pay these sums automatically,' he argued.

The 1962/63 season saw football suffering at the hands of Britain's severest winter for decades. Like most other teams, Albion managed to play only one League game between the middle of December and the beginning of March. Erratic results when the sport defrosted brought about Macaulay's resignation. Howe was about to meet his sixth – and final – West Brom manager.

Jimmy Hagan, who won an England cap during a long playing career at Sheffield United, had led Peterborough United into the Football League and to the 1960/61 Fourth Division title, although his resignation a year later came amid a series of transfer requests and talk of dissatisfaction among the players about his methods. It was not long after his appointment at West Brom that he was rubbing the Albion players up the wrong way, although the club's wages policy added even greater potential for conflict. 'We didn't compete when it came to money,' says Graham Williams. 'I was way behind other people and it wasn't just me.'

Howe and Williams were part of a group who made the club aware of their dissatisfaction in the summer of 1963, with Howe turning down a one-year contract worth £40 per week after he had asked for a two-year term. The immediate response from Albion chairman Jim Gaunt was to tell reporters that Hagan had received Howe's transfer request, but had gone on holiday, adding sniffily, 'I am available to discuss the matter with Howe, or any other players if they wish it. Beyond that I am not prepared to discuss it.'

Howe declared himself determined to leave 'regardless of whether they offer me new terms'. He added, 'I feel it will be better for my family, myself and for Albion. I don't like the way the club have handled things. They have let the matter linger over the past couple of months. I have had enough.'

Financial conflict was becoming an ever-present part of the narrative of Howe's career. 'I want to stamp on the suggestion I am an unfair money-grabber,' he said, although he was eager to stress, 'I think it is unfair of them to restrict me so far as my earnings are concerned.' By the beginning of September, there had been no resolution and Howe was operating on a monthly contract. When fans suggested raising a petition urging the club to give Howe what he wanted, he used his column in the *Sports Argus* to plead, 'Please forget the whole business. While I appreciate that attitude and good intentions I feel that the dispute is a personal matter between me and the club and that outside influences could prove embarrassing.'

By October, as winger Clive Clark became the eighth Albion player since the summer to ask for a transfer, Howe agreed to a new deal. Yet there was more disharmony to come. Having endured such harsh weather the previous season, the players went seeking a little comfort when the 1963/64 campaign entered its winter months. All they wanted was some tracksuit bottoms to make training a little more bearable. Hagan would not hear of such an idea. Having missed several games during the autumn because of fluid on the knee and a bout of tonsillitis, Howe had personal reasons for wanting to look after his health. Also, as club captain, the players looked to him to play the role of shop steward.

Williams explains, 'Jimmy Hagan's selection of players was absolutely brilliant, but he was an old guy and it was, "Do it my way or you are out." Don was opinionated with his own ideas about training methods, so there was always a clash of personalities. Don would be the first one to say what a player Jimmy must have been. Jimmy would always send somebody off in practice matches so he could play and everything he did was absolutely brilliant. But he and Don did not see eye to eye.'

In the middle of December, Howe explained to reporters that he and nine others were taking their protest as far as demanding to leave Albion. 'We are fed up with old-fashioned training methods and being treated like schoolboys instead of intelligent individuals. There is far too much unnecessary dictation and discipline, and not enough time devoted to players putting their own points of view.' Training, he said, had become a bore, consisting of constantly lapping the field. When the players had tried to speak to Hagan they had been shut down.

And then there was the issue of the tracksuit trousers. Howe would explain, 'Jim was a good manager, but he was tight. He wouldn't spend money unless he had to do. We wanted track trousers to get warmed up and when we were warmed up we'd take them off. Jim wouldn't let us have them. The lads were moaning, "This is ridiculous. We are professional players." So then the lads decided, "Let's go on strike."' Hagan, who also trained with bare legs, refused to budge.

When temperatures hit five degrees below freezing a week later and tracksuit trousers were once again banned, West Brom's 19 first-team squad members boycotted training. 'We refuse to give way,' Howe announced. 'We intend to do the same thing tomorrow if the weather is still cold and we are forced to wear shorts.'

Williams recalls, 'Don was the barrack-room lawyer. Everybody respected what he said and what he did, so he was the leader. With the iron filings in the air, the snow used to come down black. We were just in shorts and vests and plimsolls. We didn't even have a second lot of boots. One day, when it was very bad, we had to go and clean the pitch. This was all against what Don thought about. He thought we should have gone away for warm training. Horse racing was finished

– even the horses were warmer than we were. We were running round the roads of West Bromwich.'

The next day, 21 players missed training, many of them photographed standing outside the training ground in their overcoats. When they were asked back to the club that afternoon by Hagan for what they thought would be a meeting to clear the air, they were all handed a £4 voucher as a Christmas present. 'The board got involved,' Howe explained. The compromise was that players were allowed to take the field a few minutes early in tracksuits before shedding them for the usual starting time for training. 'That was good, we were happy with that, so we did our own warm-up.'

At the time, Howe was careful to adopt a conciliatory tone, writing in his newspaper column, 'As captain and spokesman for the players I have naturally had to bear much of the responsibility and also take much of the criticism … We feel satisfied that relationships will be improved and closer in the future. I must pay tribute to the chairman, Mr Jim Gaunt. He was fair with us and at our meeting listened to and saw both points of view and talked over the problem from all angles. Mr Hagan also said that if there was anything we did not like he did not mind us telling him. Now we have sorted things out a much better spirit exists.'

A footnote to the row was provided by Hagan a few weeks later when he reversed his car away from the entrance to the training ground and descended down a steep embankment into the canal. 'It just seemed to be fate,' said Howe. 'It was still freezing cold. There was a shout, "The boss has gone over." Luckily he went into the water wheels first and the front windscreen blew out.' Hagan emerged, drenched, embarrassed, bloodied on the head, but lucky that the consequences had not been more serious.

The following day, Albion were held 3-3 at home by Arsenal in the fourth round of the FA Cup, before going down 2-0 in the replay at Highbury. Without his ambition of playing in a final to pursue, Howe's fragile patience with his club was about to run out entirely, especially when tracksuit trousers became an issue again on a cold day in March. Surprised to be ordered to train outside at Spring Road in shorts rather than working indoors, Howe, Clark, Williams and Stan Jones put their clothes back on and returned to The Hawthorns. They were each fined £5.

At the beginning of April, Howe put in his third transfer request of the season. 'I am unhappy at Albion and want to leave,' he said, saying what had become evident to even the most casual Albion fan. In the dressing room it was even more obvious.

Jones recalls, 'We had great difficulty with Jimmy. For the back-four players, he was useless. His son came to one of the former players' dinners a few years ago and he came to our table and said, "How did you get on with my dad? I know he was an awkward bastard." Jimmy had these straight-line ideas. He was obsessed with full-backs marking wingers rather than doing any covering in the middle when they were on the side furthest from the ball. It was because he made his reputation in his playing career by sliding balls inside the full-backs so the winger could run on to them. I can always remember Graham Williams coming back after playing for Wales and players from other clubs saying that they used to run straight down the middle against us because the full-backs were playing so wide. That was purely because Jimmy would not have covering full-backs. We all had discussions with him, but he was like Brian Clough in saying he would listen to his players and then they would agree to do it his way. To be fair to the guy, when it came to going forward he was as good as anybody I played under.'

Williams remembered a game at Fulham, where 'it blew up'. He explained, 'We said, "Let's get the ball from the goalkeeper and let's play it out from the back." So we were having a good game and we were knocking the ball around and we came in at half-time and Don said, "Well done, lads, that's brilliant, that's good football." Jimmy came in and started pointing fingers. He pointed at Don and said, "You! If you were a good footballer you would be a forward. You're not a good footballer, you are a full-back so play like a full-back." Don could play football. He came up with some ideas and he used to say that when you were playing the ball over the top, don't kick it out, turn people round, make the ball go into the corner. He would break down teams and tell you the good points and bad points.'

Referring to 'all the upsets of the season', Howe worried that eventually they would affect his game. 'I have nothing personal against Mr Hagan,' he added. 'Our ideas simply do not mix. I developed many of my views on football under Vic Buckingham and from Walter Winterbottom, the former England team manager. They differ greatly from those of Mr Hagan.' Howe also expressed a concern about his public image. 'I don't want a repeat of last summer's events when I kept signing monthly contracts. Nor do I feel that I want to be involved as players' spokesman in disputes about training and tracksuits. I know this sort of publicity cannot be good for me as the public are bound to misconstrue many things.'

Once it became clear that this time Albion were prepared to let him go, he stressed, 'I feel there must be cohesion and understanding between the management and players. Where it does not exist there will always be trouble.' Looking back many years later, he added, 'I was 28, I had been there 13 years. I don't care who you are, it is hard to stay keen and enthusiastic when you are playing on the same path again. I just wanted to move on. I wanted it for myself, I wanted to see how other clubs trained and worked and played.'

Arsenal, managed by Howe's former England skipper Billy Wright, quickly emerged as leading candidate for his signature, with rivalry from Leicester City and further mentions in newspaper reports for Tottenham Hotspur, Wolverhampton Wanderers, Manchester City and Nottingham Forest. The Gunners' initial £40,000 offer was turned down, but on 21 April the clubs agreed a fee of £45,000 – at the time a world record for a full-back. Having arrived at the Albion training ground and begun his warm-ups, Howe was instructed by Wilf Dixon to report back to The Hawthorns, where Hagan was waiting to take him to London. Wright and Arsenal secretary Bob Wall met them at the Park Lane Hotel and, according to Howe, 'the whole transfer proceedings took only 10 minutes'.

For the benefit of the *Sports Argus*, Howe expressed 'a certain sadness' at leaving Albion after 379 League and FA Cup games and 19 goals, but said, 'I am looking forward to wearing the famous red and white of the Gunners … It has been my experience abroad that when English football is mentioned Arsenal are the first club name that comes to foreign lips. To me it is like a new lease of life. At 28, I feel a fitter and better player than when I was younger.'

He would expand on that five years later, saying, 'As soon as you walked through the gates at Highbury you felt like a million dollars. The atmosphere was terrific and I always seemed to hit top form against Arsenal. I couldn't have been more pleased when Arsenal gave me my chance. I had realised an ambition to join the greatest club in the game.'

Despite the aggravation of his last year at Albion, Howe left with a genuine appreciation for the opportunities he'd been offered by the environment at the club. 'They let me express myself,' he would recall. And even arrival in the marble entrance at Highbury helped to heighten his gratitude. 'It opened my eyes to what a great club West Brom was,' he explained. 'It showed me that what we did at West Brom was right. Being brought up properly, coached properly, playing the right way, you appreciate where you come from.'

3

LUCKY BREAK

Don struck me as a coach from the moment he arrived – very thoughtful and very concerned about the game; a deep thinker about it all.

Team-mate and future Arsenal manager Terry Neill

NOT SINCE Herbert Chapman took his modernist thinking and his résumé as a title-winning manager with Huddersfield Town to Highbury in 1925 had Arsenal looked beyond club connections for a manager. But when former goalkeeper George Swindin ended his four-year stint in charge towards the end of the 1961/62 season, it was to England's most-capped player, Billy Wright, that the club turned – even though he had no managerial experience or any tie to the club beyond having been a boyhood fan.

His reputation in the game had been earned by 105 caps and three League Championships at Wolverhampton Wanderers, while his status as a national treasure was cemented by marriage to Joy Beverley of the chart-topping Beverley Sisters – making them the Posh and Becks of their time. Having turned down previous offers of club management since retiring as a player in 1959 and taken charge of the England Under-23 and youth teams, it appeared for a time that he was being groomed to take over the national side from Walter Winterbottom. Few, then, saw any reason to doubt the wisdom of his appointment at Highbury.

Yet Arsenal were quick to demonstrate their personality under their new manager during the autumn of 1962, with a stretch of four games that included 4-4 and 5-5 draws and a 5-4 victory. Wright sought a defensive solution in the £62,500 signing of Dundee centre-back Ian Ure the following summer, but the Scotland international quickly recognised the shortcomings of the team he'd joined. 'Arsenal were desperate for success and were hoping that guys like me would spark things off,' he recalls. 'They were trying to get a wee bit of stability. But it was a slow process. We were a load of individuals; we didn't work as a team. Unless your inside-forwards, or midfield players, are working back, your defence is going to give goals away. It just wasn't a team and there was no proper leadership. George Eastham had magnificent skill and Joe Baker could score goals, but the defence and attack were like two different teams.'

Had they known it at the time, Arsenal fans could at least have drawn comfort from the debut of goalkeeper Bob Wilson, who was still teaching at a local school; the emergence of players such as John Radford, Peter Simpson and Jon Sammels from the youth team during Wright's tenure; and the establishment of George Armstrong on the wing. And those with a crystal ball would have been particularly excited by the arrival of Howe at the end of Wright's second season, a campaign that saw them finish well off the pace in eighth place.

Howe had been sold on Highbury long before he first wore the red and white shirt on an end-of-season tour of South Africa. A couple of years earlier, he'd said, 'If you talk to an Arsenal man nowadays he makes it clear that in his opinion there is no club to touch his own.'

The hotel arrangements on tour created a bond that would be significant later in Howe's career. 'We shared a room together and became great friends,' Terry Neill recalls. 'He was a few years older than most of us and I learnt from playing and training with him and sharing a room with him.'

After moving into a club-owned house in Barnet during the summer, Howe was ready to make his full Arsenal debut in a landmark game in the history of English football. 'Welcome to *Match of the Day*, the first of a weekly series, coming to you every Saturday on BBC Two,' said Kenneth Wolstenholme as he looked up at the cameras from the Anfield pitch, speaking over the pop music coming from the stadium's public address system. 'As you can hear, we are in Beatleville for this Liverpool versus Arsenal match.' As well as kicking off the season with their team as champions of the First Division, Liverpool's fans were basking in the glow of The Beatles' conquest of America. There was no more vibrant setting for the launch of the nation's first offering of regular early Saturday evening football action, albeit on the regionally restricted BBC Two, where fewer people would see the game on television than the 47,620 in the stadium.[3] 'Many people think this could be Arsenal's year,' Wolstenholme offered as he highlighted the new name of Howe in the crude graphic of Arsenal's line-up, yet the match offered viewers an accurate picture of the club's problems. Wearing their all-white change strip, they pulled back from 2-0 to draw level, only to concede a last-minute winner. Howe was given a torrid time on his debut by Liverpool's Peter Thompson, being criticised by Frank McGhee in the *Daily Mirror* for resorting to 'sometimes illegal methods' to keep the England winger in check. 'I didn't like it, but to me it was necessary,' Howe explained, ever the realist. 'You've got to get in there at him. The crowds don't seem to understand, but it's your job.'

When Frank McLintock arrived from Leicester City for an £80,000 fee in October, believing that the move would bring him the winner's medal he'd missed out on in two FA Cup finals, he soon realised that he'd been misled. 'The team wasn't properly balanced,' he remembers. 'It was a mishmash.' But he quickly recognised a kindred spirit in Howe. 'He, too, found it difficult to settle. He was an astute attacking full-back, which was relatively rare in the early Sixties. The model professional, he must have been appalled by Arsenal's lax discipline and bungled attempts at coaching. His maturity and loyalty in those early days gave him a stoical disposition towards the anarchy around

—

3 It would not be until the post-World Cup season of 1966/67 that the BBC realised the potential of *Match of the Day* and placed it in front of an audience of millions on BBC One.

him.' Arsenal would finish two places below halfway in the League and were beaten 2-1 at Third Division Peterborough United in the FA Cup.

When he wasn't convincing Wright to put Arsenal in plain red shirts instead of the white sleeves that were a reminder of the history of success that appeared to have weighed down the club since its last title in 1952/53, McLintock was agitating for a move and becoming frustrated at a manager who was 'too kind, too nice'. His view that 'we needed a manager who could kick us up the arse' is shared by Ure, who argues, 'What the club needed was discipline and we didn't get that. Players were in cliques. The star players were never criticised. Billy was in awe of the stars.'

The club did reach the FA Youth Cup Final in 1965, losing to Everton, before winning the trophy a year later against Sunderland with Pat Rice and Sammy Nelson in the side. But even inexperienced players like Radford could see Wright's problems. 'The senior players took the mickey out of Billy, who was a nice bloke. I got the impression that guys like Joe Baker and George Eastham had little respect for him. You could tell by the way they talked during training and didn't get on with what they were supposed to do.'

Happy to go along with McLintock's suggested change of kit, Wright would tell Norman Giller, his biographer, 'I got to hate the bust of Herbert Chapman in the marble halls. It was always there as a reminder of the glory years,' and he admitted, 'I discovered how comforting a drink or three could be.' Peter Storey, another future stalwart finding his way into the team, suggests, 'Billy was a nice bloke, but the pressure was too much. It all went wrong and he started hitting the bottle a bit.' Wright would eventually acknowledge, and win, his battle against alcoholism.

Having finished 13th in Wright's third year, Arsenal prepared for the new season with a shambolic six-match Caribbean tour. Howe was booked in a game that ended up being abandoned because of crowd trouble. 'We never did a day's training,' says Storey. 'We had a riot in Jamaica. Joe Baker head-butted one of the Jamaican players and the game got abandoned. In another game Joe slung his boots at Billy and said, "You do better." There was terrible friction, a terrible rift. On one side of the changing room were the big signings, and the other half was the young guys like me. We tended to get the blame for everything.'

Surprisingly, Arsenal responded by losing only twice in their first 12 League games. But then they won only six more all season to finish 14th. On 5 March 1966, the playing career of Howe, who had been made club captain by his former England team-mate, suffered irreparable damage when he collided with Blackpool goalkeeper Tony Waiters in a game at Highbury. 'It was the worst break I have ever seen,' says Sammels. 'Tony's head hit him right in the shin. I was the first one there and Don had hold of my arm so hard I thought he was going to break it; he was in that much pain. The bone was sticking through his sock.'

Neill adds, 'It was one of those instances you never forget. You could hear the crack all over the place, and poor old Pauline was in the stands. He went into hospital in west London and the next morning at least half a dozen of us went to see him. He was very philosophical about it.'

The incident proved how advanced Arsenal's treatment of injuries had become under physiotherapist Bertie Mee, who had left his practice in 1960 to enter a world he had only reached the fringes of while playing 13 League games for Mansfield Town. Howe's operation to fix his leg was the first of its type performed in Britain. 'Arsenal were at the forefront in modern techniques,' he recalled in 2004. 'I had a compound fracture of the tibia. The normal procedure in those days was to stick the leg in plaster for ten weeks and, if it was still not healing, stick on some more plaster. Bertie and Dr Alan Bass gave me the latest thing that had come from skiers. In Switzerland, instead of using plaster, they were putting a metal plate into the bone. That was real modern technology back then.'

While Howe was healing, Arsenal suffered the ignominy of drawing only 4,544 to Highbury for a late-season game against Leeds United on a rainy night when Liverpool were playing Borussia Dortmund in the Cup Winners' Cup Final live on television. 'I was sat in the paddock watching because I was injured,' recalled winger Alan Skirton. 'At one point a guy with a trumpet started playing the 'Last Post'.' Wright was sacked during the summer, and Arsenal shocked the football world when they promoted Mee from the treatment-room to the position of head coach, finally giving him the title of manager in March 1967 after an extended trial period.

Yet Wright left a legacy of which Mee, with Howe at his side, was to reap the rewards. According to Sammels, 'Billy didn't get a lot of thanks for what his work led to. Many of the Double squad were home-grown lads who Billy helped bring through. He left out Joe Baker and George Eastham, who were hero-worshipped by the fans, and brought in two youngsters, me and John Radford, to replace them. It was a brave decision.'

Howe felt that 'more was expected of Billy than some other managers because he had been a great England captain'. He continued, 'The club were bringing in new players and some of the players that Billy brought in went on to be successful in the Bertie Mee era. That's the way it often goes. One manager brings in new players and ideas and another manager gets the benefit of what he has done.'

* * *

Howe's role in Arsenal's success might have been hastened by injury, but by the time he realised that his playing days were over – when he was still short of his 31st birthday – he was already set on a course that would make him one of the most respected men in English football. Initially, he made enough on-field progress to be able to travel to play at Manchester City in September, only six months after his injury. Three days later he was in the Arsenal team that was held to a home draw by Gillingham in the League Cup, laying on the equalising goal for Tommy Baldwin. But after 74 competitive first-team games for the Gunners, his playing career was over.[4]

—

4 Howe did play in four summer friendlies in Cyprus, scoring a goal in his final appearance in an Arsenal shirt.

'I don't know whether I was lucky or unlucky,' he said, having reckoned on three more years at the top level before his injury. 'I had been struggling to get back to First Division fitness and I was never the same. One day Bertie called me in and said, "How would you like to be manager of reserves? We would just let you get on with it. We all agree that it would be a step forward." I had already done some coaching in amateur football in the Midlands, coaching a steelworks team, and I realised that after my injury I would have to drop down the divisions if I was going to carry on playing. So I agreed to do it.'

The development was no surprise to Howe's colleagues. Sammy Nelson recalls, 'They tried to introduce a provisional coaching badge for the players and we had these coaching set-ups every Monday for about six to eight weeks. Most of us just thought it was a joke. This is how you trap a ball; this is how you head a ball; teaching schoolkids. But Don really enjoyed it. He was very keen.'

Howe had already accrued several years of coaching experience, encouraged by his former England manager Walter Winterbottom. Responsible for overseeing the coaching structure around the game, Winterbottom had been influential in the introduction of two levels of qualification. The preliminary coaching certificate involved teaching the fundamentals to young players, while a more advanced qualification involved practical instruction, demonstration of skills, and written papers on the law and coaching techniques. Howe's initial enthusiasm had been more about improving himself as a player than as a foundation course for a future career. 'I think one of the most important things one has to learn in professional football is how to read a game,' he said in 1959. 'It's a bit difficult to explain exactly what is meant by this, but I suppose you could say it is the ability to know what's going on and why. Some of the best players don't have it, but I think it is something which can be cultivated through going to coaching courses.'

But for the most part, players didn't want to know. Winterbottom struggled to find many willing to attend coaching courses and sit exams. Most players of the 1950s had not given much thought to life beyond their playing careers. Those who had done so tended to think of running a newsagent, using local contacts to get a sales job or perhaps becoming a pub landlord. Most of those who ended up drifting into training and coaching did so as a way of remaining in the game and gave little thought to equipping themselves with expertise beyond the experience they had gained on the field. Football retained a general suspicion for the dark arts of coaching and 'tactics', despite the eyes that had been opened by Hungary in 1953.

It was after an England training session that Winterbottom had approached West Bromwich Albion team-mates Howe and Bobby Robson and asked, 'What are you going to do when you pack up playing, Bobby?' With no clear answer forthcoming, Winterbottom ventured, 'Why don't you both come on one of the senior professional players coaching courses at Lilleshall? You might want to begin a new career as a coach. Opportunities are opening up now for people like you.'

Howe remembered, 'Walter said to us that we would be better players if we took a coaching course. I thought it wasn't a bad idea, so I did the course and passed my exams and became qualified, with the idea that playing does not last for ever.'

Lilleshall, English football's national training centre, proved to be a breeding ground for a whole new generation of coaches. Summer courses for professional players encouraged the exchange of opinions, ideas and theories. Professional alliances and personal friendships were forged and Howe and Robson would join the likes of Bill Nicholson, Ron Greenwood, Dave Sexton, Malcolm Allison, Joe Mercer, Jimmy Hill, Alan Brown and their former boss Vic Buckingham as men whose future careers were shaped in the Shropshire countryside.

According to Winterbottom's biographer, Graham Morse, 'Walter encouraged young professional players to think of coaching as a career and a cadre of around 20 were appointed as FA staff coaches. They became known as his disciples and spread the message of coaching at local, national and eventually international level. In this way a new breed of managers emerged which began to change attitudes to coaching in League clubs.'

One of the most influential figures at Lilleshall was Allison, whose dissatisfaction at the coaching methods at West Ham United had encouraged him to take his team-mates under his wing and spend afternoons discussing tactics with them in a café near Upton Park. Along with Sexton, John Bond, Noel Cantwell, Frank O'Farrell, Malcolm Musgrove and Jimmy Andrews – all to become successful managers and coaches – he moved the condiments around the tablecloths to make his point and ended up taking over training sessions from manager Ted Fenton. By the 1960s, he had retired from the game after losing a lung through tuberculosis and began one of the sport's great coaching careers.

As his reputation as a football intellectual and innovator grew, Allison was regularly asked to act as one of the FA course instructors at Lilleshall. 'People like Malcolm and Dave Sexton were the ones we looked at most closely on those courses,' said Howe. 'Every club sent at least one person – even Bill Shankly used to come – and Malcolm showed us what we should be working at. Malcolm loved to be inventive and be the first to try things. He had great football knowledge, could make sessions interesting and had a terrific sense of humour.'

McNab adds, 'I remember Don saying that when he was at Lilleshall in the mid-60s Malcolm Allison was doing stuff we had never even dreamt about. He was innovative and creative, a great thinking man.'

In turn, Howe would become an inspiration to future generations of coaches and managers; men such as future England manager Roy Hodgson, who says, 'I was an incredible admirer of Don. He, Bob Robson and Dave Sexton were, for me, the Holy Trinity of the coaching world as I was growing up and trying to become a coach myself. At the time when we were doing our coaching badges, these guys were way above us so it was very satisfying to get to know them and to get a chance to learn from them and to take something of the wisdom they had accumulated. Every time I would come back to England during my years at Halmstad or Malmo, Don would always invite me to Arsenal. I am grateful to Don for what he did for me.'

Tactics in football were nothing new. Even the first-ever England team, taking on Scotland in 1872, had employed a tactical approach to the game, albeit a 1-2-7 formation that must have looked haphazard. What was still relatively novel in the 1950s, however, was the notion that teams should actually plan and strategise in order to maximise performance within whatever shape they adopted on the field. This was particularly true in England, where clubs in the late 19th and early 20th centuries had been run by professional businessmen who formed a board responsible for finance, administration and team selection. They employed a club secretary to act as liaison between the board and players, considered their social inferiors – mostly to share details of selection and travel arrangements. As the sport grew in popularity in the years approaching the First World War and the task of running a club became greater, more responsibility passed to the man who held the role of what was now termed secretary-manager. It was only when these men realised how frequently, and casually, they were held up to the fans as scapegoats that the idea developed that perhaps they ought to make some effort to make their teams better.

By the time Britain emerged from conflict in 1918, the alien concept of coaching began to find a home at the more enlightened training grounds. For decades to come there would still be plenty of clubs where an old-fashioned trainer would focus on getting players to a peak of physical fitness and care little about working with the ball or devising game plans. Yet there were some managers for whom the game of football presented a cerebral challenge; an opportunity to strive – sometimes alongside a coach – to outwit the opposition, to teach players how to play the game and execute tactics rather than simply run themselves into the ground from Monday to Friday.

Chapman, the man whose bronze bust would intimidate future Highbury managers, was one such man. He even had the self-assuredness to suggest in 1934 that the club manager should select the side, rather than the directors – and had earned enough respect to have such demands taken seriously. Having concluded a modest playing career, he abandoned plans to become a mining engineer when offered the role of player-manager at Southern League Northampton Town. After a subsequent spell at Leeds City, he led Huddersfield Town to the FA Cup and successive First Division titles, prompting Arsenal to approach him to replace the sacked Leslie Knighton. While Huddersfield were going on to win a third successive title, Chapman was in the process of revolutionising the game in the wake of a change in the offside law.

Having seen goalscoring stifled by teams exploiting the need for three players to be between an attacker and the goal for him to be ruled onside, the FA and Scottish FA successfully lobbied international lawmakers to reduce the requirement to two players. With the offside trap now more difficult to execute, Chapman was innovative enough to see the need for a stopper centre-half to negate the advantage the game's forwards now enjoyed. The act of pulling back the No.5 to play between the two full-backs, rather than in midfield, established the WM formation in football's structure. It also led to the first application of the 'Boring Arsenal' label that Howe would have to contend with four decades later.

As well as coming up with practical solutions, Chapman was one of the first managers to coach his team, encouraging players to study and practise tactics and to discuss the game with team-mates. He introduced pre-match team talks and urged his men to contribute their own ideas, none of which was typical of how English football clubs approached Saturday afternoons.

A former amateur goalkeeper and Football League referee helped move English football even closer to the kind of environment Chapman desired and from which Howe would benefit. Stanley Rous was appointed secretary of the Football Association in 1934, a year that had begun with the sudden death of Chapman after he'd won the League twice at Arsenal, as well as an FA Cup. The second of those Championships was the first of three consecutive titles for the Gunners.

Rous would hold his post for 28 years, during which time he brought a more enlightened approach to the role than his predecessor,

Sir Frederick Wall. Writing in *The Ball is Round*, author David Goldblatt described him as 'the leading force of bureaucratic modernity, technical innovation and cosmopolitan openness. In insisting on such developments as regular and standardised teaching for coaches, players and referees he was 20 years ahead of the rest of the country.'

In 1946, Rous manoeuvred the appointment of Winterbottom – an RAF wing commander during the war with responsibility for training PE instructors – as the FA's director of coaching. Although he had the dual responsibility of manager of the England team, it was developing the manner in which the game was taught that he saw as the more meaningful role. Howe, who worked under him in both capacities, would say, 'Walter was a great man; started many good things off; opened us up to continental football; told everyone that if we didn't get a grip, bring new things in, that we'd fall behind. He'd warned us about it, and then the Hungarians and then Real Madrid came along and showed us how to play. Walter knew what was coming, but we were stuck in the old WM formation, the old-fashioned styles. Managers wouldn't listen and we suffered for years as a result. He was very forward in his thinking and he was a big influence on me and Bobby Robson, and many others from that era.'

According to Ron Greenwood, writing in 1982, 'Many people in the game have no idea how much English football owes to Walter Winterbottom. He launched our coaching system and gave it impetus and status; and his influence has reached on down through the years … many of our best coaches, including Don Howe, Dave Sexton and Malcolm Allison, really acknowledged their debt to Walter.'

Interestingly, the love of coaching that Howe developed under men such as Winterbottom never extended to a desire to inflict on his own sons the kind of regime imposed on Alan Ball by his father, who would tie his right leg to a drainpipe to force him to kick with his weaker left foot. 'My dad never ever pushed us into anything,' Rob Howe explains. 'I did actually have a trial at Arsenal but he felt that if you're going to make it you would do it on your own and not do anything to influence it. David wasn't interested in football – he was a musician – but the rest of us used to play football and my dad rarely watched us because he couldn't be there. He used to encourage us to play and was supportive but was not going to force you to do it. We never felt we were having to live up to his standards on the field.'

* * *

Aware of his own limitations but having seen the best coaching minds at work while supporting Lilleshall's courses as a staff physiotherapist, Bertie Mee had made the appointment of the correct right-hand man a priority when given the job of Arsenal manager. Sexton, a former forward with several London clubs who had gone on to work under Tommy Docherty at Chelsea and was now coaching at Fulham, had little hesitation in accepting the offer to become Mee's first-team coach. 'I was trying to get my coaching badge at Lilleshall on a course run by the FA,' he explained. 'Bertie was one of the staff there, giving us talks about the physiotherapy and the medical side. I struck up a good friendship with him. I liked Bertie and because he was an intelligent man, I felt I couldn't go wrong. Plus, of course, Arsenal was a huge club. With Bertie's background, he gave me my head as a coach, which doesn't always happen in our business.'

The appointment helped to ease any doubts Mee's players harboured over his surprise promotion. 'When Billy Wright was manager there were no real tactics and the training was totally different,' Simpson recalls. 'Just a bit of running and five-a-side. Dave was fantastic. He was one of those coaches who encouraged you so much.'

Bob McNab, who arrived at the club in the early weeks of Mee's reign, described the dressing room as being 'in a bit of upheaval', with players such as Eastham and Skirton on their way out, and Baldwin about to cross London as part of a deal that would bring George Graham from Chelsea. 'Players were looking over their shoulder and appeared a bit insecure. After a while, things started to improve, in large part to the influence of Dave Sexton and Bertie's discipline, which set standards much higher.'

Arsenal finished the 1966/67 season with a 12-game unbeaten run that took them to seventh position, having conceded only 47 goals, compared to 75 the previous season. 'Dave started working on closing down as a team, like a chain reaction,' recalls McLintock. 'The right-back would push forward; the right-sided centre-half would push over. We always used to try to keep the line. As soon as the ball was cleared and the forwards pushed upfield, we would all push up as well.'

Meanwhile, Howe had enjoyed his first season leading the reserves in the Football Combination in the role of captain and coach. 'Bertie laid down some ground rules,' he explained. 'He said he wanted the young reserve players to work harder. He wanted them back for training in the afternoons, sometimes as a group, sometimes as individuals. I said, "Fine", and then got on with it. And there was no interference from Bertie. We would have meetings on Monday and Friday, but he left everything to me. It wasn't because he was not interested; he just believed in letting people do their jobs.'

As a side venture, Howe also followed a path taken by many other up-and-coming coaches in offering his services to the annual Varsity Match. The likes of Allison, Buckingham, Greenwood, Nicholson and Joe Mercer had all been associated with the game and Howe took responsibility for the fortunes of the Dark Blues against their rivals from Cambridge. After a 3-0 defeat against an FA Amateur XI at Eastbourne, *The Times* warned, 'It is obvious that Don Howe, the Oxford coach, has a lot of hard work ahead of him.' Five weeks later, his first experience of coaching at Wembley Stadium ended in a 1-0 defeat in the Varsity Match in front of a crowd of 17,500. Interestingly, given what we now know about Howe's coaching career, *The Times* blamed Oxford's fate on an insistence on withdrawing one of their midfield players to mark a dangerous Cambridge forward. 'This tactic left Oxford unbalanced in that they played five defenders and it probably cost them the match,' was the paper's damning verdict.

In little more than a year's time, Howe would be back at the national stadium. This time he would be coaching Arsenal's first team, the result of a chain of events set in motion by Chelsea's club tour in the summer of 1967. Former Gunner Docherty, who had left Highbury in 1961 to become coach and then manager of Chelsea, had exploded after seeing two of his players sent off during a game in Bermuda, making a derogatory comment to the local match official. The remark earned him a one-month ban from football. In October, the man who had led 'Docherty's Diamonds' to finishes of fifth, third and fifth in the First Division and to the most recent FA Cup Final – as well as winning the League Cup in 1965 – resigned his position at Stamford Bridge, depressed at the direction in which his career was heading and worn down by confrontation with the club's directors. Chelsea persuaded Sexton to return to the club, making him one of the game's youngest managers at 37. 'It was a difficult decision to make,' he admitted. 'I was reluctant to break the bond between me and Bertie and I had worked with all the younger players. I left Arsenal with a heavy heart.'

Mee spoke of Sexton's desire to 'paddle his own canoe', but the players were less understanding. McLintock, who had been appointed club captain, recalls, 'We were furious when Bertie let Dave go. Maybe he couldn't have stopped him, or maybe he should have done more to keep him there, but it was the first time we had found somebody we felt could do what was a very difficult job.' Neill recalls McLintock 'going mad at me and saying Bertie should never have let Dave go'. Neill replied, 'Frank, he has got to make his own way and make his own decisions. He has an opportunity to progress in management.'

Mee's acceptance of Sexton's decision was partly down to recognising that he had the perfect replacement lined up, although Howe's elevation to chief coach did not immediately quell the unrest. McNab remembers, 'We all felt a great sense of loss after Dave left. I heard many times the players feeling the club had no ambition. The first couple of weeks under Don were strained, with quite a number of players sulking and not putting much out in training.'

Not only did Mee have what Wilson described as the 'self-belief to give power to someone and not feel as though they will threaten you', he also had confidence enough in Howe to leave him to win over the players rather than intervening on his behalf. And Howe had no qualms about showing former team-mates that he was now someone to be respected and obeyed. A couple of weeks after his appointment, he became frustrated at what he was seeing during a training session in the Highbury gymnasium and brought proceedings to a halt.

'Right,' he yelled. 'I have fucking had enough of you lot. I am Don Howe. Dave Sexton has gone. I am the coach and from now on you will do what I say. Right, come on! We are going to do double laps!'

Radford recalls, 'The players weren't really putting it in properly. I remember Don just blowing his top. He stopped everything, sat everyone down and gave us the biggest bollocking we'd ever had.' The shock tactic worked. According to McLintock, 'From then on you could tell he was in charge. We had been so pissed off. Don grabbed us by the scruff of the neck and gave himself a good kick up the bollocks as well, knowing that he had got to start acting properly. He just got better and better as a coach.'

4
LAYING THE FOUNDATIONS

This defensive tag people hang on us just isn't true. They are fooled into thinking it because we have had so few goals scored against us. This is because we have a good defence, not because we are defensive-minded.

Don Howe, speaking in 1969

DON HOWE had been chief coach at Arsenal for only a month, and already the methods of his team were being questioned. In the space of two games against Burnley the Gunners had three men sent off: Bob McNab in a League Cup quarter-final at Turf Moor, and Frank McLintock and Peter Storey in the First Division three days later. To critical observers, this was an indication of a pragmatic approach that, while not out of step with the developing nature of the English professional game, was not what people expected to emerge from the elegant traditions of Highbury. Chairman Denis Hill-Wood was forced to defend his men by telling reporters, 'I will not tolerate dirty players at Arsenal and I do not believe we have one on the club's books.'

The Burnley matches had been preceded by a 0-0 draw against West Ham United, a notable result in that it halted a run of four League games since Sexton's departure in which Arsenal conceded ten goals. After winning their replay against Burnley, Arsenal reeled off three wins and three clean sheets to climb to sixth place in the table. While no one can be exact about the date of Howe's explosion in front of his distracted players, results suggest that it had some effect on performance. And now Arsenal were about to return to Wembley.

They had last played at the national stadium when beaten in the 1952 FA Cup Final, almost a decade before the inception of the League Cup, the brainchild of League secretary Alan Hardaker, who saw it as a way of capitalising on clubs' growing demand for football under floodlights. In 1967, the tournament was granted a Wembley final, rather than the two-legged contests of its early years, while the granting of a place in the European Inter-Cities Fairs Cup for the winners moved it up the priority list of most clubs. Mee had watched London rivals Tottenham Hotspur and West Ham triumph in the European Cup Winners' Cup and wanted some of that excitement for his players. 'It is important for the climate of the club,' he said, before the two-legged semi-final against Huddersfield Town. 'The players take on new-found status.'

A 3-2 win at Highbury meant there was still much work to do when Arsenal travelled to their Second Division opponents. But having conceded after 17 minutes, they scored three more goals to win 6-3 on aggregate and book a place in the final against Leeds United. It was a game that marked the start of an era-defining run of success for the Yorkshire club, making them the team against whom all English sides of the period would measure themselves. It also laid the foundation of bitter rivalry.

Even with the award of a Wembley final, the League Cup was still disregarded by some in the game. Manchester United, the club that defined the mid-1960s in the way that Leeds would characterise the latter part of the decade and the first part of the next, had not even bothered to enter for five years after playing in the inaugural tournament in 1960/61. For Arsenal and Leeds, meeting early in March 1968, it meant everything. The Gunners had an opportunity to end 15 years without a trophy; for Leeds, victory would prove that they could actually get across the line in a close race. Since Don Revie, a former

Footballer of the Year at Manchester City, had become manager and led them out of the Second Division, they had finished as runners-up in the League twice and lost in the finals of the FA Cup and Fairs Cup.

The manner in which they had battled – a word used advisedly – for football's leading honours had either been a blight on the sport or merely a modernist approach that recognised the need for organisation, professionalism and uncompromising ruthlessness, depending on which class of philosophy one belonged to. Even a stylish passer such as Johnny Giles, signed from Manchester United in the Leeds promotion season of 1963/64, could be a cold-blooded menace to midfield opponents, admitting, 'You had to establish a reputation that would make people think twice about messing with you.' No other Leeds player of the era better encapsulated the light and dark of a team that, when it chose to, could be uplifting in its performance. Once the League title was won, as it would be in 1968/69, Revie would encourage his team to emphasise the more sublime side of their dual personality, with players such as Scottish winger Eddie Gray casting spells over the opposition. But until they had that first trophy in the cabinet, the win-at-all-costs approach prevailed in a team driven by their fiery captain, Billy Bremner, and bolstered by the uncompromising defensive methods of Jack Charlton and Norman Hunter.

Arsenal's recent publicity ensured that few were expecting a festival of flowing football at Wembley. In the edition of the *Football League Review* that was included as part of the official Wembley programme, Mee hinted at what lay in store by saying, 'If … we get tensions boiling over on occasions, if we get incidents, these should not be misinterpreted as anything more than the consequence of the hard and professional approach.' But even Mee probably did not foresee a match that *Charles Buchan's Football Monthly* would describe as a 'complete and cynical disregard for the £90,000 paid by real football supporters'.

Mee and Howe had two major selection issues to resolve, preferring winger David Jenkins to George Johnston and leaving Northern Ireland international and former club captain Terry Neill on the bench after he had missed only one game all season. Howe felt more comfortable with the defensive pairing of Ian Ure and Peter Simpson. Neill missed the pre-game introductions to Princess Alexandra and, after the game, refused to collect his medal.

The only goal came after 18 minutes, a volley by left-back Terry Cooper after Arsenal felt that Charlton, in his usual position under the crossbar at corner kicks, had forced goalkeeper Jim Furnell to the ground. The match never opened up. George Armstrong missed a chance to equalise, but Arsenal were accused of lack of urgency in getting men forward. A goal up, Leeds were happy to use midfield players Paul Madeley and Jimmy Greenhoff as supplementary full-backs. It was tedious and tetchy, with a brawl breaking out after McLintock charged into Leeds goalkeeper Gary Sprake. The photograph from the game that was most widely published was not of the goal or the trophy celebration, but of the two groups of players poised to launch into each other like participants in the wrestling that was airing on ITV's *World of Sport* as the match was being played.

Leeds celebrated the final whistle in blissful relief and would soon be adding the Fairs Cup to their breakthrough achievements. Arsenal fans booed them on their lap of honour, while Desmond Hackett typed up a *Daily Express* report that said, 'This League Cup Final will make history only as a game so bad it was little short of scandalous.'

Mee and Howe encouraged their players to celebrate their achievement in reaching the final, while John Radford recalls the game as an important learning experience. 'Leeds at that time were dominating and bullying people. Losing to them in the League Cup was a good game for us in some ways because from then on we started to get a little bit like that ourselves and we were probably the first side to stand up to them. Reaching Wembley that year was really the changing point. We just started getting stronger from then on.'

Howe would admit a few years later, 'I was influenced a lot by the early Leeds team. I used to think it was legitimate to, well, intimidate players, even referees.' On a separate occasion, he argued, 'Football is a game of physical contact. And our players are taught to accept physical contact – and threaten it. I say threaten because football is full of kidders, people who look as if they can dish out tough play but never actually do so.'

Arsenal's intent, and Howe's influence, was clear for all to see during a 1968/69 campaign that began with a 2-1 win at Tottenham Hotspur, achieved by resolute defence and swift counter-attack. After winning seven of their first nine games – including an impressive 4-1 beating of champions Manchester City – the unbeaten Gunners sat on top of the League when they visited Leeds towards the end of September. More goalmouth shenanigans involving Charlton contributed to a 2-0 win for the home team. Further evidence of how intense the clubs' rivalry was becoming would be offered in the return game in the spring, when it took only five minutes for Bobby Gould to tangle with Sprake. The goalkeeper laid out the Arsenal forward with a left hook that Henry Cooper would have been proud of as he'd defended his European heavyweight title against Italian Piero Tomasino a couple of weeks earlier. This being an era when little short of actual bodily harm would get you sent off, both players were merely booked. 'It was the most brutal game I ever played in,' said Gould. 'But all the matches against Leeds were gigantic. Facing them was one of those occasions when you had to pack the boxing gloves in your kit bag.'

Howe's recollection of contests against Leeds around that time was: 'They were shocking games. Everybody was too professional. We all knew how to stop the game and hold the momentum if one team got on top. The games against Leeds were not for the supporters. They were for the coaches and the players.'

According to Sammels, 'I remember Don Howe saying once, "You know we are playing Leeds today. You know what it's going to be like. Is there anyone who doesn't want to play?" They had very skilful players but they were very intimidating.'

The harder edge Arsenal were developing in response was evident two days after the Sprake incident when McLintock made the bold decision to headbutt Ron 'Chopper' Harris' at Chelsea and Howe ended up having to drag his players away from referee Norman Burtenshaw at the end of a 2-1 defeat. But that addition of steel, along with Howe's reorganisation of basic defensive methods, meant Arsenal more than halved their number of goals conceded – from 56 to 27 – in finishing fourth as Revie's Leeds won their first title.

Howe had viewed predecessor Dave Sexton's introduction of a man-to-marking system with scepticism, although any type of strategic approach to keeping the ball out of the net had been an improvement on the previous state of affairs. 'I respect Dave as a fine coach but I didn't agree with all his methods,' said Howe in 1969 in the first edition of the *Arsenal Football Book*. 'One of my first jobs was to introduce the zonal system of defence, which has paid dividends for Leeds and Liverpool. Each player has his slot in the system. The old idea of man-for-man marking has been thrown overboard. Now we put a player in the position which suits him best and he takes on the opponent who comes into his territory.'

Howe had made his decision during a pair of pre-season friendlies in Germany, saying to Mee, 'I don't like the way we have players running around with their forwards, allowing themselves to be dragged all over the field. I'd like to change it.' Mee's response was, 'Right. Get on with it', a phrase that became familiar to those working for him. 'That was Bertie's big saying,' Howe remembered. 'He felt that if you spent too much time talking about things it was not productive.'

According to McNab, 'It was a very brave decision, since only Don and myself had experience with the zonal system and the other defenders were not convinced that we should change. We'd had a bit of success with the man-for-man system. I loved David, but I didn't like playing for his defence. I could understand why he did it because they had been such a mess in defence. If you give someone an assignment and say, "Right, mark him" and that fellow scores, you know whose fault it is. Personally, I thought it was a mindless way of playing football. I would just switch my brains off in the dressing room before the game.

'I knew we could do better – my problem was convincing players like Peter Simpson and Peter Storey, who had never won anything. I think I drove Don mad. Pat Rice always says he remembers Don and I debating it in a bar for hours and hours. It was a brave decision to change a system that had got us to the League Cup Final, which was the first hint of success they'd had for years. I was flattered to see that Don said he was happy to play the zonal system because he had me on the field to manage it. I think I did that. I was a thinker, while Frank was very emotional, someone who would beat the drum. And the lads listened, even though I used to slaughter them sometimes.'

Playing alongside McNab was Simpson, who admits, 'It was difficult to make the switch at first because you had to start using your head. Not being the brainiest of people I found that difficult! We got it off pat in the end, but we had the players for it.'

McLintock was still an energetic force in midfield, but when Mee and Howe decided a year later that he could be a more reliable presence in the No.5 shirt than either Ure or Neill, he became a key part of the system. 'Don and Bob McNab helped me a lot,' he explains. 'Especially with holding the line and not running into the corner flags. I would get dragged in sometimes. You go with someone and you know they are taking you into a false position, so I learnt to just back off two or three yards because you don't want your centre-halves getting in positions where there are holes up the side of you. If I drifted a bit too far one way, Bob would shout, "Get fucking back here and stop dragging me across." It wasn't just, "Frank, don't go as much as that." He would let you have it and it made me pick it up more quickly.

'We used to pass men over. If my centre-forward was running out to the right wing I could have ended up running into corner flags and we would be pulled all over the place. So when the centre-forward started his run I would go with him for five or ten yards and then the right-back just used to come and get him. Peter Simpson would do the same with Bob on the left. It was carefully mapped out and Don was a great help, as was Bob, who was a great tactician.'

Arsenal's defensive performance saw them better the previous lowest number of goals conceded in a 42-game First Division season, 28 by Huddersfield 44 years earlier – although it was a sign of the new realism of English football that champions Leeds (26 conceded) and runners-up Liverpool (24) were even stingier. 'If people thought our games were not exciting then it was a condemnation of what was going on at the time,' says McNab.

In a single season, Howe had established the reputation as a defensive organiser that was to become the defining feature of his coaching career – and, at times, a millstone. That conflict is best summed up by his quote at the top of this chapter. And the exasperation was still clear in his voice when, in 2001, I interviewed him for *Seventy-One Guns*. 'It was that jealousy of Arsenal that still exists today,' he said. 'You are always going to get people who criticise you for the way you are playing and the success you are having. If you get to the top in any sporting life people want to find things wrong. It is professional jealousy, but it never affected my way of thinking.'

According to Sammels, the team's improvement 'was wonderful for us even if we were criticised by people who thought us a dull, defensive side with little or no flair. That, of course, did have some truth at the time. Bertie and Don knew that we had to build a solid foundation to tighten the defence and stop giving goals away before we thought about becoming inventive.'

When Howe was asked, a year into his new role, whether his training sessions focused on defence at the expense of all else, he insisted, 'Nothing could be further from the truth. In fact, the accent is on attacking in training sessions. Eighty per cent of our time is devoted to working out attack moves. Our defenders often asked me, "When are you going to spend some time on us?"'

McNab supports that argument, explaining that Arsenal's aim was to get men forward. 'When we had the ball, Pat Rice or I would go forward. Geordie [Armstrong] would make a run and clear space for me and I would be like a midfield forward. People had never seen that. It just evolved, we never really planned it, although we did a lot of practice at getting out of the back into midfield with the ball. I would go down the wing and Peter Simpson would come out wide on the left, or he would go forward and I would cover him. People didn't understand it. I regret that they never filmed our games of one-touch in training. Everyone criticised us because they thought we were defensive, but our two centre-backs were the key in people breaking forward. We were effectively playing three at the back even in those days.'

Howe himself said there was little to be gained by throwing men forward with abandon simply in an effort to find more goals. 'All that will happen is that the other team will pull back six and seven players to stop you,' he argued. 'You on the other hand are weakened at the back and less able to check a counter-attack. I tell the boys to try and make it four or five up front whenever it is possible to do so.'

Howe preached a simple philosophy, believing that 'the basis of the modern game is to create space in attack and deny space in defence'. To achieve the first part of that equation most training sessions would include a period of shadow football, without opposition, in which 'players are instructed to spray passes to certain areas of the field'.

And when he put the emphasis on defensive preparation, Arsenal's use of the offside trap – another legacy handed down to Graham – offered further ammunition for the critics. But what could appear crude in the middle of the match concealed a sophisticated preparation. 'When forwards used to make their runs we bent our run with them,' recalls McLintock, hard-pressed to think of other teams capable of such execution. 'We used to make a run with them and when they thought they were going to be okay, then we would step up a yard. Norman Hunter, for example, would bring his foot back and you'd get the call, "Hold, Frank," and Allan Clarke or Mick Jones would be ten yards offside. When they started the run they thought you were trying to catch them up, but you were just pretending, not going as fast as you could. In the meantime, the full-backs were taught to stay two yards ahead of us centre-halves because we might come up quickly and catch them off guard. We played the offside trap with just the two of us, keeping the full-backs slightly ahead of us, and it really worked great.'

Meanwhile, Mee had enough military-style pragmatism in his DNA that, for all his demands of Arsenal personnel to 'remember who you are, what you are, and who you represent', he was happy with the results that Howe was producing, even if the methods might not have pleased the aesthetes. While Matt Busby had seen Manchester United become champions of Europe with a happy-go-lucky style unencumbered by team instructions, Mee knew that without talent such as George Best and Bobby Charlton he was more reliant on Howe's ability on the training ground.

'It comes back to the competition of the modern game,' he said. 'Success is demanded by the fans, the directors, all of us – and I have to produce an adaptable set-up within which success can be achieved. Sometimes it is hard to reconcile principles that may be dear to me, but situations have to be coped with in this as in any other job.' He acknowledged the influence of Revie's team when he added, 'One would accept that Leeds have done the right and proper thing and hope that we are on the same lines.'

Mee told interviewer Jeremy James for BBC's *Man Alive* documentary series that even though footballers should view themselves as entertainers, it was 'difficult to decide whether the public want entertainment pure and simple or whether they want a winning team irrespective'. His conclusion was, 'If they can have an entertaining team as well that's fine, but primarily winning is the first requisite from the spectators' point of view.'

It was that kind of attitude that allowed Howe to deploy a pragmatic approach. But while he was busy fixing the defence, much media attention had fallen upon Arsenal's efforts to increase their goalscoring. Names such as Southampton's Martin Chivers and Swindon Town's Don Rogers had been linked to the club before a club-record £90,000 bought Bobby Gould from Coventry City, where he had scored 24 goals in their promotion campaign under Jimmy Hill. An honest tryer who made up in enthusiasm what he lacked in finesse, Gould's transfer during the 1967/68 season might not have offered the long-term forward solution that Arsenal hoped – he was gone from the club before the Double season – but it did begin a connection with Howe that would see their careers intertwined on and off for a quarter of a century. 'I believe Bertie had lined me up on the understanding that Dave Sexton was going to be here,' Gould ventures. 'I don't think Don had a contribution in taking me there.'

Gould says he was 'frightened' after his first encounter with Howe. 'I had never seen so much running in my life. It was a dramatic change from Coventry. Don was starting to play the football they now call the press. Don started it in 1968. If the goalkeeper gave the ball to the right-back then me or the left-winger had to close him down. We would still be running in the 80th minute. By the time I had done that I was fucked. It wasn't my game. I liked flick-ons and to sit in the penalty area. I just couldn't come up to the running quality that Don wanted, whereas big John Radford was phenomenal. When I was transferred to Wolves, Bill McGarry took me out on the pitch and said, "If we're kicking that way I don't want to see you in our half." I said, "Gaffer, that is music to my ears."'

While Arsenal were going well in the 1968/69 First Division campaign, Gould put them on their way to a 6-1 win against Scunthorpe United in the third round of the League Cup and scored in a five-goal performance against Blackpool that sent them into a semi-final tie against Tottenham. The success of the Gunners' neighbours during the 1960s – the Double, two more FA Cups and England's first success in Europe in the 1963 Cup Winners' Cup – had served to emphasise Arsenal's struggles and intensify the desperation of their fans to experience some kind of success. Victory in the semi-final would be symbolic, as well as securing a place in another Wembley final.

The high stakes were perhaps to blame for Arsenal being part of another contest that was not for the faint-hearted. It took 88 goalless minutes at Highbury before Radford, who had earned a first England cap a few weeks earlier, seized upon a mistake by Spurs full-back Joe Kinnear to score the only goal. The second leg at White Hart Lane was a bitter, brutal affair that prompted a headline of 'The Shame of London' in more than one publication. As the battle on the field became increasingly nasty, police had to keep the peace on the terraces.

One of referee John Gow's first actions had been to separate scuffling players after Spurs defender Mike England appeared to stamp on Bob Wilson. The goalkeeper was later decked by Peter Collins, prompting team-mates to throw their fists about in retaliation. Radford admits that he 'could easily have been sent off' for punching Cyril Knowles in a later incident. Amid the mayhem, Jimmy Greaves levelled the tie with the 25th goal of what was his last great season. Only four minutes remained when Radford headed home George Armstrong's corner to put Arsenal into a final against Third Division Swindon Town.

Rebuilt by former Yorkshire miner Danny Williams after relegation from the Second Division and the sale of forwards Mike Summerbee and Ernie Hunt to Manchester City and Wolves respectively, Swindon had beaten First Division Coventry City and Burnley on their way to the final. Few gave them much chance of making Arsenal their third top-flight victims in the tournament. They were happy just to be there, weren't they? Even if the sight of Wembley on an eve-of-final visit did bring them down to earth.

The place was a mess. Instead of lush green grass, the playing surface was pure slop. The presence of the Royal International Horse Show on the turf the previous summer – a diary date that would be repeated later in the year – had destroyed the pitch. Torrential rain had not helped and England's game against France a few days earlier had only been played after hundreds of gallons of water were pumped away. Unable to get a roller on top of the soaked surface, the ground staff were only able to replace divots.

Such energy-sapping conditions were not what Arsenal needed after battling to get several of their players to something approaching full fitness after eight of them contracted a chest infection in the days before the final. As players went to bed unable to breathe properly, the club's league game against Liverpool was postponed. Under Howe, the Gunners had become one of the fittest teams in the country, but now they feared what might lay in store in a testing final against fired-up opponents guaranteed to run until they dropped. 'I got out my bed on Thursday and went to Wembley to look at the pitch on the Friday,' Sammels explains. 'There were planks all over the pitch. It was a bog.' Ure recalls that 'the water was up over my shoes' and believes that any other game than a showpiece would have been postponed.

Arsenal trainer George Wright, responsible for the players' wellbeing, had his worst fears confirmed on the day of the game. 'In the morning they had all these jet driers on the pitch,' he remembered. 'It was a right mess. The players took the field with tracksuit tops on and when I went to collect them I was up to my ankles in mud.'

Even so, few saw anything other than an Arsenal victory, with Hackett announcing in the *Daily Express*, 'This is like Arkle at his peerless best running against game selling-platers.' But as any racegoer could have told him, the heavier the going, the more the thoroughbreds were likely to struggle.

Swindon goalkeeper Peter Downsborough produced the game of his life at one end of the field, while Rogers made Arsenal pay for their reticence in the transfer market at the other. 'He was stopping everything,' says Ure of Downsborough. 'He would be diving one way and the ball would hit his heel or something.' Tragically for Ure, his ill-judged attempt to get the ball back to Wilson let in Roger Smart to give the underdogs the lead. 'Bob was shouting for the ball and Ian kept on dribbling it back,' recalls McLintock. 'He was probably a bit worried about the surface. All of a sudden he gave it to Bob from about five yards away and it bounced off him and they put it in the net.' It was not until four minutes from time that Downsborough booted the ball against Gould, who reacted promptly to head the rebound into the unguarded net.

Arsenal might have been reprieved, but now their recuperating players faced another tiring half hour. 'As soon as 90 minutes were up, someone blew out my candle,' says McLintock. 'I couldn't lift my legs.' Howe attempted to take matters into his own hands. Pointing to the mud-soaked yellow shirts of his players, he pleaded with referee Bill Handley to abandon the contest. Swindon's players, the white of their kit no less soiled, felt brighter and lighter with what they were witnessing. 'I remember seeing Don Howe going berserk,' said defender Joe Butler. 'Obviously they were worried.'

The relatively clean outfit of Rogers showed how peripheral to the action he had been until extra time began. But the solid 5ft 10in forward was about to enter folklore, forcing the ball home following a corner as half-time of the additional period approached. With time almost up and Arsenal already facing up to a second Wembley defeat in two years, Rogers raced clear from halfway, veered in from the right and beat Wilson from an acute angle. 'And that is that,' announced ITV's Brian Moore, commentating for the following day's *The Big Match*. Moments later it was. McLintock, now a four-time Wembley loser, was photographed wandering in a daze among the Royal Engineers' band, an image that summed up Arsenal's day.

Unusually, long-serving club secretary Bob Wall would later criticise Mee and Howe for looking to win the game in extra time. 'That was a mistake,' he wrote. 'I should have advised them to close up the game and look for a replay. The virus left us physically weak and tactically vulnerable.'

Mee responded with stoicism. 'We are not going to hold a massive inquest, nor are we going to shake up the team.' Nor did he need to. The players who would take the club to its successes of the next two seasons had all been at the club since late 1966 – a further endorsement of the much-maligned Billy Wright's long-term contribution to Arsenal's fortunes.

Howe believed, however, that some of those players could be utilised more effectively. George Graham, who had lost his place as a striker to Gould, was reintroduced to the side in a deeper position. 'Bertie and Don had an idea that I could play in midfield and come late in the box and maybe get a few goals,' Graham recalls. 'So I took on a new role and enjoyed it.'

That allowed for the reassignment of McLintock at the heart of Arsenal's defence, a suggestion first taken to Howe by chief scout Gordon Clark, one of his former West Bromwich Albion managers. McLintock explains, 'It was a dangerous thing to do, but Don and Gordon said they thought I would extend my career and do better for the club if I didn't play as someone who was driving forward the whole time.'

McNab, who was sceptical about the move, adds, 'To say I was not enthusiastic about it would be an understatement. Frank had shown nothing to give any indication he would have the discipline to become a centre-back. But, once you know Frank, you know anything is possible. He became so comfortable.'

When McLintock had proposed a toast of thanks to Mee and Howe for the success of the 1968/69 season, Mee responded by warning them that fourth place was not good enough and told them, 'Some of you may fall by the wayside, but we are going to the top.' Indeed, McLintock's positional switch, which became permanent during the next season, allowed Arsenal to sell Ure to Manchester United, while Neill went to Hull City to become player-manager.

John Roberts arrived from Northampton as centre-back cover, while December 1969 found Arsenal on the kind of flashy, headline-grabbing shopping spree they had hardly been known for under Mee's thrifty stewardship. Unproven winger Peter Marinello arrived in a £100,000 transfer from Hibernian, making an immediate impact with a brilliant individual goal on his debut at Old Trafford. 'The actual buying of the player was left to Bertie,' said Howe, explaining how the procurement of new talent worked in their partnership. 'We both always knew the areas of the team that needed strengthening and I might know who we were looking at, but when the time came to buy I had no input. Bertie listened to what Gordon Clark said about players he had looked at. Often I would just hear that so-and-so was coming to the club.'

In the case of Marinello, his long dark hair and pretty-boy vulnerability made him perfect fodder not only for the newly launched *Shoot!* magazine and its target market of football-mad schoolboys, but also publications such as *Jackie*, aimed at their record-buying sisters. While Marinello's image vied for space on bedroom walls with David Cassidy, it proved unfortunate that his feats in his first Arsenal game had been achieved in direct opposition to George Best, making burdensome comparison inevitable. Every clothing deal he signed and newspaper article he wrote as he made the most of the commercial opportunities in London gave Mee pause to doubt the wisdom of his signing, while the pressure increased on Howe to get the best out of him. Yet by the time Marinello married his 19-year-old girlfriend

Joyce Murray in the summer of 1970, a ceremony besieged by weeping adolescents, it was already clear that the dependable George Armstrong had seen off the challenge to his place on the flank, just as he had with the former Tottenham winger Jimmy Robertson, who was on his way to Ipswich in March 1970.

Arsenal had already found room for one maverick talent that season in former Holloway schoolboy Charlie George, who had graduated from the North Bank to a debut on the opening day of the 1969/70 at the age of 18. George's entrance ended in a 1-0 defeat against Everton, who would end up as champions, while a follow-up 0-0 draw at Leeds had the crowd chanting, 'We want football!' By October, it was clear that Arsenal were not going to build on their fourth-place finish of the previous season and Mee's position was thought by those in the media to be under threat after a slow handclap greeted a home draw against Sheffield Wednesday. Stoke City manager Tony Waddington claimed that Arsenal's defensive tactics at the Victoria Ground could have been carried out by 'ten navvies'.

It was to Europe that Arsenal looked for salvation, disposing of Northern Ireland's Glentoran in the first round of the Fairs Cup and then getting past Portugal's Sporting Lisbon, helped by an important first-leg penalty save by Geoff Barnett, signed for £35,000 from Everton after Wilson broke his arm. Howe took the charge of a goalless draw at French club Rouen when illness forced Mee to stay at home, Sammels scoring a late winner in the return leg to put Arsenal into the last eight.

By the time European competition resumed after the winter break and Arsenal prepared to fly to Romania to face Dynamo Bacau, Howe and Mee had made some important decisions about their squad. David Court and Robertson were left behind and a ruthless Mee explained, 'I regard them as virtually departed from the club. And there are others who will follow them later.' The old hands, Sammels and Radford, scored goals set up by newcomers George and Eddie Kelly respectively and the Gunners banged in seven goals in the return at Highbury.

The semi-final and final were due to take place in successive weeks in April, after the League season wrapped up early to allow the England team to prepare for the World Cup finals in Mexico. Arsenal were to face Ajax Amsterdam, beaten finalists in the European Cup a year earlier. The newly crowned champions of Holland possessed one of the world's most exciting young talents in Johan Cruyff and were about to embark on a hat-trick of European Cup wins. So when Arsenal brushed them aside 3-0 in the first leg at Highbury, it was the first real evidence that this team was capable of great things; certainly more than the 12th-place finish they had achieved in the First Division. Only 17 minutes had been played when George fired in a fierce shot and, with Storey subduing Cruyff, a period of Ajax pressure was repelled. Needing another goal, Howe and Mee decided that their best option was to send on Armstrong to reclaim his position from Marinello, who was thus condemned to the sidelines for the historic months that followed. Armstrong set up Sammels to force the ball home with ten minutes to play. Four minutes later, Graham was pulled down and a nerveless George stepped up to score the third goal from the penalty spot. In Amsterdam, Arsenal prepared for a return game that would put them into a third final in successive seasons and after Gerrie Mühren's 18th-minute goal they produced what Mee described as 'a fine defensive performance' to secure their place.

One week later, Arsenal seemed taken aback by the fierce atmosphere of the 30,000-capacity Parc Astrid Stadium, home of Belgian side Anderlecht, who had upset Inter Milan in their semi-final. McLintock recalls, 'They just knocked the ball about and were very patient. But all of a sudden it's, boom, a goal. You're thinking, "Lucky bastards." They go back to the same tempo again, probing, probing, probing. It lulls you into a false sense of security. Suddenly another goal, two nothing down, and you feel as though you have been doing well.' Anderlecht pressed patiently and scored a third, the magnitude of lead that no team had ever squandered in a European final.

Howe would recall, 'There were not as many substitutions in those days and it was one area where Bertie and I would perhaps not always agree. You never had long to discuss things and we would sometimes have a difference of opinion.' This time, however, they agreed to send on the powerful 18-year-old Ray Kennedy instead of the limping George and launch a more direct assault on goal. With seven minutes left, he rose to meet Armstrong's cross to head a potentially valuable away goal in the event of a draw after two legs. The goal lifted the mood of the dressing room, with Bob Wilson recalling McLintock emerging from the showers 'like Mel Gibson in *Braveheart* – by the time we left we were all convinced we could win'.

Yet it was not until the day of the second leg that the tournament's organising committee finally ratified that away goals would continue to count double in the final, meaning Arsenal needed to score two goals without reply to win rather than to force extra time. Victory would see them follow Leeds and Newcastle United as the two previous winners of the competition, while the following night Manchester City would lift the European Cup Winners' Cup in Vienna – although barely noticed by a nation watching Chelsea beat Leeds in the replay of the FA Cup Final at Old Trafford.

Mee, who harboured a level of distrust towards the football media, agreed to allow *Daily Telegraph* feature writer Patrick Marnham access to Highbury's inner sanctum on one of the biggest nights in the club's history. Describing the scene at the team talk at South Herts Golf Club in Totteridge at 5.30pm, Marnham described Mee reminding the players 'what this game means to your careers and this club':

> Then Howe talks over the game as he wants them to play it. 'First 15, I want you forward … Their best two forwards can be bullied. Well bully them. Hit them hard and do it quick. And when you've done it, pick them up. Let the crowd see it was an accident. I don't want any messing with the offside trap. I want to cover at the back. Don't let Mulder start running at you. He can take off on a run and go straight past a lot of you. I've got a lot of respect for him.' Howe talks quickly, using gestures, pacing out attacks, giving them moves he is describing. The team watch him intently.

At Highbury, Marnham witnessed Howe making 'various suggestions' an hour before kick-off and getting into lively debate with McLintock and Graham. And as kick-off approached with 51,612 in the stadium, he noted, 'In the dressing room, you can still hear very little of the din outside. Howe is still talking to anyone who will listen.'

The atmosphere generated by the occasion was exactly what had made Howe so excited about joining the club six years earlier. That he had never experienced it as a player was more than compensated for by the satisfaction he felt as the team he had prepared for the biggest night of their careers took the field in pouring rain. The discipline he and Mee had preached was never more important than in the early stages, when they withstood Anderlecht's pressure and refused to leave themselves vulnerable by chasing the game too soon. It was vindication of Howe's ambition of 'trying to prepare the players for those split-second decisions which can change the course of a game'. After 26 minutes, Armstrong delivered a corner, McLintock touched it back and Kelly, barely born when Arsenal last won anything, smashed the ball in from 20 yards. Still one up at half-time, Howe went to work in the dressing room. 'Don took over,' said Wilson. 'Animated in his shirt sleeves and braces, he was positivity personified.' He reminded his players, 'One will be enough; two will do nicely.'

With the momentum and the frenzied crowd behind them, Arsenal swept forward. There were 19 minutes remaining when McNab put in a high ball from the left and Radford, arms wide as if to remain airborne as long as possible, connected with an unstoppable header. Two minutes later, Sammels, a man who had attracted his share of criticism from the Highbury crowd during the down times for the club, raced after George's pass to fire the third goal. Who needed the ruling of the Fairs Cup committee now?

At the final whistle, 17 years of relief came cascading around the Arsenal squad as fans scrambled over the concrete moat surrounding the pitch. In the dressing room, Howe watched players toss pieces of muddy, champagne-soaked kit through the open windows to the fans on Avenell Road. The pictures of winning teams from years past –

removed from the players' meeting room on Mee's instructions to avoid the idea that the club was living in the past – could now go back on the walls, with new images to go alongside them.

McLintock recalls, 'On the night, as a team, individually and collectively, we couldn't have played any better. Everyone was on fire and the crowd was really behind us. Winning that cup was so important; the first trophy in 17 years. We were becoming a good team and now we had the confidence to go with it.'

Part of that new-found faith was directed towards the management team of Mee and Howe, as Graham explains. 'The Fairs Cup win gave the players the confidence that what Bertie and Don were doing must be right. When you are teaching people to absorb what you are putting across and you have success with it, they think, "I like this teacher. I am going to work even more."'

For Howe, the success was nothing less than he had expected, having confidently predicted at the start of the season, 'Make no mistake. The next two years will be fantastic at Highbury.' He didn't know the half of it.

5
DOUBLE DEALER

Neither we nor anyone can imitate them. Far more practical for us is to stick to our own particular strengths. The English [managers] will again find the pressures at home too powerful for change and adventure, so that when the curtain goes up on another long season today we need not expect anything new.

***The Times* on Brazil's 1970 World Cup win**

THE SUMMER of 1970 made an indelible mark on football fans around the world, much like the impact of Hungary's visit to Wembley in the autumn of 1953 on English observers. Don Howe had witnessed both the mighty Magyars and the brilliant Brazilians, whose samba around the opposition in Mexico had won them their third World Cup. The likes of Pelé, Jairzinho, Tostao and Gerson captivated the globe with their goals and their glamour – even Pelé's near misses would go down in history. England, beaten in the quarter-finals by West Germany after surrendering a two-goal lead, were the only team to hold the eventual winners to fewer than three goals when they went down 1-0 in a memorable contest in the group stages.

It meant that as the new season began in England all the talk was of the manner of the Brazilians' success, of attacking football, of flair. Even the *Radio Times* prefaced the new season with an article headlined 'Can the ball-player come back?' Peter Marinello was one of four players interviewed, insisting that he would play his own game. Of course, how much opportunity he would get would be largely down to his coach. Howe hinted that Highbury had caught the mood of Mexico 70 when he said, 'We will be looking towards the young players to give us more flair' – which must have been music to Marinello's ears. But then Howe remembered that the football fields of England bore little resemblance to the Jalisco Stadium in Guadalajara. 'We all admired the Brazilians, but the game must be adapted to suit your conditions. There is more physical contact in our game and that hinders individual flair. Most managers will continue to do what will bring success.'

When Charlie George suffered a broken ankle in scoring in a 2-2 draw at Everton on the opening day of the new season, it allowed Marinello a return to the first team. But his opportunity to 'play his own game' lasted just one match. It was another player introduced in the second game of the season, Ray Kennedy, who would form a prolific partnership with John Radford that helped shape the greatest season Arsenal had ever experienced.

Kennedy, previously rejected by Port Vale manager Sir Stanley Matthews, was little known beyond north London when he emerged to national prominence with his goal as a substitute against Anderlecht. But even though he'd made only a couple of starts in the First Division, Howe and Bertie Mee were fully aware of his potential. Steve Burtenshaw, who coached the reserves following Howe's elevation, explains, 'Bertie and Don did what they would always do with a young player they were thinking of moving up. They asked me, "Do you think he can handle it?" I would always just give them a straight "yes" or "no" and if I said "yes" you could bet your life they would give him his chance. I was absolutely 100 per cent sure Ray had enough ability.' It also helped that 'the reserves played in the same way as the first team, and the youth team'.

The manner of the first team's attacking approach was set in stone after the Gunners' opening home game, in which Radford scored a hat-trick against Manchester United. 'Suddenly the chemistry was right,' Howe would reflect at the end of the season. 'Kennedy and Radford struck up a brilliant understanding.' They were the first goals of a combined 47 the duo netted in all competitions that season, Kennedy overcoming a mid-season dip in form after an aborted attempt to shed some pounds. Allowed to return to his fighting weight of 13 stone-plus, Kennedy explained, 'The club put me on a strict diet to try to quicken me up. I lost half a stone and felt as weak as a kitten. So Don Howe ordered me to start eating again. The result has been that I am much happier with my game. I need that weight in the penalty box.'

Whether the success of the Radford-Kennedy combination was enabled by Arsenal's direct style of play, or whether it was their happy union that encouraged Howe to pursue such methods, is a chicken-and-egg question that is hard to answer definitively. Either way, the method proved effective enough for Arsenal to score 20 League goals more than they had managed the season before. The final League table would mean that every single one of them counted.

And the system was a lot more sophisticated than mere hit-and-hope. 'We used to come back and work in the afternoons, it wasn't just off the cuff,' says Radford. 'Don Howe would come and do a lot of work with us, showing us the kind of movement he wanted. It was all in-and-outs – one player going for the ball and the other making a run in behind him. We also did a lot of coming towards the ball and spinning off. We used to work endless hours at that. At the time, teams weren't playing with sweepers. We used to try to draw defenders in and then spin off them and play balls over the top. People used to say we were just knocking balls over the top but it wasn't like that.

'There were lots of different ways of doing it, it was not just straight balls. You could play different angles or have one man going for the ball and another spinning away – me blocking Ray's defender, him blocking mine, to get people away and to get a yard of space. We did a lot of near-post ball work, where the first one is spinning off and getting in the way of the centre-half as the other is coming past. We scored a lot of goals at the near post.'

Goalkeeper Bob Wilson used to marvel at what he saw on the training ground. 'Don Howe did things in such a simple way,' he says. 'He would put things on the board and you would say, "Christ, I see what you mean." Things like playing into space, the value of getting in behind defences. He was a really good teacher with a teaching plan.'

Bob McNab claims, 'If people could have made videos of [Radford and Kennedy] playing up front in practices with Don Howe, they would be used as coaching videos. You couldn't believe what they did. It was a nightmare when Don used to go two-on-two and change defenders every few minutes. They were both so big and quick. It was mesmerising. They would dummy it, flick it through and sidefoot it in the goal. You couldn't defend it. I'll never forget a session after they signed Jeff Blockley a couple of seasons after the Double. They never failed to score. Fifteen goals in fifteen attempts. We were killing ourselves laughing.'

Meanwhile, Howe was not just an architect, drawing up schemes from a distance. His method of coaching was to be in the faces of his players when he felt it was needed. 'Don was an excellent coach,' says Eddie Kelly. 'He was always one for a good kick up the arse, but he was someone you could talk to. Don's knowledge of the game was superb and he could talk to you. He had been at the top. The whole system was top notch.'

Wilson felt that Howe's great strength was not just an ability to read the game, but to 'read it through the eyes of every player on the field. You could stand eye-to-eye and argue with him and there would be spit flying everywhere, but we always had great respect for him.'

Peter Simpson, a quiet man who could often lack confidence, says, 'Don would scream and shout if you weren't doing what he wanted. I always thought I responded to the likes of Dave Sexton more than Don because I didn't like people shouting at me. But, there again, I needed a gee-up sometimes.'

There were few days in Howe's tenure as Arsenal coach that angered him more than a 5-0 defeat at Stoke City in late September. In midweek, Arsenal had completed a physically and emotionally draining Fairs Cup tie against Lazio, winning 2-0 at Highbury after a 2-2 draw in Rome a week earlier had been followed by the infamous street fight between the players at the post-game banquet. Mee and Howe had decided to give their men an additional night in their own beds by travelling to Stoke on the morning of the game and had given no extensive team talk.

Aware that they might have contributed to the team's struggles on that day, Mee and Howe excused their men an extensive inquest, leaving them to work out for themselves what had gone wrong. Kelly recalls, 'I think Bertie and Don felt we might be fed up with listening to them and thought it would be better for the lads to have a chance to say how they felt. Frank McLintock led the meeting and he insulted a few of us. One or two had a go back. It was a vicious meeting but it was really good, much better than if thc manager or coach had taken it.'

Howe recalled three decades later, 'We used to have regular team meetings if things were not right. We had a little room half-way down the tunnel at Highbury, on the way out to the pitch. We used to have real up and downers in there. We'd had a real beating but the players responded the right way. It really was a slating match but it was a man's way of dealing with it.'

And, according to McLintock, Howe was the more approachable part of the management duo when players had issues to get off their chests. 'For all his intensity and dedication, [Don] wasn't as one-dimensional as the boss. Don knew how to be a sounding board for all our gripes and could help to rationalise disputes when our hotheadedness threatened to find a target in the person of our manager.'

The response to events at Stoke was a run of 14 unbeaten League games, during which Arsenal kept nine clean sheets. After they lost consecutive games against Huddersfield and Liverpool, George was fit to return to the starting line-up in a home win against Manchester City and would inject his own kind of magic into many of the most important games in the latter weeks of the season.

Prodigiously gifted in both feet, George was self-assured to the point of cockiness. When Wilson, playing for Arsenal as an amateur, had taught him PE at Holloway School he was regularly greeted by his pupil with, 'How you doin', Bob?' It was that streak of independence, which turned to rebelliousness as his career advanced, that meant it was down to Howe to form a connection with George. 'Charlie didn't have much respect for Bertie because football-wise he was limited,' Simpson explains. 'He respected Don and he got the best out of Charlie. Bertie was a disciplinarian and Charlie is not the sort of person who takes to that very easily.'

Howe said, 'I don't know what it was between Charlie and Bertie, I never got caught up in any of that. But Bertie was the boss, the disciplinarian, and that is never easy. He never flinched from his responsibility. One or two would have a moan back but most of the players respected it.'

After George's two-goal performance at a muddy Maine Road beat Manchester City again to put Arsenal into the quarter-finals of the FA Cup, Mee decided to make a dressing room speech that has lived in the memory of his players. 'Bertie and Don sat everybody down and I could see that Bertie was getting quite shaky about the whole thing,' is Wilson's recollection. Although Leeds still held a sizeable lead in the table, Mee told his men they had a 'chance here to put your names into the history book for always' but that they had to 'make football the priority of your life, at the expense of your family, your wife and everything else'.

The defence of the Fairs Cup was soon eliminated from Arsenal's calendar with defeat to FC Cologne, a tie that effectively ended the Gunners career of Sammels. Taking more abuse from the Highbury crowd than ever, he admits, 'I was in a terrible mental state. I was awful. I remember Don Howe saying to me at half-time, "Come on, it's not your night." I was substituted and I could understand it.'

A George header beat Leicester City in the quarter-finals of the FA Cup, meaning Arsenal faced Stoke City at Hillsborough in the last four. They fell behind 2-0 in the first half via a lucky ricochet off centre-half

Denis Smith and a blunder by George, whose ill-judged backpass set up John Ritchie. According to Wilson, the half-time break 'illustrated the brilliance of Don Howe as a coach and Frank McLintock as a captain'. They were, he said, 'wild men, urging, cajoling, bullying … they demanded inspiration from a team on its knees'.

Sure enough, Storey volleyed the Gunners back into the game early in the second half before Jimmy Greenhoff missed an opportunity to give Stoke an unassailable lead. Even so, Arsenal were still losing when they were awarded a disputed corner inside injury time. McLintock's header from Armstrong's delivery was palmed away at the post by Wales midfielder John Mahoney. England goalkeeper Gordon Banks, still angry that the corner had been awarded after he felt he had been fouled, put his weight on to his right foot as Storey rolled the penalty to his left to keep alive Arsenal's hopes of the Double. Graham and Kennedy duly scored in a 2-0 replay victory at Villa Park.

In the meantime, Leeds had been faltering, seeing a seven-point lead gradually eroded. On 17 April, George half-volleyed a goal in front of the North Bank that beat Newcastle United. Coupled with dramatic events at Elland Road it sent Arsenal to the top of the table. Having won only two of their previous six matches, Leeds were a goal down against West Bromwich Albion when referee Ray Tinkler ruled that Albion midfielder Colin Suggett, clearly in an offside position, had not been interfering with play when Tony Brown broke past him into the home team's half to lay on a goal for Jeff Astle. The Leeds players screamed at the official; fans advanced on to the pitch to join the protest; BBC commentator Barry Davies declared that Leeds 'have every right to go mad'; and manager Don Revie ended up trudging back to the dugout with a rueful look to unforgiving gods. Leeds lost 2-1 and Elland Road would be closed by the FA for the start of the following season.

Howe was in the mood for some fighting talk. 'For eight months we have been chasing them, but now they have to catch us. We must be favourites, but we will not be celebrating any championships tonight. To be sure of the title we need seven points from our five remaining games. Six would probably be enough, but we can't let up.'

One of those games was against Leeds. Their Highbury contest back in September had seen referee Iorwerth Jones requiring a police escort after a 0-0 draw in which Kelly had been sent off for exacting retribution on Billy Bremner. And the game at Elland Road on the final Monday of April was even more contentious. Victory would have given Arsenal their first League Championship for 18 years, with two games still to play, and even a draw would make it a near formality. Yet Jack Charlton was ruled onside as he scored the Leeds winner in injury time, after Bremner's cross precipitated a series of blocks and scrambles. Wilson and McLintock confronted referee Norman Burtenshaw and George hoofed the ball into the stand, causing Mee to instruct his players to calm down. As Arsenal's bus pulled away from the stadium, a sheepish McNab confessed that he may have played Charlton onside.

While Leeds were beating Nottingham Forest on the final Saturday of the season, Kelly was sent on as a second-half substitute for the injured Storey and scored the only goal at Highbury against Stoke. That the Scot was playing an important part in the denouement was partly down to Howe's intervention earlier in the season. 'I wasn't in the team and I was getting the hump. I wasn't training properly. Don asked to see me in the boot-room. I didn't know what it was about and he proceeded to give me the biggest bollocking I have ever had. He said, "Eddie, you are a fucking disgrace. Look at the state of you. You are 20 years old and you are walking around being miserable because you are not in the side." I said that it was the way I felt. I thought I was good enough to be in the team. He said, "You are one of the best players we have here, but your attitude is one of the worst and until you get that sorted out you will be in the reserves."

'He almost got me by the throat. He said, "Peter Storey is not as good as you as a football player but as a competitor and in terms of attitude he is 100 per cent better. That's the way our team works. It is up to you to get yourself in the team and make sure you are not the one left out." I was a bad trainer. I knew my attitude was crap. I was strolling about and Don said I was not giving them a chance to put me back in the team because I was just sulking.'

Storey's misfortune meant a place for Kelly in a finale to the League season that no scriptwriter would have dared suggest. A point behind Leeds, who had finished their fixtures, Arsenal went to White Hart Lane on a Monday night knowing that a draw against Tottenham would leave the contenders locked together on 64 points. If it was 0-0, Arsenal would maintain their superior goal average; yet any scoring draw would give Leeds the edge. Third in the table, Spurs would be determined to hang on to their status as the only team in the 20th century to do the Double, having won the League and FA Cup ten seasons previously.

Howe felt confident that he had seen something in Tottenham's play to be exploited. 'If there is one thing I can always remember about matches it is the tactics,' he told me in 2001. 'We knew Bill Nicholson liked a bit of man-to-man marking, with a touch of zonal. He liked his centre-halves to mark the centre-forwards wherever they went. So we told John Radford, "Play wide on the left or right and [Peter] Collins, the centre-back, will come out with you." John pulled him all over the place.'

Having already achieved 24 clean sheets during the season, the question of whether Arsenal should settle for a 0-0 draw or go for victory was not one that Howe sought to address. 'Nobody ever knows how many goals you will score. You send your team out with tactical ideas and motivation. Sometimes you score three and sometimes you can't score at all, which is when, as a coach, you have to change things around. You just try to get the team right, every individual player right and the shape right – and then you send them out. From there it might surprise you.'

Howe had little chance for a last-minute tactical talk after the thousands of fans locked outside White Hart Lane made it impossible for the Arsenal team bus to reach its destination, forcing the players to turn up on foot only half an hour before kick-off. The 51,992 inside the ground were the only ones able to follow events as they happened; this being an age before live television coverage and a time when even live radio commentary of League games was restricted to the weekends.

Nor were there highlights later in the evening, coverage being limited to clips on the television news and score updates on local radio.

A combative game was still goalless with four minutes to play, the better chances having fallen to the home team. Then Spurs full-back Cyril Knowles came under pressure and George was able to get in a cross that was cleared to the Arsenal left wing. Armstrong gained control and delivered the ball perfectly to Kennedy, whose header from ten yards out squeezed underneath the crossbar. Arsenal were ahead but had riled their opponents into a counter-attack that threatened to rob them of the title. Referee Kevin Howley allowed an additional four minutes for stoppages, leaving Wilson to recall, 'For the eight minutes after the goal, all hell broke loose. They came piling back and the atmosphere was extraordinary.'

When the whistle went it was like Highbury a year earlier, the fans engulfing their players. 'Doing it at Tottenham was incredible,' says McLintock. 'That night in the Fairs Cup at Highbury and winning the Championship at Tottenham were the two greatest nights of my life. The Championship was the hardest thing of all to win. The emotion that night and the feeling I got were everything I had always dreamed of.'

Howe was insistent that the players should let their hair down while the FA Cup Final against Liverpool was still five days away. 'Don said that, as we had won the most important thing, it was all right to have a drink,' remembers Graham, who headed with team-mates to the White Hart pub in Southgate. 'We had a right few that night.'

After a day off to nurse aching heads and limbs, Arsenal, now eight-time champions of England, were back in training on Wednesday. Howe was on hand when a meeting about ticket allocations threatened to turn ugly, as Storey recalls. 'Bertie came in and said, "You will be sitting with us," pointing at me. Don said to him, "You can't say that, he might be fit." It wasn't until the Friday the ankle suddenly felt better and I had a fitness test.'

Howe had been forced to intervene between Mee and Storey a few weeks earlier when the player earned an England call-up to face Greece in a European Championship qualifier the night after Arsenal were due to face Burnley. Mee asked Storey and McNab, also called up, to withdraw from Sir Alf Ramsey's squad. 'You can't ask them to drop out of the England side,' Howe interrupted.

'If Don hadn't spoken up, I might have had to pull out and I don't think I would ever have got picked again,' says Storey, who went on to win 19 caps.

Howe might not have been afraid of standing up to and contradicting Mee when he felt it was merited, but he was always keen to emphasise his respect for his boss's understanding of the sport. 'A lot of what's said about him is unfair,' he said. 'People didn't give him enough credit for his football knowledge. There was never a time when he couldn't join in and make points to players. His football intelligence was very high. His strength was that he let people get on with their jobs, but we knew we couldn't get away with anything by saying something and thinking that Bertie wouldn't understand. A lot of managers would have been too proud to bring in people like Dave Sexton and [future coach] Bobby Campbell and me. He had no ego.'

Mee's expertise and eye for detail gave Arsenal an edge at Wembley. It might not have been as important as Liverpool's Emlyn Hughes would contend in future years, but the thin air-tex yellow shirts that Mee dressed his team in were a lot more appropriate than the long-sleeved thick cotton red jerseys that absorbed the early May sunshine and made life uncomfortable for their opponents. What with the lush green grass, it was all a far cry from Arsenal's previous Wembley occasion two years earlier. This time Howe didn't make a plea for abandonment when the game went into extra time, even though an additional half hour in their 64th match of the season would offer one final test of the Gunners' resolve. And when winger Steve Heighway's shot from the left wing beat Wilson at the near post after two minutes, it looked as though it might be one game too far.

Kelly had replaced Storey in the second half, with Howe telling him, 'Eddie, you could win this game for us if you start going at them through the middle of the park, attacking their centre-backs.' With four minutes left in the first period of extra time, Radford hooked the ball into the penalty area and Kelly swung his right leg at the ball. Graham also flicked out as it trundled past Liverpool goalkeeper Ray Clemence and it would need the next day's highlights on *The Big Match* to prove that the goal belonged to Kelly. Having moved elegantly around Wembley, Graham would have to settle for his man-of-the-match award.

After the teams changed ends, Arsenal found their hero in the shape of their former North Bank boy. George had been having a quiet afternoon until receiving a square ball from Radford and teeing up a shot that screamed past Clemence's right hand from 20 yards. 'A lot of people were tired,' he says, 'but I could always hit the ball from anywhere. I may have been the only one capable of scoring a goal like that.' George celebrated his Double-winning goal by lying on his back, arms outstretched; an enduring image to cap an historic season.

Looking back on the 1970/71 season, Mee put his team's achievements down to '100 per cent efficiency and endeavour' and argued that 'our greatest qualities are confidence and character'. Howe echoed that assessment. 'The features of the Arsenal players which I believe made them nearly invincible last season were their character and their spirit,' he said, pointing to 'the way they picked themselves up after a shock defeat'. They were apposite citations after the last four League victories of a triumphant campaign had all been '1-0 to the Arsenal', as fans would sing in future years.

As unapologetic as Howe was about the methods of his team, the inference from some of his post-season comments was that he was sensitive to criticism. He sounded not unlike Don Revie unleashing his team after their first title in 1968/69 when he said, 'Winning titles apart, the next thing I want for Arsenal is to mould them into an entertaining side as well as a successful one. Don't get me wrong, I think a manager and coach's first duty is success. That is what matters most. You must be successful for your own sake and your family's – and your supporters. They demand success. But I am aware that Arsenal don't always play entertaining football to watch as far as the committed are concerned. But with the confidence of the Double behind them I think Arsenal will develop along those lines.'

Howe also appeared to be relishing the opportunity of chasing the biggest prize in club football, describing the League as 'the first hurdle along football's glory road', and adding, 'The second hurdle is the European Cup.' There was certainly no suggestion that Howe would not be responsible for planning that particular challenge. And when Mee stated that 'it has been my job to create the [team's] elusive qualities by the organisation of the staff' it was clear that his decision to make Howe part of that group had been inspired.

'When Don was 28 he was like 35,' says McLintock, the man who lifted the Cup at Wembley and then fell asleep on the steps of Islington Town Hall during the following day's celebrations through sheer exhaustion. 'He was that kind of father figure. I love him, have great respect for him. He won us over, made us such an efficient team. We could play against anyone and they would be huffing and puffing and we never felt we were in any danger.'

There is no bigger admirer among the Double winners than McNab, who used to go to games with Howe. 'I loved being with Don,' he says. 'I wasn't afraid of people thinking I was creeping; I was just very comfortable with him. I liked to sit and talk to him about the game. George Graham's practices when he was manager at Arsenal? Don's practices. There is no great mystery to it all.'

No mystery maybe, but a certain level of dependency. Just how much Arsenal owed to Howe's influence might have been impossible to quantify fully, but McLintock was in no doubt. 'The old line that a good team depends solely on the quality of the players at a manager's disposal is still trotted out regularly. But our team's decline disproved that; without Don Howe at Arsenal we were no longer able to replicate the intensity that had led to our dominance.' He concluded, 'When it came to coaching [Bertie] had relied so strongly on Don, his right-hand man, that without his influence things inevitably started to deteriorate.'

Or, as Joni Mitchell had been singing when Arsenal had won their first trophy for 17 years, 'Don't it always seem to go; that you don't know what you got 'til it's gone?'

6

MAN AT THE TOP

Howe is a self-confessed man of ambition. And ambitious men don't like living in the shadows.

***Daily Mirror*, 23 June 1971**

DON HOWE was going nowhere. 'The decision is made,' he announced in a column for the *Daily Mirror*. 'My future lies at Highbury.' Arsenal fans and players breathed a sigh of relief. Club captain Frank McLintock had said, 'It will be an absolute choker for us if Don leaves.'

Events at Old Trafford had made Howe the focus of football conversation, one of the few stories to turn sporting attention away from the British Lions' bid to win a series in New Zealand for the first time and the efforts of the England bowlers to contain the broad bat of Pakistan's Zaheer Abbas. This was an age when football, unless there was a World Cup going on, really did fade from consciousness during the summer. Mentioned briefly as a potential Manchester United manager after Sir Matt Busby stepped aside for the second time, Howe began to generate headlines when Leicester City manager Frank O'Farrell was given the task of succeeding the great man, a task that had already proved beyond Wilf McGuinness.

Having been guided back to the First Division by the genial Irishman, Leicester now found themselves without a manager for the new campaign. Howe returned from a day at Royal Ascot to find that chairman Len Shipman had called his Arsenal counterpart, Denis Hill-Wood, and been granted permission to discuss the position with him. 'What else could I say?' said Hill-Wood. 'I hope Don doesn't leave us, but we couldn't possibly attempt to stop him speaking to Leicester.'

After a week of speculation, during which Howe said he was 'flattered and touched' by the reaction of the Arsenal players, the *Daily Mirror*, which, fortuitously, had signed up Howe for a series of articles on Arsenal's achievements of the previous season, was able to splash the headline, 'Why I'll stay at Arsenal'. While their own writer, Ron Wills, warned Gunners fans that Howe remained ambitious for management, Howe appeared to be thinking only of a new campaign at Highbury. 'I think the Double is on next season,' he said. 'Arsenal could do it. So could Leeds. So could Chelsea, Everton, Spurs, Liverpool. I think it will become much more commonplace in the future.' While showing some prescience in highlighting the competitive nature of the season to come – and the greater frequency of teams winning League and Cup in the same year[5] – Howe did not foresee his own role in the coming campaign. Admitting that he would have missed the players he had coached to the pinnacle of the English game if he'd departed Highbury, he said, 'My efforts are now 100 per cent on what I can help Arsenal achieve in the 1971/72 season.'

Hill-Wood denied that Howe was to be rewarded with the title of manager, with Bertie Mee becoming general manager. Interestingly, that was exactly the move that Manchester City would make a few weeks later in an apparent effort to accommodate the ambition of Malcolm Allison, the one man who could rival Howe's coaching reputation in the English game. Like Howe, Allison had guided his club to success in the League and in cup competitions at home and in Europe – all while working under manager Joe Mercer – but now felt that his boss was welching on an agreement to move aside. Meanwhile,

---

5 One point would separate the top four teams as Brian Clough's Derby County won an exciting First Division title race, with Leeds denied the Double when they lost at Wolverhampton Wanderers on a dramatic final night two days after beating Arsenal in the FA Cup Final.

Hill-Wood declared, 'Titles mean little to me at Highbury. As chief coach and assistant manager, Don runs the tactical side. Bertie and Don turned out to be one of the greatest partnerships in football and what they call themselves is their business.'

Yet Fred Street, a former NHS physiotherapy colleague of Mee who was about to arrive at Highbury from his first football job at Stoke City, suggests, 'At that time, Bertie was God at Highbury after winning the Double and he had the sort of personality and ego that did not need too much encouragement before going a little over the top in his demands. It probably contributed to the departure of Don. He ruled with a mix of military discipline, fear and pompous lower-middle-class high-ground morality. He conveyed it all with an articulate tongue that could bamboozle a lot of backroom staff who were grateful for the job and in fear of the sack.'

When West Bromwich Albion decided to part company with Alan Ashman, three years after he led them to the FA Cup, it made available a job that would prove irresistible to Hawthorns old boy Howe. Even though Albion had boasted the First Division's top scorer for the past two seasons in Jeff Astle (25 goals in 1969/70) and Tony Brown (28 in 1970/71), finishes of 16th and 17th place meant the end of Ashman, who was away on holiday when the story leaked out. Howe was also enjoying the Majorcan sun with his family when he emerged as the leading candidate for a job, reportedly worth £9,000 a year. The timing and nature of what Howe had said to Arsenal before heading to the holiday village of Santa Ponsa would be a bone of contention and cast a cloud over the end of his first period at Highbury.

Hill-Wood initially told reporters, 'Don and I had a long talk, with me trying to convince him how valuable he is at Highbury. Possibly it was too late. It looks as if his mind was made up before he went on holiday.' Howe, who had worked without a contract at Arsenal even though he had been offered one a year earlier, was tracked down at the swimming pool and was suitably cagey. 'If Arsenal or West Bromwich make an official statement then I might have something to say. At the moment I must keep silent.' Which was as good as confirming the story. 'Someone has spoken when it would have been better if they had not,' he added. Arsenal went on record to say it wasn't them. It was all getting a bit messy; a situation that got worse when stories emerged that Howe would take trainer George Wright and youth-team coach Brian Whitehouse with him to The Hawthorns. Mee stated, 'I would be very annoyed if they took George as well. That could lead to a row.'

Hill-Wood weighed in by saying that Howe would be 'very foolish to take the job', adding, 'I think he'd be crazy to go there.' He also said that his coach had 'a lot of explaining to do about why he hasn't contacted us'. When Howe's resignation was confirmed, he felt compelled to defend himself. 'I believe that I have acted honestly and openly with Arsenal … I did everything I could to keep them in the picture. I tried several times before I left for my holiday to contact the chairman, but without success.'

A day later, on Friday, 9 July, Howe was introduced as Albion's manager, expanding further on the apparent breakdown in communications with Arsenal and suggesting that an inability to get Hill-Wood to meet him before he went on holiday implied indifference on his employers' part about his future. 'The more I thought about it the more I knew I was doing the right thing. Albion could give me the chance to be my own man.'

Arsenal secretary Bob Wall appeared to have drawn a line under the affair by stating, 'It has all ended amicably. We wish him well.' But the 'he said, she said' narrative had not yet been exhausted. A couple of days later, Hill-Wood announced, 'The whole thing is disgraceful. How could he remain as our assistant manager without letting us know he was leaving? Then he induces two other members of the staff to go with him. It has made me furious. If he thinks this is blackening his character then he is right.'

Howe was not going to let that go without a response. 'I can't stand aside and let this man pull me to pieces without presenting my side of the affair,' he hit back. 'In the first place I did not induce Brian and George to join me. When they learnt I was leaving they both came to me and asked if I wanted them. The chairman knew about Albion's interest and yet again I couldn't get anyone to show me any interest. In the end I was forced to take the initiative. I reached the point where I felt that Arsenal wanted me out of the way.' Howe said he shared his intentions with Wall before leaving for Majorca, and added, 'I asked to see the chairman on my return. Once again the chairman was unavailable. Always unavailable.'

The unseemly row over his exit was unworthy of Howe's achievements and the club's status as Double champions. It certainly made it unthinkable that he would be welcomed back at Highbury a few years later to further cement his place in the history of the club. Three decades later, Howe told me he had not discussed his departure from the club with Mee, nor did he ever hear from him in the aftermath of his appointment as Albion manager. 'I really don't know what Bertie's reaction was because we never talked about it,' he said. 'I had a chance to go back to my old club as manager and I went. Bertie didn't ring me up to talk about it and I didn't call him.'

The lack of communication undermined Mee's subsequent public insistence that, 'I will miss him from a personal friendship point of view,' but is in keeping with Howe's comment that 'Bertie used to accept things, so I am sure he just got on with things without me'. He continued, 'Bertie and I had a good working relationship, but he was a bloke that I worked with; he wasn't a bloke I went out to dinner with. I have always been grateful for him giving me the chance to work with Arsenal and giving me the chance as first-team coach. But this was a great opportunity for me.'

Albion's recruitment of Wright and Whitehouse had Hill-Wood spluttering that 'loyalty is a dirty word these days'. But Howe had made clear his admiration for the work of Wright, his new assistant manager, in discussing Arsenal's recent success. 'There were times when I went home on a Saturday night worried that a player would not be fit for a midweek game. But George worked wonders. He was often on duty for eight hours on a Sunday.'

Wright recalled that his decision 'didn't go down well' with Mee, a man with whom he had once shared a house as they pursued their careers in physiotherapy. 'But,' he continued, 'I was going to get promotion and an increase in salary. Bertie offered me the same money to stay but I told him I was going because I was getting promotion. He said, "Don't be ridiculous. It is only West Brom." I don't think he ever forgave me. We met on other occasions, but there was a bit of coldness there. We never swapped Christmas cards.'

* * *

Highbury was behind Howe – for now, anyway – and he was back where it had all begun more than 20 years earlier. 'Albion have always been a part of me,' he said as he took charge, saying that the job offer had 'changed things overnight' for him. 'They taught me the game so maybe it's right that I try to give something back. Albion have tremendous potential. If I can get the same spirit going there as at Highbury there is no reason why we shouldn't do well. I want to make Albion the biggest and best club in the country.'

In an interview with *Shoot!* magazine, Howe acknowledged the hard work ahead. 'I must concentrate on the team, six days a week at least. I'll spend Sundays at home with my family in Wolverhampton but any manager knows that Sundays can quickly erupt into chaos if his team have been involved in a "happening" the day before. I wouldn't be a manager if I couldn't give it my all.'

And in the rival *Goal*, he reiterated his motivation for taking the job. 'At Highbury I had got to a level where I could progress no further,' he said. 'If you stay as a number two you never know if you are good enough to make it on your own. I'm now in a position to extend my own ideas.'

Centre-back John Wile, one of Ashman's last signings when he joined Albion from Peterborough United and destined to become a long-serving skipper of the club, remembers, 'There was a certain amount of surprise because we didn't expect Alan to be leaving, even though the team weren't doing fantastically. I was sorry for Alan because I thought he was a lovely fellow, but I was absolutely delighted because Don at that time was given a huge amount of credit for what

Arsenal had achieved and to get him at the Albion was fantastic. We would be working with a coach who had shown he was the tops.'

There was an opportunity for Howe to win a trophy before the League season even began. The Watney Cup had been introduced in the summer of 1970; an eight-team event featuring the two highest-scoring teams in each division not to have won promotion or qualified for Europe. On the wave of post-World Cup excitement, the first tournament attracted big crowds and had seen Derby County pound Manchester United 4-1 in the final. This time, United had gone out in the first round to Third Division Halifax Town, who hosted Albion at The Shay in the semi-final. Albion won 2-0 with goals by Colin Suggett, but they caused raised eyebrows by having three players booked – a high number for the era. 'The new, get-tough philosophy of new manager Don Howe angered the Halifax crowd,' the *Birmingham Post* recorded.

Colchester United, the Fourth Division side who had shocked Leeds United in the previous season's FA Cup, were Albion's opponents in the final in front of 19,009 at The Hawthorns. A remarkable match saw the home team 3-2 up at half-time, only to fall behind 4-3. Jeff Astle scored a last-minute equaliser and disappeared among the fans behind the goal in an explosion of excitement that said much about the status of the tournament in its first couple of seasons. 'He and everybody else in this town will believe in fairies,' said BBC commentator Barry Davies over the din. Yet it was Colchester who had the happy ending when Ray Wilson and Len Cantello missed during the penalty shoot-out. The match was exactly what had been envisaged when an experimental law was introduced whereby players could only be offside if inside or level with the penalty area. It offered West Brom's fans little indication of the frustratingly dour months that lay ahead and, according to the local paper, was a warning for Howe of the 'magnitude of the task' he had taken on.

All seemed well when Albion won 1-0 at West Ham United to kick off the League season, a performance in which, one report said, 'West Ham had to trace a difficult path through a midfield filled with hard-working forwards, chasing back and jostling for position. Albion made themselves hard to beat.' Then Everton were overcome 2-0 at The Hawthorns, with Brown scoring his second goal in two games. In the *Sports Argus*, Tom Duckworth – a cheerleader from Howe's playing days – wrote, 'It is a long time since I have seen an Albion side so well organised, particularly in defence.'

Wile explains, 'There was an immediate change from the type of coaching and training we had been doing with Alan. There is no question I became a better player. There was much more individual coaching and work on how the team was set up for you to do your job properly, in terms of positional play and integrating with other players. The training regime had been a little bit old- fashioned. You warmed up and Jeff Astle would come out with a bag of balls over his shoulder and say, "Right, old 'uns versus young 'uns." Suddenly there was a lot more emphasis on physical training and becoming fitter and running and weights and gym work. And there was afternoon work, which we had never been used to.' Significantly, he adds, 'This approach wasn't popular with everyone.'

The first midweek fixtures of the season had been notable in that they marked the launch of what the media quickly called the 'Refs' Revolution', a zero-tolerance policy on tackles from behind and less violent crimes such as dissent and deliberate handballs. Players and managers were soon complaining that the tough streak that characterised the English game was under threat and asking why they had not been given prior warning of the Football League's intentions. Amid the bickering that went on for the first few months of the season, a George Best-inspired Manchester United stormed to the top of the table, while the skills of some of the sport's more esoteric performers – men such as Alan Hudson and Peter Osgood, Tony Currie and Rodney Marsh – had more space in which to flourish.

At Albion, Howe had no inclination to attempt anything too exotic. It might be overstating things to claim that his team was unsuited to the style of football that the League bosses were trying to promote, but the fact is that Albion failed to win any of their next nine games.

Defensively they were still solid, but they scored only six goals in their first 11 matches – Brown's five and one by Wile. Astle had missed games because of appendicitis and after he returned he was quickly dropped, claiming that Howe had told him he was 'not trying hard enough'.

Astle would feature only sporadically over the next few seasons because of chronic knee problems. 'He never really got fit enough,' Howe would recall. 'He would have been ideal for me because I wanted to get the ball into the forwards early and then play around them.'

Wile adds, 'Jeff was a big player in every sense and to lose someone of his ability was a huge blow. Jeff always offered a get-out ball and he contributed his own goal tally. When Jeff wasn't there it affected Tony [Brown] particularly because he got a lot of his goals linking up with Jeff.'

Howe sought a solution by signing a player he had previously discarded at Arsenal. Bobby Gould, who had scored 24 goals in all competitions in his season at Wolverhampton Wanderers, was surprised to find Howe offering to spend £66,666 to take him to The Hawthorns. 'I drove there and I looked at Don and said, "Why me?" He said, "Because you are brilliant in the dressing room. It's a strange dressing room here." When I asked about the football he said, "Oh, that will be all right."' Gould was initially viewed as Howe's spy, but insisted that he never passed any dressing room information back to his manager.

'The players were struggling to adapt to Don following the more carefree style of Ashman,' he recalls. 'The lads were being driven much harder in training and it's fair to say there was a bit of a dressing room backlash. You couldn't meet a nicer guy than [goalkeeper] John Osborne and even he was riled enough to moan, "He has only gone and stopped our table tennis in the afternoons." Another day the Spring Road training ground was waterlogged and we thought we'd be sent home early but Don built fences on the track by laying brooms over two spread-out buckets and had us racing round and jumping them like horses.'

Gould's memory is supported by Wile, who says, 'Players at the latter end of their careers had probably trained in a certain way for years so it was difficult for them to adapt to the way Don wanted us to work. It meant there was a big turnover and some experienced players were moved on.'

Club captain John Kaye was bought by Howe's old Arsenal buddy Terry Neill at Hull City, while goalkeeper Jim Cumbes went to Aston Villa. Howe's former Albion team-mate and FA Cup-winning captain Graham Williams also discovered that he did not fit into the club's plans, having joined former manager Ashman on the coaching staff. 'I was assistant manager for a day,' recalls Williams, who would leave to become player-manager at Southern League Weymouth. 'I was in the office and the telephone rang and the secretary said that Don Howe was our new manager. Don kept me on but said the players were still using me as club captain and that was making life difficult for him. They were coming to me and telling me about their problems. Don wasn't sociable because he wanted to change the system and there was no real enjoyment. If players were laughing or joking in the dressing room, Don didn't like that and he stopped it.

'Don asked me if I would play again because we were having problems in the full-back position. He said, "The only way we're going to keep you is if you come back and play." I couldn't come back. It would have been difficult to get fit enough. He sacked me, and he cried. He rang me when he got home and apologised to me and my wife Heather.'

The most eye-catching transfer news came when 21-year-old midfielder Asa Hartford was sold to Leeds United for £177,000. 'I've admired him for two years,' Leeds manager Don Revie told a press conference staged when Hartford arrived in Yorkshire. Summoned to his pre-transfer medical examination, Hartford told the Leeds club doctors that he had been diagnosed with a heart murmur as a child but it had never impeded him. The doctors carried out an electro-cardiograph test before sending him to specialists, who discovered a tiny hole in the heart. The deal was off; perhaps his career was over. After reporting back to The Hawthorns, Hartford was told by Howe, 'I'll make you the best coach in the country. It's not the end, son.'

Indeed it wasn't. At Birmingham's Queen Elizabeth Hospital, heart specialist Dr Paul Davison confirmed that although Hartford did have a hole the size of a pinhead in the upper part of his heart he could continue playing. 'Everyone at the club agrees that Asa Hartford stays an Albion player from now on,' Howe declared. 'The deal with Leeds was an exceptional one. It was a huge fee and we decided to take a chance.' He dismissed suggestions that the club would be unable to sell their 'damaged goods' even if they wanted to. 'There could be doubt in some other clubs' minds now, but this has not influenced our decision. We have seen him train after what must have been a very worrying weekend for him and he has shown no ill-effects either physically or mentally. He was always in front, as always, and everyone could see how fit he was. No one works harder in training or playing.'

Hartford returned to the Albion team to face Nottingham Forest, having been selected for Tommy Docherty's Scotland squad, and found himself being told off by Howe at half-time for trying too hard to impress. 'He had a go back at me and I know he was the old Asa because he doesn't take a telling off easily,' Howe said after the match. The 4-1 defeat was the second in a run of seven consecutive losses that saw West Brom reach Christmas at the bottom of the First Division.

Meanwhile, the difference in being a manager as opposed to coach was becoming obvious to Howe. 'You are concerned with so many jobs that it is difficult to spend as much time as you would like on the training pitch with players,' he explained. Wile believes that Howe 'needed a hand on his shoulder', while Gould noticed a stark change in the man he had known at Arsenal. 'He was like a ghost,' he remembers. 'This wasn't the Don Howe I knew. It was his first management job and there was the pressure of going back to your home club and the players didn't know Don the way I did. Now he was having to do the whole shebang, which wasn't him. He was a coach.'

More than 43,000 were at The Hawthorns on 27 December when Brown scored a fifth-minute goal against Liverpool. It produced an important victory that Howe hoped 'could be the turning point'. He had been wrong about a lot in his first few months at Albion, but this time it was an accurate prediction.

Albion's form improved enough to win eight and draw three of their next 16 games, securing their place in the top flight. Along the way, Howe was named as the First Division's manager of the month for February. At the end of the season, Albion occupied 16th place and Howe reflected, 'The players' character really showed through. The defeat of Liverpool gave the lads confidence and they really began to believe in themselves. Up to Christmas, every player who was worth a first-team chance got one. After that, and having assessed their abilities in match play, it was a question of slotting them into the right positions.'

One such player was Gordon Nisbet, a former goalkeeper who had played in seven different jerseys for Albion before being given the right-back position just before Christmas. Within weeks he had been selected for the England Under-23s. 'We played a pre-season friendly at Stafford Rangers and I played up front with Jeff and banged a couple of goals in,' he explains. 'All the lads were saying I was going to get in the first team. But Don said, "You will never be a centre-forward. I see you as a right-back. I will work with you." He worked with me in the afternoons, and I got into the first team. I think he thought of me as being a bit like himself; I was quick and had some pace.' Having played more than 600 senior games for Albion, Hull City and Plymouth Argyle, Nisbet concludes, 'I put my career down to him.'

Howe's verdict on the first season in his new job was, 'I think Albion have a great future. It may take us four years. The whole club has been reorganised, including training, travelling and coaching methods. When I first came here Albion were regarded as an easy touch away from home. Nobody can say that now.' It was true that Albion had reduced the number of goals conceded by 21, but there was dissatisfaction among the club's followers at what they had sacrificed at the other end of the field. If they were going to be at the wrong end of the table, they might as well play more watchable football along the way.

Nisbet recalls, 'It was up, back and through. That was Don's thing. Up to the front men, back to the midfield and through to the forwards again. We worked a lot on that; hitting the ball long, hitting the ball down the line. I was lucky Jeff Astle was up front when I started because you could hit the ball anywhere and he would take it. He was brilliant. It was a big loss when Jeff was injured. We had other good players, but Jeff was Jeff.'

As Gould remembers, 'Don tried several centre-forwards but he couldn't find a John Radford. He wasn't going to change his philosophy and his knowledge of what had been successful at Arsenal, but it wasn't going to be successful at West Brom.'

Brown finished as top scorer again with 19 League goals but had been uncomfortable trying to fit into Howe's direct style of play. 'Everything would be straight up to the big two front men and then played off them, but we didn't have the personnel to play that way,' Brown told Albion historian Gavin McOwan. 'Don tried to convert me into an out-and-out front man but I couldn't play like that, holding it up, shielding the ball. That was not my game. I had to be running on to the ball. He had all these charts on the wall with all these zones which players weren't supposed to go out of, based mainly on not giving anything away. The problem was that it stopped us scoring as well.' As future signing Joe Mayo remembers, 'Don tried to coach Tony Brown into running backwards and forwards and he probably had the worst spell he'd ever had. Some players you have to give license to.'

According to Wile, Howe's tactical approach 'created tension with the group'. He explains, 'Younger players who had a lot to prove were more readily accepting of new ideas and were happy doing everything Don told them. But the older group wanted to play a different way and the two didn't go together. We had very creative players like Bobby Hope, and Tony Brown used to get up to support the front people, but Don wanted us to be more direct and the midfield players had to change their game a lot. He wanted them to work back and it didn't fit them. Tony was expected to track back and win tackles. He was deadly in their box but he was equally deadly in our box. We had to chase about covering up for him. Tony, being the honest lad he is, did everything Don wanted him to do but it detracted from what he was good at.

'Don's approach was that this was how we were going to play and he was going to get the players in who would play that way if you couldn't do what he wanted you to do. The big talking point today is the high press and winning the ball back early, but Don was trying to get us to do that; to press high up the field and get the midfield and the front players on the opposition as soon as they got the ball. The players we had just weren't the type to do that.'

While acknowledging Howe's achievements at Highbury, Williams admits that the methods he employed there had taken him by surprise. 'As a player at Albion he'd always wanted to play football all over the pitch. It was a surprise to see him knocking long balls up to the front and fighting for the second ball. It wasn't the football he was teaching when he'd played at West Brom. But it was a style of football that suited Arsenal.'

Howe's second season at Albion got off to a horrible start – no wins in seven games – and failed to get much better. They ended the season with only nine wins and finished bottom of the table. Only Norwich City scored fewer and conceded more goals than Albion, who ended a 24-year run in the First Division.

Early in 1973, Howe confessed to the *News of the World*, 'Most of the Albion fans are against me. I have got to accept that. And how can you blame them? I've achieved nothing so far … who's going to slap my back and say, "Good lad, Don"? They'd have to be mad.' In his interview, Howe confessed, however, that he was growing weary of the constant comparison with his achievements at Arsenal. 'Honestly, the circumstances are so different it is not true,' he said, pointing to the work done before him by Dave Sexton and the players at his disposal at Highbury.

After a 4-0 home defeat against fellow strugglers Crystal Palace, Howe found a group of 30 angry fans waiting outside the ground to make their feelings known. Rather than running for cover, he invited them into the dressing room and spent half an hour chatting. 'It was something I welcomed,' he explained. 'They were down-to-earth supporters – the kind who follow us week-in and week-out. It was a frank discussion and I told them what the club's position was. I think they know now that nobody wants Albion success more than I do.'

The game had also been witnessed by Walsall striker Mayo, taken to The Hawthorns with colleague Bobby Shinton to finalise a £17,000 transfer after his own club's game was called off. 'Bobby knew we were going over so that West Brom could sign one of us,' Mayo remembers. 'I thought it was going to be him. It was the only time I ever went into the boardroom. Jim Gaunt, the chairman, had obviously been drinking and it just seemed like a normal day to them. "Oh, we lost," a "who cares?" sort of thing.'

Mayo would not make his Albion debut until the following season but his signing was another indication of how Albion's line-up had continued to move on from that which Howe inherited. Before the end of the previous campaign, Howe had made what would prove to be an important long-term signing for Albion in spending a reported £55,000 on forward Alistair Brown from Leicester City. The club then began their relegation season without Scottish midfielder Hope, a crowd favourite, who was sold to Birmingham City because Howe felt that 'one match he would do it, one match he wouldn't do it'. They subsequently parted company with Suggett, sold to Norwich, and Gould, whose nomadic career found a next stop at Bristol City. The most significant arrival was Rangers winger Willie Johnston, signed for a club-record £138,000 in mid-season, while a £50,000 bid to sign former Wales centre-forward Wyn Davies from Manchester United did not succeed.

McOwan's historical take on the signing of Johnston was that as a player who was 'completely undisciplined, a real showman and sometimes quite brilliant' he was not an obvious fit for a Don Howe team. Yet that ignores Charlie George's similarly maverick presence in the Arsenal Double team and that it was only after Howe's departure from Highbury that George encountered regularly the behavioural problems that blighted the remainder of his time at the club. Howe was not unable to accommodate the individual within his systematic approach to the game.

Johnston's talents could not prevent the inevitable, however. When future West Brom centre-forward David Cross scored the only goal on Norwich City's visit to The Hawthorns, ITV commentator Hugh Johns declared, 'It might just be the death knell for West Bromwich Albion.' There were still two games remaining, but relegation became a mathematical certainty when they were beaten 2-1 at home by Manchester City in the next match. 'Afterwards I thought Don Howe was great,' said goalkeeper John Osborne. 'There was no blame on the players. He started talking about what could be done.'

The fans who wrote to the *Sports Argus* were less forgiving. 'Since Don Howe took over, the emphasis on defensive play has transformed an enigmatic side of some talent into the dreariest in the First Division,' went a letter by D. Crump from Dorridge. 'Had we gone down fighting, playing attacking football, it would have been more in character and less shameful of the great players in the Albion teams of the past.' Another reader, hiding behind the initials T.E.M., argued, 'Mr Howe has had a disastrous two seasons. If he had been in a similar situation in industry the shareholders would not have been pleased with the results.'

Yet chairman Gaunt insisted that Albion 'will not panic' and lived up to his word by giving Howe the chance to put things right. 'Jimmy Gaunt was brilliant, very helpful,' Howe remembered. 'There was no interference; the board was first class.' But, for now, Second Division.

7

LOSING HIS STRIPES

Don Howe was a fantastic coach, but there are certain Albion players who wouldn't agree with that because he tried to change the style that they played. You can put a few of us in a room and we will argue until we are black and blue about the guy.

Former West Bromwich Albion striker Joe Mayo

IF THERE was a salutary lesson to be learnt on the perils of moving from a successful coaching career into the manager's office, then it was present at the second match of West Brom's return to the Second Division in 1973/74. We have noted previously that Malcolm Allison shared Don Howe's ambition to be his own boss and had made that move at the same time. 'People knock Malcolm Allison for the way he handled the Joe Mercer affair at Manchester City,' Howe would say. 'I know how he must have felt, I don't think I'd blame him.'

Now the men who had dominated the discussion about successful coaches in the late 1960s and early 1970s were in opposition on the touchline as West Brom hosted Crystal Palace in football's second tier. Allison's conversion to management had been no less problematic than Howe's. He had been poised to win the First Division with Manchester City in his first season in charge, only for his impulsive purchase of Rodney Marsh to upset the pattern and chemistry of his team, causing them to stumble over the final few weeks. And as the 1972/73 season unfolded, he fell out with his directors over a variety of issues and experienced an increasing pull to return to London. He quit City with the intention of steering Palace away from relegation, only to accompany Howe down to the Second Division. And, like Howe, there was to be no immediate return. In fact, while Howe and Albion would be frustrated in their efforts to mount a serious promotion challenge, Allison and Palace plummeted to the Third Division.

There were clearly different forces at play in the respective challenges they faced in replicating coaching success as managers. Allison, for example, had become a different person since his success at City had cast him in the role of 'Big Mal', the larger-than-life media personality beloved by the cameras.

Without the calming influence of Mercer beside him, his ego had gone unchecked, his whims unchallenged – as evidenced by the Marsh transfer, considered ill-timed by most City players. Howe could never be accused of that.

Yet there were some shared traits, the biggest one being the difficulty to acknowledge that methods that had served them well previously might be unsuited to their new surroundings. Several Palace players of the time believe that Allison simply forgot that his new group of players were not as gifted as Colin Bell, Francis Lee and Mike Summerbee and that his way of coaching and constructing a team could not follow his Maine Road template. Don Rogers, who had joined Palace from Swindon Town, explains, 'From the day I first met him to the very last day when I left, all he wanted was for people to play football. We probably went too much that way too early, instead of getting rid of it and playing in their half. The fact that Malcolm changed too much too quickly had a lot to do with our problems, but you couldn't argue with it at the time because he'd had such success.'

Even Allison would admit to seeing a look of confusion on players' faces at his methods. 'Malcolm thought he was still at Manchester City,' says striker Alan Whittle. 'He didn't evaluate the club he was coming to. Mal was a great coach but had no success as a manager.

Malcolm thought we could get through with pure skill, but he should have realised he needed a little more.'

Howe was similarly guilty of trying to fit his new players into a style of play that had worked previously for him, albeit vastly different to Allison's. It made it easy for observers such as Randall Northam in the *Birmingham Post* to simply accuse Howe of having 'failed to inject flair and a sense of adventure into his team' and of being scared to risk losing a game in order to win it. According to goalkeeper John Osborne, Howe's 'revolutionary ideas' did not suit a group of largely young and inexperienced players. 'The system they are playing is not working, the players have not really got hold of it,' he said, even though skipper John Wile's belief is that it was the older members of the squad who were most unsettled by the different style required of them.

Terry Venables, Howe's future boss with England, had been close enough friends with many at Arsenal to understand how much he had been 'idolised by those young players at Highbury' and the extent to which they responded to his methods. His observation was that 'Don had a group of seasoned players at West Brom who were not ideally suited to what he wanted to do. Instead of breaking himself in gently or doing what he had to do gently, I think it was a case of "I've proved myself, I've just done the Double. My way is right." There was a battle on between them and he never really got it going at The Hawthorns.' Venables felt that perhaps Howe had been too 'unbending' and unwilling to compromise.

As in the case of Allison, Howe had players who sometimes struggled with what appears to have been an oversophisticated – overcomplicated if you like – approach on the training ground. 'He had all these systems and training exercises, but it all just seemed too complex,' said Len Cantello, while Tony Brown recalled, 'It was all drills and sessions … I am sure it was clever stuff but it didn't work at the Albion.'

Centre-back Alistair Robertson wrote, 'Don was a great coach, years ahead of his time. The problem was some of us weren't! He was trying to make us do stuff we just weren't ready for. Today's players would lap it up but back then it was early days for that kind of coaching, and players struggled to adapt.'

Wile says, 'I watched Don do coaching sessions that were fantastic in the way they were set up and in what he was trying to achieve. Equally, there were other times when you thought it was a bit too much.' Joe Mayo, only 20 when he signed for the team he supported as a boy, enjoyed advancing from the primitive training sessions he'd experienced at Walsall. But even he recalls, 'Football is a simple game if you've got the right players, but sometimes, if you make the training too sophisticated, it's not simple and players would have been confused if they didn't get what he was trying to put across. I think Don confused the life out of Willie Johnston because he was one of those players who you just gave the ball to and let him get on with it.

'We used to have two different kinds of Wrigley's Spearmint chewing gum. Don would put it on the table and we were always the white and the opposition was the green. He would get Willie and say, "Come here, this is what I've got to show you," and Willie's brain went. He just carried on doing what he was doing. Before the games people used to stick an extra bit of chewing gum on the table to confuse him as well. Sometimes when I was on the bench with Don he would go ape if Willie wouldn't do what he was told.'

Mayo makes no secret of his admiration for Howe. 'He taught me more about the game in a couple of seasons than I learnt in all the time I had been playing football. He signed Ian Edwards and he tried to get us to play together. We used to do so much work; one going short and one long. And if there was an incident in a game, Don would have a coaching method to work out how you should be dealing with it. A lot of what we worked on was what we did when we didn't have the ball; closing people down and pushing teams into areas where we had our strengths.'

As relegation had loomed, Howe said, 'More important than tactical issues is the attitude of your players. I've got gifted players here, but they're not as dedicated as they ought to be.' But a few months after leaving Albion, he confessed, 'I went into the Albion job thinking

I'd do the Double again in the shortest possible time. Perhaps I wasn't adaptable enough and perhaps I frightened the players off by trying to put too much into their heads.'

And three decades later, he was still expressing frustration that 'I just couldn't get the team to take on what I thought was the modern way of playing football', although Wile suggests, 'Don wanted to get there too quickly. I think he might have been better swallowing a bit of what he wanted to do for what he could do with the players he had.'

None of which answers the question of whether Howe was simply not cut out for management. Unlike Allison, whose problems were partly those of personality, Howe's issues were mostly created by tactical decisions; the introduction of a playing style he would presumably have adopted had he joined Albion as coach rather than manager. But he also admitted that there were some man-management issues, from which he might have been protected with someone to act as a buffer between him and the players.

'He demanded that you gave everything that you had,' Wile continues. 'The way that he did it was getting on top of you. It was a complete change of what had gone before at the club. Don was always open to discussion, but more often than not the discussion was, "I will tell you what is right and I will tell you what we're going to do."'

Howe said the Albion players didn't respond to a 'nose into your face' method of communication – 'the direct approach when you tell a player, "You didn't play well, son."' At Arsenal, where there were other strong characters such as Bertie Mee and Frank McLintock to support and encourage the players while reinforcing Howe's messages, such devices had worked. Yet, at Albion, Howe wondered if the players doubted whether he was trying to help them. 'I would definitely approach it differently,' he admitted with the benefit of years of hindsight. 'It was go, go, go and training all day. I would definitely not do that.'

As club captain, Wile often felt himself caught in the middle of the differing opinions at the club. 'I was a big disciple of Don's and I thought what he was trying to do was the right way to go. But I disagreed with the way that he was going about it and I tried to put myself in a position between the two groups. I could say to people, "It is to our benefit to try and do what he wants to do." But towards the end I was finding it difficult to be 100 per cent supportive. I will admit that.'

Wile recalls that 'it blew up' when he and Osborne were told to report back to the gymnasium in the afternoon because Howe had been dissatisfied with how they had performed in the morning's physical training session. 'My argument,' says Wile, 'was that if you stick me out on a Saturday I will do a good job. If you are asking me to run 800 metres in two minutes I might do it 30 seconds slower, but I will still do a hell of a better job than younger players who might do it in one minute and 30 seconds and are getting all the praise. I thought the balance was wrong.' Recalling that Howe introduced a game of head tennis, Wile continues, 'I had lost it by this time and every ball that came to me I just volleyed into the ceiling. Don and I had a discussion afterwards and I said I felt that the emphasis was being put on some things that weren't the right things. That was towards the end of the season that Don left. I thought we weren't making any progress.'

According to Mayo, 'If you had done something wrong you were back the next day running. Don used to run the balls off you. But everybody makes mistakes. Don hated to lose but he didn't get that we hated it as well. If you have had a bad result and feel bad, it is not the best thing if next day you are doing however many laps around the pitch. Players would rather just get on with the next game; you can't bring the last one back and you can't harp on about it. You just show your mettle in the next one.'

Mayo remembers an occasion under Howe's successor, Johnny Giles, when Albion lost 7-0 at Ipswich Town and the manager's response was to stop the team bus at an off-licence and remind the players it was his birthday. 'He filled the bus with booze and we all had a drink to his birthday. I would love to have seen Giles working with Don Howe as his coach. Don could have coached us in the week and Gilesie could take over on Friday, give us the tactics and look after the team on Saturday. I think that would have been perfect.' The players would have been sheltered from the consequences of Howe being, as Mayo puts it, 'the world's worst loser'.

After beating Palace to make it two wins out of two, Albion went ten games without victory, undermining their promotion effort before it really got started. They did climb into the top four by the end of 1973, and a 3-1 win at Aston Villa in early March left them poised for a final push. But then they won only once in the final ten matches to finish eighth. Hartford, whom Howe had persuaded to stay for the promotion bid, was allowed to return to the First Division with Manchester City. Howe had also agreed to let Tony Brown go to Palace, but that move was blocked by the Albion board.

That summer also found Howe deciding the future of a nervous Hawthorns apprentice called Bryan Robson. Rather than putting the young midfielder on a train back to the northeast, Howe offered him a contract worth £28 per week, plus a £250 signing bonus. Even as a trainee, Robson had been fully aware of Howe's influence; his demand for high levels of fitness and rigorous training permeating all playing levels at the club. 'The sessions I'd put in back at my old school gym went a long way towards preparing me for an apprenticeship at The Hawthorns,' Robson explained. 'Don Howe had left me in no doubt about what I had to do, although I didn't have a lot of direct contact with him in those first couple of years.'

Howe would be gone from the club by the time an 18-year-old Robson made his first-team debut. 'Although I hadn't had a lot of dealings with Don he had always been very supportive and I was grateful to him for giving me the job,' the future England captain would recall. 'The more contact I had with him the more I appreciated what an outstanding coach he was, certainly one of the best I've ever worked with. It's probably true to say he was more cut out to be on the training pitch, working with the players, rather than having to contend with all the other parts of managing. If anything, he liked coaching too much. He was so intense and enthusiastic that I sometimes wondered whether he didn't overtrain his players.'

The Second Division had an unfamiliar look in 1974/75, with Manchester United, relegated only six years on from being champions of Europe, trying to find their way back to the top flight. In fact, it had been a strange few months for English football. After the national team had failed to reach the World Cup finals in West Germany, Sir Alf Ramsey was fired and Leeds United's Don Revie given the role. Howe had been among the names mentioned as potential England candidates, but his struggles at West Brom meant that he was never a serious contender. In a move that would ultimately touch Howe's career, former Derby County manager Brian Clough was chosen to replace Revie at a club whose methods he had previously delighted in holding in public contempt. Clough lasted 44 days before being replaced by Howe's old England rival Jimmy Armfield.

The impact of all that lay ahead. For now, Howe began another promotion attempt with a couple of defeats before a run of nine unbeaten games, including a 1-1 draw against Manchester United, who would lead the division from start to finish and whose fans celebrated by wreaking havoc around the country. It was Aston Villa and Norwich who progressed to promotion in United's slipstream, while Albion were always just off the pace on their way to a sixth-place finish; an improvement, but not enough to save Howe's job.

'We can't go up now,' he admitted after defeat at Blackpool on the last day of March. A week later, Howe was told that his four-year contract would not be renewed at the end of the season. He chose not to stick around for the last four games. 'I've been working 12 to 16 hours a day for Albion, often putting football before family,' he said. 'When you have done that for four years and this happens, it does hurt.' He also felt that the success of local rivals Villa, who had won the League Cup as well as promotion, and Birmingham City's re-establishment in the top flight worked against his chances of being given more time at Albion – sentiment with which club chairman Bert Millichip disagreed. 'This has been building up over 12 months,' he said. 'I think he will have success in football but we never appeared to have a really entertaining team.'

The story goes that the players discovered what had transpired when Howe marched into the dressing room, tore his charts off the wall and stormed out. There were those happy to see his back disappearing from view. 'Without doubt the era was the worst I played in in 20 years at the Albion,' Tony Brown said in Gavin McOwan's club history. 'The whole place had lost its spirit. The players just didn't enjoy playing.'

Howe's parting message was, 'I have given the club a future,' referring to the influx of new blood in the first team. But he also warned that Albion needed additional experience. Expressing the same sentiment that would come to haunt BBC pundit Alan Hansen two decades later, he argued, 'You don't win anything with youngsters.'

What Howe felt he missed at Albion was the influence of a veteran able to pull the strings on the field. He envied the on-field leadership available to his successor, former Leeds man Giles. 'People ask me, "Why is it you didn't do it at West Brom?" That is easy. Johnny Giles took over and he was lucky because he'd got Johnny Giles playing for him. I hadn't got the playmaker. People looked at me and said that is an excuse. That was not an excuse because Johnny was still good enough and fit enough to go out and play.'

Mayo concludes, 'When Giles came in he didn't change the team much and he got us out the division right away. I always felt bad for Don about that because he had worked so hard and Gilesie comes in with a different approach altogether. We never did any serious running or sprinting; we just played five-a-sides most of the time and then you could do some heading or shooting. The morale was so much higher under Giles. His philosophy was if you lost the game it wasn't the end of the world. We can get it together and do it next week.'

Giles would lead Albion to promotion in his first season, with Wile recalling, 'He was still a world-class player. When you have him in the team it makes a hell of a difference. But in the first few weeks under John nothing changed. We were doing the same things and he was relying on the coaches who were there. We weren't playing well. Then suddenly he took more responsibility in training and we went on a fantastic run. Don was a very technical coach and with John it was more about the way you set up the team. Not basic, but a lot less emphasis on the technical side of coaching. The players that Don inherited weren't suitable for the way he wanted to play, and the players that John inherited, plus himself, were perfect for the way he wanted to play.'

Howe's four years as West Brom manager remained the biggest disappointment of his footballing life. 'I worked harder during that period than anywhere,' he concluded. 'It was my club and I wanted success there more than anything – more than anywhere else I've been – and I couldn't get it. I worked my socks off, put everything in and it didn't go right. I think the work I did was ultimately fruitful, some good came from it for the club, but I couldn't get results to save my life. I took a lot of stick, fair enough, but I still did all I could.'

Son Rob recalls, 'Obviously at West Brom it wasn't a great time at the end. We used to go to those games and there would be chanting of "Howe out" and that was not a pleasant thing. He always said his biggest mistake was that he thought he knew everything when he went to West Brom and he didn't. Having done the Double with the Arsenal he thought he knew what was required to be successful. I don't think he had any regrets, but it was an eye opener for him.'

* * *

Howe's exit from West Brom meant he was out of work for the first time since first arriving at the club a quarter of a century earlier. It was a state of affairs that did not go unnoticed in Turkey. Galatasaray would make their biggest impact on English football when, in 1993, their fans greeted Manchester United for a Champions League game with a giant banner reading, 'Welcome to Hell'. But long before that the Istanbul club had been developing a thing for English managers, winning three successive titles in the 1970s under Brian Birch, one of Manchester United's original 'Busby Babes' of the 1950s. They also had a season under the leadership of former Reading manager Jack Mansell.

With the role vacant in the summer of 1975, club president Selahattin Beyazit persuaded Don Howe to take the job for a while. The British press seemed confused as to whether Howe was manager or 'consultant coach', an ambiguity not helped by the fact that he remained living in England and travelled home frequently between spells of duty in Istanbul. 'The only thing my mum ever said no to Dad on was when we had a chance to move to Turkey,' says Rob Howe. 'He wanted to go and he asked us kids if we wanted to go and we said yes, but my mum said no. It was the only time. She was always very supportive of him, even though she is not interested in football or the football life. She never wanted to go to any of the dinners and used to go to the games reluctantly in the early days. When she had us she had an excuse not to go so she stopped.'

By the end of October, Howe had overseen only one victory in six League games – albeit his team had only lost one as well – and looked set to exit the UEFA Cup after losing the home leg of their second-round tie against Torpedo Moscow. He was back home while England were losing in Czechoslovakia to end their hopes of qualification for the European Championship finals and send Don Revie's reign as manager into a tailspin that would finally reach its crashing conclusion almost two years later. While that was the event that captured the headlines, there was interest enough in Howe for the morning papers to speculate that he would go to Revie's old club, Leeds United, to work under Jimmy Armfield following coach Syd Owen's departure for Birmingham. Although he was operating without a contract at Galatasaray, Howe responded by saying, 'I am due to fly back to Istanbul at the weekend.'

Yet later the same day the stories were confirmed. Howe was back in English football, ironically at the club whose rivalry had helped define his achievements at Arsenal.[6] 'This is a great appointment for me

---

6 Howe would make one final contribution to Galatasaray the following summer when Beyazit, seeking advice about a new manager, told him that Malcolm Allison, recently sacked by Crystal Palace, and Arthur Cox, former Sunderland coach, were the two names recommended to him. 'You have got two good blokes there,' Howe replied. 'They both know the game but they are every different personalities. When Malcolm is in work mode he is intelligent and will work hard for you, but he does like to put himself about – he likes a drink and he likes the ladies.' Allison must have sounded like someone Beyazit could get along with and he spent more than a year working in Istanbul.

because I will be working with players of tremendous calibre,' he said. 'As a manager I was not able to spend the amount of time I would have liked in this direction because of the other responsibilities involved. But as chief coach of Leeds I will be able to devote 100 per cent of my attention to the players and this is one of the reasons I am looking forward to the job so much.'

Noting the battles between him and Armfield for the right-back position in England's Under-23 and senior teams, he added, 'Jimmy explained that it was necessary to have teamwork behind the scenes as well as on the field. Instead of competing with each other we will be working together and it should be a great experience.'

Armfield had rescued the previous campaign from the early-season wreckage of Brian Clough's ill-fated spell at Leeds, leading them to the European Cup Final. Despite the controversial nature of their 2-0 loss against Bayern Munich in Paris, where a series of refereeing decisions went against them, the game was assumed to have been the last hurrah for the team built by Revie and was expected to precipitate a period of rebuilding, or even decline. Armfield thought Howe's exile in Turkey was 'a waste to English football' and viewed him as the man who could help him fight what many saw as the inevitable. 'I felt the players needed someone who was a complete contrast to me; more verbal, more outgoing, and we were a good combination,' he would explain. 'I've never been frightened of bringing in top people and certainly didn't regard Don as a threat to my own position.'

Howe met with the Leeds players at their hotel in Derby, where they had arrived for what would become an infamous match the next day, when Norman Hunter and Francis Lee were sent off for swinging roundhouse punches at each other in front of the *Match of the Day* cameras. A 3-2 defeat left them in seventh place after only one win in the previous four matches, along with a League Cup defeat by Notts County.

Coincidence or not, results improved immediately. Duncan McKenzie, the talented and unpredictable forward Clough had signed from Nottingham Forest, scored twice in a 3-0 win against

Newcastle United. After a goalless draw against Middlesbrough, Leeds scored ten goals in beating Birmingham, Everton and Arsenal. While the Leeds players had railed against the arrival of an old enemy in Clough, the input of another former foe in Howe was welcomed. 'At the beginning of the season we were not playing well or enjoying our football,' said forward Peter Lorimer. 'Since Don Howe joined he has motivated us with new ideas and worked so well with Jimmy Armfield.'

McKenzie, who had spent so long trying to fit in among the Revie loyalists at Elland Road, finished 1975 by scoring two more in a 4-0 win against Leicester City, taking his tally to nine goals in the nine games with Howe as coach. He was named by the *Daily Mirror* as player of the month for December. 'I have been helped so much by Don Howe,' he said. 'I know where I am going now. I conform in the middle of the field, but around the area I can do it my way – score goals and entertain. He told me my job was to get into scoring positions in the box. He said if I didn't get the ball he would want to know why from others. Now I am enjoying my football again.'

Yet McKenzie also stressed, 'We worked harder in his first month here than we had in the previous 12.' It restored to Leeds the kind of professionalism for which they earned renown under Revie and which, according to Lorimer years later, had gone missing. 'The lack of discipline was becoming almost total. Footballers need only an inch to take a mile, and in Jimmy Armfield we had a manager who could be manoeuvred.'

Howe might have been an old adversary, but there were no grudges borne on either side and he was welcomed easily by powerful dressing room characters who were not afraid to put him straight on occasions. Howe's approach to half-time was that a coach 'must not indulge in generalities. He must confront individual players.' But he recalled, 'I remember once at Leeds when I was coach I said to the team at half-time, "You're not getting your tackles in." Billy Bremner, who could hardly be accused of that, replied, "Who isn't getting their tackles in?" It taught me a lesson. The coach has to name names.'

A 2-0 win in the first League game of 1976 was their fourth consecutive clean-sheet victory and left them only one point behind joint League leaders Liverpool and Manchester United with a game in hand. Yet an unexpected 1-0 home defeat in the fourth round of the FA Cup against Malcolm Allison's Crystal Palace – on their way to reaching the semi-finals as a Third Division side – triggered three more defeats without scoring. For the rest of the season, Leeds remained just adrift of the title battle developing between eventual champions Liverpool and Queens Park Rangers, finishing in fifth place, just failing to qualify for the UEFA Cup.

Europe seemed the least of their concerns when they began the 1976/77 season by winning only one of their first eight League games and slumping to 19th in the table. Ironically for Howe, the first match of the season pitted Leeds against newly promoted West Brom. 'First game up and there was Don sat on the bench,' laughs Mayo. 'We thought it was a great result to go up there and get a 2-2 draw and the three amigos – me, Tony Brown and Willie Johnston – all did well and felt we showed him what we could do.'

Leeds also lost 2-1 to Stoke City in the second round of the League Cup, despite a goal by Tony Currie. The £250,000 signing of the elegant Sheffield United midfielder, one of the best long-range passers in the game, was part of a steady makeover of the side. Giles had long since departed; Bremner signed for Hull City for £25,000 in the second month of the new season; and Hunter left for Bristol City for £40,000 a few weeks later. That trio, more than any other players, had given Revie's team its identity. Hunter believed that Howe 'had a big influence over who should be moved out and who should remain', adding, 'I loved Leeds and I didn't want to leave. I didn't know whether the boss wanted me there or not and that is never a good situation for any player to be in.'

McKenzie had gone to Anderlecht for £200,000 and the man earmarked to replace him up front was Ray Hankin, a powerful young forward who had come to prominence during Burnley's rise from the Second Division to a position of challenging for the title in 1974/75.

Relegated a year later, Burnley continued their policy of selling their best young players by allowing him to move to Leeds for £172,000. Hankin, who had turned down a move to West Ham United because he wanted to keep his family in the north, arrived at Elland Road suffering from a knee injury and battling with his weight. According to Eddie Gray, 'Ray was one of the most exiting strikers I have played with. However, Don Howe … who was something of a perfectionist, used to tear his hair out at Ray's level of fitness. The fluctuations in Ray's weight became a bone of contention. Don would insist on him being weighed every day.' It was the knee that proved more problematical than his metabolism, however, and Hankin played only four League games in his first season at the club – although he did bounce back to score 20 League goals in the following campaign.

Leeds never cracked the top five and stumbled along to a tenth-place finish, their lowest since Revie's side arrived in the top flight 12 years earlier. The FA Cup, however, kept the season alive, with Leeds navigating a none-too-easy course past Norwich City, Birmingham City, Manchester City and Wolverhampton Wanderers into a semi-final against Manchester United at Hillsborough.

Fans were perched in the trees to get a look at Leeds taking on the team who had been beaten in the previous season's final by Second Division Southampton and were trying to live up to manager Tommy Docherty's post-match promise to the fans that they would return to Wembley a year later. After a quarter of an hour, their outspoken manager's boast was almost a reality. After eight minutes, Leeds conceded a goal that infuriated Howe when they failed to clear a corner and the ball fell via Frank Gray's shin for Jimmy Greenhoff to score. The second goal wasn't much better, their inability to deal with Gordon Hill's hopeful hoof into the area allowing the ball to bounce nicely for Steve Coppell to fire home.

Allan Clarke missed an immediate opportunity to pull one back and centre-back Gordon McQueen fluffed another just before half-time. But Leeds scored midway through the second half when Joe Jordan was sliced down by full-back Jimmy Nicholl, and Clarke squeezed his penalty past Alex Stepney. But despite the persistent threat of Currie, it was Manchester United who advanced to Wembley, where they would end Liverpool's bid for a Treble – four days before the League champions beat Borussia Monchengladbach in Rome to lift the European Cup.

Yet, with football being an intricate spider's web of cause and effect, the fate that awaited Docherty ended up playing a large part in the next phase of Howe's career. With the bubbles from the Wembley champagne barely flat, the United boss admitted to the tabloids that he had been conducting an affair with Mary Brown, the wife of club physiotherapist Laurie Brown, and was leaving his wife Agnes to set up home with her. After a couple of weeks of outrage and debate, Docherty was fired. The fact that he and Mary would be a lasting item rather than a brief fling lent weight to his assertion that he had been 'sacked for falling in love'. Even so, it left United looking for a new manager.

Their choice was Dave Sexton, former FA Cup winner as Chelsea manager, unexpected First Division runner-up with Queens Park Rangers and, of course, Howe's predecessor as Arsenal coach. Gunners manager Terry Neill, who had left his post at Tottenham Hotspur to take over from Bertie Mee in the summer of 1976, had been trying to execute an ambitious plan to tempt Sexton back to Highbury to work as his first-team coach. The men had remained close, often travelling to Europe together to watch matches, and Neill sensed that Sexton had become unhappy at Loftus Road. Meanwhile, he acknowledged that his first season at Arsenal 'was filled with problems and I realised that I needed someone like Dave to work with me'.

When Arsenal departed for a pre-season trip to Singapore and Australia, Neill believed Sexton had agreed to a switch, although not in time to make the trip. But one morning in Singapore, Neill found a telex waiting in his hotel, reading, 'Regret unable to resist the challenge of managing Manchester United – Dave Sexton.' Disappointed but understanding Sexton's decision, Neill instead turned his attention to his friend and former team-mate Howe, calling him on his return from

Australia, having first checked with Armfield and been told, 'I know you two go back a long way and I wouldn't stand in his way.'

Neill continues, 'When I rang Don he asked if I thought there would be repercussions at Arsenal. But the old man – as we called Denis Hill-Wood – had said that if it was what I wanted then there would be no problem.' Neill knew of the ill-feeling when Howe had departed Highbury six years earlier but established in discussion with Hill-Wood that the directors accepted there had been various communication problems.

Leeds returned from pre-season games in Denmark and Holland to find that speculation about Howe was rife, forcing Armfield to say, 'We shall do everything we can to keep Don here.' Yet he knew there was nothing in his power to prevent Howe accepting an offer reportedly worth £15,000 a year – a decent amount for an assistant manager at that time. On 9 August, Howe's appointment was confirmed, with Hill-Wood putting those previous accusations of 'betrayal' behind him and declaring, 'We have made him a very good offer indeed. It has always been our policy to get the best. It will be a popular choice among the players.'

8

BACK IN THE HIGH LIFE

We would have got relegated if Don Howe hadn't come, even though we had quite a few good players and had the nucleus of a good team, Don came in and steadied a really rocky ship.

Former Arsenal midfielder Alan Hudson

DESPITE HIS long history as a player at Arsenal, Terry Neill had been a surprise choice to replace Bertie Mee after he ended his decade as manager in the summer of 1976. Neill's two seasons at Tottenham Hotspur as successor to Bill Nicholson had hardly been a tale of success, needing a win against Leeds in the last match to avoid relegation in 1974/75 before a rise to ninth place the following season. There had been talk of Miljan Miljanić, Real Madrid's Yugoslav head coach, going to Highbury, while an influential group of Arsenal players, led by Alan Ball, made no secret of their desire to see coach Bobby Campbell promoted. Yet it was Neill who, at 34, became Arsenal's youngest manager, having previously been the club's most junior captain.

For a while, Arsenal had continued to contend for honours after Howe's departure – runners-up in the FA Cup in 1971/72 and in the League a season later – but had then gone into swift decline. While Neill's Tottenham had been narrowly avoiding relegation, Arsenal also struggled, relying largely on the performances of goalkeeper Jimmy

Rimmer and goalscorer Brian Kidd – both signings from Manchester United – to keep them out of the bottom three. Key members of the Double team, such as Ray Kennedy, Charlie George, Frank McLintock and George Graham, were sold long before Neill became manager, while his first season at the club saw the phasing out of Peter Simpson, Peter Storey and John Radford.

Neill marked his Highbury entrance in 1976 with the kind of financial splash that would have made Prime Minister James Callaghan envious as the country went to the International Monetary Fund for an eye-watering $3.9 billion loan in an attempt to prop up a flagging economy. Malcolm Macdonald, a £333,333 signing from Newcastle United, made his debut on a sunny Saturday typical of that baking hot summer; the extent of London's drought having just been evident to sports fans as they watched the West Indies demolish England on the parched field of straw that was The Oval cricket ground. Arsenal brought the gloom, however, and managed to subdue the chants of 'Supermac' coming from Highbury's North Bank by losing 1-0 to a Bristol City team that had not played in the top flight for 65 years.

Macdonald would soon be joined by another of the most high-profile characters of 1970s English football. In December, Arsenal capitalised on Stoke City's need to replace an uninsured roof at the Victoria Ground by giving them £240,000 for Alan Hudson, one of the decade's most dynamic and creative midfield forces. Still only 25 when he joined Arsenal, Hudson had been part of the exciting Chelsea team of the early 1970s – cup winners at home and in Europe – and helped turn Stoke into unlikely title challengers before financial pressures forced the sale of their top players. In the spring of 1975 he'd at last played two England games, teaming up with Alan Ball to help England beat world champions West Germany before being dumped by Don Revie.

Hudson looked forward to slotting into a midfield that included Liam Brady and his former England team-mate. Yet Hudson and Ball would never play in the same Arsenal team. Hudson had been suffering from an abdominal injury that delayed his debut until the first match of 1977, by which time Neill had sold Ball to Southampton. 'For some obscure reason, somebody thought Alan Hudson and I would be too much in the same side,' Ball recalled. 'That could be one of the greatest soccer mistakes of all time.'

Similarly, Hudson harbours regrets over what might have been. 'If Terry hadn't sold Alan Ball that could have been the best midfield in the game,' he argues. 'I don't care about Ball, Harvey and Kendall at Everton. Alan was the best one-touch player I had ever seen; 'Chippy' Brady was a left-sided player with that magic left foot; and I could do other things. Alan was magic to play with and he was so difficult to play against because you went to tackle him and the ball had gone because he was so quick.'

Arsenal went on to finish eighth in Neill's first season – Macdonald's televised Highbury hat-trick against his former club being the highlight – but Brady recalls agreeing with Neill's belief that something else was needed. 'Terry needed to shake things up as regards to coaching and training,' he says. Neill felt his first-team coach, Wilf Dixon, was better suited to recruitment and scouting. 'I believed in myself,' Neill says, 'otherwise I wouldn't have taken the Tottenham job, where I took over from a wonderful man in Bill Nicholson. I didn't mind rolling my sleeves up, but I knew I didn't know everything. There was never any fear of bringing in someone like Tommy Docherty, as I did at Hull, or Don Howe; someone you can lean on.'

Hudson could not help but feel pessimistic during the summer of 1977. His mood stemmed largely from the rancour at the club, much of it revolving around him and Macdonald. If the Highbury that Howe had left six years earlier had been plunged into turmoil by his departure, then the atmosphere he found on his return was even more fractious. Arsenal's five-match tour was nearing its end when Macdonald and Hudson were left out of the final game in Adelaide and sent home, although Hudson felt that as the squad was returning the next day the early banishment was Neill's way of making a public example of them. Macdonald and Hudson – along with George Armstrong – could be said to have enjoyed themselves to the full during the tour, and

Neill's patience broke when the duo were found having a steak and a drink after a lunchtime arrival at their Adelaide hotel following an early-morning flight. They missed an afternoon training session but claimed that Neill had neglected to tell them about it and pointed out that chairman Denis Hill-Wood had been the one buying their gin and tonics, a drink recommended by club medical staff to help players sleep after a long flight. Armstrong, meanwhile, argued that he should be sent home too as his behaviour had mostly mirrored that of Macdonald and Hudson, whose images were splashed on the front of the *Daily Mirror* under the headline 'SOCCER'S BAD BOYS'.

Amid rumours of unrest in the squad about payment for the tour and the treatment of Macdonald and Hudson, the *Mirror* suggested, 'Neill has to patch up the cracks or completely rebuild his team.' Arsenal initially announced that the pair had been suspended for two weeks and placed on the transfer list, only for Macdonald to meet Hill-Wood at the chairman's Hampshire home to clear the air and secure his future at the club. Hudson, too, was staying, although Armstrong moved to Leicester City to team up with McLintock, the new manager at Filbert Street. Goalkeeper Rimmer, bound for Aston Villa, was another who never saw the start of the League season, his place taken by Pat Jennings, signed for £45,000 from relegated Tottenham when they decided that Barry Daines was their goalkeeper for the future.

This was the unsettled environment into which Howe arrived a few days after the squad returned from Australia. 'Terry was trying to change things around and it takes a bit of time,' Brady explains. 'He wanted to bring his own players in and he wanted to release some players and that always causes some upheaval.'

Macdonald's statement that news of Howe's appointment 'got a tremendous reception from the lads' was mostly true, although not in the case of Hudson. 'When I first got to Stoke there was a guy there called Peter Hewitt,' he remembers. Hewitt was reporting for the *Stoke Sentinel*, having covered Howe's playing career for the *Birmingham Mail*. 'He told me, "Whenever I went to see Don Howe to interview him, he always had a coaching manual with him." I thought he wouldn't be my cup of tea.' Yet Hudson ended up acknowledging that Howe's return was 'Terry pulling the greatest stroke of his time at Arsenal'.

Macdonald recalls older Arsenal players 'talking him up to the highest' and was looking forward to Howe's arrival. 'Wilf wasn't getting through to any of the players. He had an old-fashioned style of doing things. It wasn't helped by the fact he had been the coach at Everton and Bally didn't rate him. So the door was open for Don and he changed the mood of the dressing room immediately. It was quite electrifying.'

Brady has a similar recall, calling Howe's appointment a 'masterstroke' and adding that his thoughts of an early departure from the club were replaced by a desire to 'get down to work to grasp Howe's methods'. He continues, 'Don pretty much had a blank sheet of paper and Terry told him to get on with it. Results, team spirit, good atmosphere at training; all those things began to happen. You came off the training field thinking, "I worked hard and I learnt what is going to make me improve as a player."' In his 1980 book, *So Far So Good*, Brady describes Howe's initial impact in a revealing passage printed here with his permission:

> Players such as myself, Malcolm Macdonald, Alan Hudson, George Armstrong, Trevor Ross, we all had an axe to grind with the club. Howe cannot have found his task an easy one when he arrived. And how odd it must have seemed to him when you consider the strong and successful united squad he left behind with Bertie Mee.
>
> So the fact that Howe won over the whole squad in a matter of days speaks volume for his talent as a man-handler and a coach. And now we had a clear and defined situation. We saw Terry Neil, about things such as wages, transfer requests, contracts etc. And we worked with Don Howe on football and nothing else. Howe left none of us in any doubts as to what he demanded from us as professionals – loyalty, discipline, hard work and consistently high standards in all that we did. These demands sound very grand. And I have

> no doubt that any coach could make them. But getting a whole squad, many members of which were close to leaving the club, to respond to those demands is another matter.
>
> A number of things struck me about Howe from the start. He is not a man who indulges in small talk. He speaks his mind openly and to your face. He has no favourites and in his eyes no player is too big to be verbally taken apart if he steps out of line. Everything at Arsenal stepped up a gear. Everyone became punctual for training. Lateness meant being disciplined and excuses were not invited. Contrary to popular belief, Howe does not fine players. But then he does not have to. Being on the receiving end of his anger is far worse than having a set amount of money deducted from your wage packet. Training was harder. Everyone worked harder.

Howe's workday would begin with a regular staff meeting. 'We had a good team, including Fred Street, and we had meetings before training with all the coaches of all the teams,' Neill explains. 'People like Don and Wilf were not yes men. They all felt comfortable speaking their mind but in the end the buck stopped with me. That was the only way it would work; a close-knit team with respect all round. Similarly, I spoke to Don and a lot of my backroom staff about transfers. We were a team; there was no bossy attitude about it. Don and I were adults and had been on the football scene a while and done a few things as players, so there were never any real disagreements.'

Many was the day when Neill would return home from the London Colney training ground and immediately pick up the phone to Howe. 'Sandra, my wife, would say, "But you've been with him all afternoon,"' Neill laughs. 'We got almost telepathic. He would say, "I was just about to ring you." Our wives would say, "Why don't the two of you get married?" In a football sense, we were.'

Arsenal's 12 players on the opening day of the 1977/78 season included only five who had featured in the first match a year earlier, so perhaps it was no surprise that their campaign began inconsistently.

Their most impressive early performance was the 3-0 Highbury defeat of a previously unbeaten Nottingham Forest side destined to win the title in the season after Brian Clough had led them to promotion. A week later, defeat at Aston Villa saw Howe demonstrate his fierce side. 'Don was so easy to get on with and he made life easy for everyone, but he wasn't afraid to call out a player,' says Hudson, who'd played his first game of the season at Villa Park. 'He had a real dig at me. I had a shin splint or something and he thought I was making excuses and he also tore into Liam and Malcolm. He wasn't worried about reputations.'

Macdonald would incur Howe's wrath on New Year's Eve after a loss at Everton ended a five-game unbeaten run that had seen Arsenal rise to third place. Howe accused him of gesturing to the crowd when things didn't go his way, instead of helping to win back the ball. At the team's next training session Howe initiated a routine where team-mates would hit long balls into the corners beyond Macdonald, who then had to turn quickly and get back in to the action. Hudson recalls, 'He had Malcolm on his knees chasing balls that he had no reason to chase. Don spotted these problems and could sort them out.'

According to Brady, 'Howe recognised the weakness in our style of playing almost solely to Malcolm's strengths. Malcolm was told plainly that he would have to work harder as a team man and contribute more to overall play.'

Meanwhile, Howe and Neill encouraged the players to find their own voices. 'We sought their opinion,' says Neill. 'The players of that era and just before were accustomed to being dictated to and shouted at by the management, whereas Don and I would come in at half-time and while the players were having a cup of tea we would ask if they wanted to have a few words first. We welcomed their suggestions sometimes. Willie Young would hold his corner. The players have got to think for themselves. They can't be on the field thinking, "What did the coach say we should do?" They had to mature as players and decision makers.

'They didn't agree with us at times. I would have to threaten to take Willie round the back of the stand. Thankfully he never accepted it because he would have beaten ten bells of shit out of me. We could spout off our philosophy and tactics, but we weren't kicking the ball. They had to make decisions, and Don and I had to hand them the freedom to make those decisions.'

Hudson, who had been quickly won over, continues, 'Don was the only coach I have ever taken any notice of. I don't believe good players need coaching, but Don was different. He would never tell you what to do or how to play. He knew you could play, and it was the not so talented players he would help. He was a great organiser. When we went out we knew what everybody was doing. If they didn't do what they were told when the other team had the ball then they wouldn't have fitted in. He was very thorough.'

According to Hudson, Howe was responsible for getting the best out of Brady, who had entered a period when he undoubtedly became one of the English game's most influential performers. 'Before Don arrived, Chippy was allowed to get away with anything he wanted on the field. He thought all you had to do was get the ball and dribble. Don wasn't having it. He tried to make the point to Brady that he was far too predictable to become the truly great player his magnificent ability deserved.'

Brady himself explains, 'Don had a really inspirational way with players. He challenged you to make yourself better and had no hesitation in telling you what you needed to add to your game to get better. He was very knowledgeable about the individual requirements for every position and also what was needed as a team. I wanted to play centre of midfield and he would say it is OK playing there and doing the things you are good at, but you have to do the things that you are not good at; like chasing back and picking up players. You had your responsibilities defensively and they were the kind of things he pushed me to improve if I was going to be important to the team.'

Jennings quickly recognised that Howe's ability to address what each player needed was one of his greatest assets. 'He can get the best out of the whole squad,' he said. 'Players are individuals and each has strengths and weaknesses. Each needs individual help. Don can provide that by using the rest of the squad in his endless variety of coaching routines.'

He described Howe as a 'hard man but a fair one' and acknowledged his ability to retain the respect of players without becoming 'too familiar'. He explained, 'We still know he is in charge. He knows all the tricks and can spot a player taking it easy very quickly. He has no time for shirking. He gives everything to his club and players and he expects the same in return. Don has a great sense of humour … but when it's time to work you know you've been through a training session.' He concluded his appraisal by echoing the familiar praise for Howe's varied training sessions, saying that 'the players become absorbed in his ideas and his tactical knowledge'.

An important game in Arsenal's season came in January, when they hosted Manchester City in a League Cup quarter-final replay, a week after a 0-0 draw at Maine Road. Forced to omit the cup-tied Alan Sunderland, signed in the autumn from Wolverhampton Wanderers, journeyman midfielder John Matthews was preferred in the No.8 shirt to Hudson, who was on the bench after two months out of the team.

'That game against City was one of the funniest things,' laughs Hudson, who was sitting behind Howe and Neill in the dugout, next to kit man Tony Donnelly. 'It was a freezing cold night and I had a towel wrapped around my feet. I didn't have my boots on. After about half an hour City were pounding us, with Asa Hartford running the midfield. We couldn't get the ball off them and Don turned to Terry and said, "Make a change." I didn't want to go on then because my stomach used to play up after about an hour on the field so I wanted to wait until half-time. Don turned to me and said, "Alan, you're coming on." So I said to Tony, "Come on, let's go in the dressing room," because my feet were fucking freezing. Tony was crying with laughter and I said, "Put my feet under that hot tap." I was sitting on the end of the bath and I asked Tony to come in and rub my feet down.'

At half-time, Howe was finally able to make his change, telling Hudson he was going on for Matthews. For the next 45 minutes, Hudson was everywhere, picking up possession all over the field, and helping his team to an eventual 1-0 win, secured by a Brady penalty. 'They were murdering us that night, and then that was a great 45 minutes for me,' Hudson continues. 'The Arsenal fans had finally seen that I could play because I was awful before that.'

Arsenal's League Cup run ended with a narrow two-leg defeat against Liverpool in the semi-final, but Hudson's introduction sparked a run of performances, particularly at Highbury, that featured a fluent style of football virtually unrecognisable from the Double team. For critics of Howe, it was proof that his teams did not have to be one-dimensional defensive automatons. Hudson and Brady began to fulfil the promise of their partnership; Macdonald was on his way to a 26-goal season; and at the back even the former figure of fun, Young – who followed Neill from Tottenham – was proving an effective foil to the cultured centre-back play of teenager David O'Leary.

Brady explains, 'With the players he had in the Double years, Don was pretty direct because he had big players like John Radford and Ray Kennedy up front who were brilliant target men. But we kept the ball on the ground. We had players like Hudson and Graham Rix, with Malcolm up front, so we played on the deck. David O'Leary was a footballing centre-back and brought the ball forward and Sammy Nelson was an attacking left-back so we played in a very attractive and offensive way.'

Macdonald adds, 'It was fabulous; a joy to be playing in. And all the time I would see Don putting his arm around people's shoulders and quietly talking to them and feeding them a bit of information or a suggestion here and there on how to cope with the player they were up against that week. He made it a very personal thing. I found him absolutely amazing. I would have loved to have played in an England side with him.'

Having been introduced to the England team by Sir Alf Ramsey, Macdonald's most notable international appearances were under Don Revie, scoring in the 1975 victory against West Germany and bagging all five goals against Cyprus a few weeks later – all under Revie's threat of being dropped if he didn't find the net. 'Don Revie would never have tolerated someone like Don Howe working with him,' says Macdonald. 'He had to have a henchman, not so much a coach.'

In the spring of 1978, Arsenal scored at least three goals five times in a sequence of six home games and found themselves in the FA Cup semi-finals, where they would face Second Division Orient. But Howe was not fully satisfied with the team's form and, after drawing 1-1 at Birmingham City, he opted for an extraordinary approach to driving the Gunners players towards improved performance. On the day before a home match against West Bromwich Albion he gathered the squad in the 'halfway house' meeting room off the Highbury tunnel. Instead of discussing the opposition, as was customary in these team talks, he turned towards Macdonald.

'Our recent performances hadn't been great but I had been scoring goals,' the striker recalls. 'Don pointed at me and gave me the biggest and longest bollocking I had ever had. His voice was raised, which was unusual, and every time I went to say something he told me to shut up and listen. I'm sitting there thinking, "What the fuck is going on here?" I could see the embarrassment that the other players were feeling at having to witness this. Seriously, it went on for an hour and he absolutely slaughtered me as if I was a novice. I was seething.'

Howe finished with, 'I hope to see a difference tomorrow,' and walked out, leaving stunned team-mates to approach their colleague. 'They sheepishly came over and said, "Bloody hell. Thank heavens it wasn't us." Anyway, we went out the next day against West Brom and I knocked them all over the place and got a hat-trick [in a 4-0 win]. All the players were really working, so well organised and looking to get me in.'

As Macdonald left the Highbury pitch, he was approached by Howe. 'You can stick that fucking hat-trick right up your arse,' he barked at his coach.

'But it worked, didn't it?' Howe smiled back.

Macdonald finishes the story. 'He told me to come into his room before I showered. "Let me explain why I did what I did yesterday," he said. "The side hasn't been playing well and I was getting the impression that a lot of the players were being detrimentally affected by the lack of performance and were getting nervous about it. But you were still scoring goals, so I realised that if I was going to get my point across I had to find the one man who would fight me and react in the right way. The bollocking you got was for everybody, but I embarrassed you all into improving." He understood how each player ticked and came up with a way to get them to react. It is something you can only do once and you have to pick your moment and your person to do it with. Don picked it perfectly.'

Two weeks later, Arsenal's 3-0 win against Orient at Stamford Bridge meant they had scored 17 goals in five games to reach Wembley, and were considered strong favourites to beat Ipswich Town, whose years of consistency in the First Division table had deserted them as they hovered just above the relegation places. Nevertheless, Ipswich had overcome many of Howe's old players when they beat West Brom, now managed by Ron Atkinson, 3-1 in the other semi-final at Highbury.

Another of Howe's former charges, Joe Mayo, had been a member of the Orient team that surprisingly reached the last four before offering little resistance against Arsenal. 'The game was such a nightmare for us,' he recalls, 'and Don sat on the bench made it worse for me. We didn't play like we could have and they got two poxy goals.' The goals to which Mayo refers were first-half strikes by Macdonald that went in via deflections off defenders Bill Roffey and Glenn Roeder.

With seven goals in the Cup run, Macdonald was proving too valuable for Arsenal to allow him to take time off to sort out a cartilage problem in his right knee, excusing him from training but delaying surgery. 'I'd put my foot down and felt this horrible pain in my knee and realised I had torn a cartilage,' Macdonald explains. 'The next match was the third round of the FA Cup. Terry sat me down and said, "Let's see if we can get a bit of a run going. If we get knocked out in the third round we will get you straight into hospital." We won in the third round and I kept going; we won in the fourth and I kept going – and so on through to the final.'

It meant that he was one of several players about whom the Gunners had fitness concerns in the build-up to the final, including skipper Pat Rice, Brady and Sunderland, who had missed seven games with a stress fracture before returning a week before Wembley. If all were fit, then Sunderland's presence in the team was expected to mean either Hudson or Rix missing out, an issue that led Howe to blowing his top in the days leading up to the match.

Hudson explains, 'Don saw me in the tunnel and said, "You look a bit concerned." And then he said, "Sleep well tonight, you are definitely playing." Bob Driscoll from *The Sun* and I were friends and used to go drinking and I spoke to him that night. Just before he put the phone down I said, "I am playing, Bob. Don told me today." I never thought he would print it but all over *The Sun* the next day was that Hudson was playing. It was all out of context.

'I went in the next day and Terry said Don was going mad. I walked into his office and he took his jumper off and shaped up to me and I thought he was going to hit me. He said, "I will never ever speak to you again. I tried to help you and that's how you repay me." I said, "Mate, I am sorry. I would never do that." After the game he got hold of my arm and said, "I spoke to Bob Driscoll and checked your story out and it all adds up." He said it was all forgotten. I really admire that about him.'

Given all the injury worries – even Brady admits he should not have played on his bad ankle – it was perhaps surprising, and harsh, that the fighting-fit Rix, scorer of a lovely individual goal in the semi-final, was the player who missed out on selection. Brady recalls, 'I had to have injections before the game just to get me out there and it didn't work. With Malcolm's problems we went into that game two men down, which was really why we didn't perform.' Macdonald, as disappointingly anonymous as he had been in Newcastle's defeat against Liverpool four years earlier, admits that Ipswich could have won by five goals. 'They didn't half play well; they were brilliant,' he says. *The Times* reported that Ipswich 'outplayed, outran and outwitted mighty Arsenal in a triumph for the good things that football these days tends to forget'.

Paul Mariner tormented Young and hit the bar after the big defender was caught out on an ill-judged foray upfield. Brian Talbot and John Wark controlled the middle of the pitch and Howe, chewing gum vigorously as he sat in his red tracksuit on Wembley's distant benches, was powerless to change events. 'For all the encouragement and good advice Terry and Don gave us at half-time, Ipswich seemed to have the bit firmly between their teeth,' remembered Brady, who gave way to Rix midway through the second half. With Wark twice hitting shots against the post, the surprise was that it took Ipswich until the final 13 minutes to win the game, when Young struggled to clear the ball in the box, allowing Roger Osborne to become an unlikely Suffolk hero. If there was any consolation for Howe on such a miserable day, it was to be found in the happiness of his great friend Bobby Robson, the Ipswich manager, with whom he chatted amiably as they watched their respective groups of players go through their on-field celebrations and commiserations.

With one League game left, the Arsenal squad reconvened two days later. Howe led a review of the final in which each player was invited to suggest what had gone wrong. After half an hour he reached Hudson.

'I blame him for not picking the right team,' the midfielder announced, pointing at Neill.

'You are a disgrace, Huddy,' shot back a wounded Neill.

'I know I am but you picked the wrong team and Don asked me to speak, not you.' Addressing Sunderland, he added, 'No disrespect to you, but Rixy was the man in form and should have played.'

It was the final, irretrievable breakdown in the relationship between player and manager. Hudson was soon bound for the Seattle Sounders in the North American Soccer League. 'I didn't want to go but I couldn't get on with the manager,' he explains. Coincidentally, he came across the Arsenal squad at Heathrow Airport as he waited for a flight to the US and had a final conversation with his coach.

'Please, Alan, don't leave,' Howe pleaded. 'You'll lose yourself over there.'

'I am sorry, I've signed the papers and I am off,' Hudson replied. 'But I appreciate everything you've done for me and you've got me on the straight and narrow.'

Decades later, Hudson concludes, 'I love the man.'

* * *

The new season saw Arsenal make a slow start, dropping to 13th when they lost to champions Nottingham Forest in mid-September. The most memorable Highbury moment of the first few months was provided in unlikely fashion by Young, who chipped in a stoppage-time winner against Yugoslavian side Hajduk Split in the UEFA Cup; a contest that had seen Howe and Neill getting confused on the sidelines as Arsenal faced up to an exit from the competition on away goals. 'I was accused of substituting the wrong lad,' Street recalls. 'With a few minutes to go, Terry told me to take off the Australian forward, John Kosmina, who had gone on as a substitute at half-time. I put up John's number and off he came. Don shouted at me, "Fred, you have brought the wrong player off." I said, "Don, I have brought off the player the manager told me to. You two get together and stop acting like Laurel and Hardy."'

Yet Arsenal had risen from another nice mess to reach second place in the First Division table by mid-February, losing only twice in a stretch of 21 League games. To the delight of Arsenal fans, the run included a 5-0 pre-Christmas win at Tottenham, whose summer capture of Argentinian World Cup winners Osvaldo Ardiles and Ricardo Villa had made White Hart Lane the epicentre of English football and heralded a new wave of overseas signings. Arsenal were at various stages of the season linked with Ruud Krol and fellow Dutch internationals Willy and René van de Kerkhof, but their major foray into the transfer market kept them closer to home, with the £450,000 signing of one of the men who had undermined them at Wembley, Ipswich and England midfielder Talbot. Brady remembers, 'Don recognised they needed to get a strong player in alongside me. Brian Talbot could run all day, which would help me.'

The winter of 1978/79 was one of the most significant in the modern history of the nation. Labour Prime Minister James Callaghan, who had decided against calling an autumn general election that he would probably have won, found the unions waging war against his government's pay policy. From refuse collectors to grave diggers, public workers went on strike. As the rubbish piled high in landmark sites such as Leicester Square, the image of Britain that the world saw was one of decay and unrest. A vote of no-confidence in the government paved the way for a May election that saw Margaret Thatcher's Conservative party ride into power.

Reflecting the economic and social hardship of the so-called 'Winter of Discontent', the snow arrived on New Year's Eve and stuck around until the spring, creating havoc with the football fixture list. For Arsenal, their third-round FA Cup tie against Second Division Sheffield Wednesday, consisting of five games, was no less gruelling than Callaghan's war of attrition with the unions, although *Monty Python* star Michael Palin described it in his published diary as 'a golden ring of light' in such dark days. In the wake of defeat to Ipswich, Neill had assured his team they would be back at Wembley the next year. But they needed Brady's late equaliser to save them in the Highbury replay against Jack Charlton's team, before slogging through two more drawn matches at Leicester and winning the fourth replay 2-0 at Villa Park.

Brady, who would be named Player of the Year by the Professional Footballers' Association, felt that Arsenal had been 'swept along through a terrible winter by our own ambitions and the convictions and the coaching of one man' – meaning Howe, of course. He explains, 'Don would game-plan for opponents, even though we had our way of playing. He knew the strengths and weaknesses of the opposition and he would go through all those things with us before the game. Even in training he would say, "Let's work on this today because on Saturday it might pay dividends." He was thorough and totally prepared. And in the Cup games we came to the fore, even if we didn't quite have the strength in depth to challenge for the League.'

Arsenal returned to Wembley after an FA Cup run that included victory at Forest in the fifth round and a 2-1 defeat of Wolves in the semi-final without Brady, who this time made no attempt to play when he was badly injured. Once again, Howe would find a familiar figure in opposition in the final: Dave Sexton's Manchester United.

Arsenal won only two of their final 13 League games and dropped to a final finishing place of seventh behind champions Liverpool, the quest for the FA Cup overtaking all other concerns. This time, Macdonald had not been a factor, his creaking knees sidelining him after three League games. His return to some semblance of fitness did, he hoped, make him a contender for a Cup Final comeback.

'I was given the OK by the medical people prior to the final and Terry was weighing up whether to play me or Alan Sunderland up front with Frank. Terry had been talking in a manner which made me believe that he was going to play me and when the team was named I thought, "Well, what was all that crap about?" Don saw my face and after the team meeting he walked me out into the gardens of the hotel and he picked me right up. He knew Terry wasn't the best of communicators at times, and he smoothed everything and made sure I understood it was all for the good of the club. He asked me, "Do you really feel 100 per cent that you can go out at Wembley and give us everything we know you can do?" I said probably not and he said, "Well, at least you are honest with yourself."'[7]

Prior to kick-off at Wembley, Howe reminded the Arsenal players, 'We got beaten here last year and we let an awful lot of people down. This year we are going to make up for that.' According to Brady, 'Don gave us a lot of confidence. No one went into that game thinking, "We lost last year, what's going to happen this year?" We went in thinking we were going to win and that was down to Don's coaching and Don's inspiration.'

Brady was as influential on this occasion as he had been ineffective a year earlier. His surge towards the United penalty area opened the way for Talbot to open the scoring, and his weaving journey into the box and delicate right-footed cross set up a Stapleton header that gave Arsenal a 2-0 half-time lead. 'Terry and Don did their best to keep feet

---

7 Macdonald made a goalscoring return to the team against Chelsea two days after the final, although it proved to be his swansong. While playing in Sweden to recover fitness during the summer he was fitted with a specially designed knee brace. Told by the FA he could not wear it in England, he realised he was doomed without it when attempting Howe's 12-minute running drill during pre-season training, breaking down two thirds of the way through. 'It was like running barefoot on broken glass,' he lamented.

firmly on the ground, reminding us that we needed to hold onto the initiative and hit more goals,' Brady explained.

The additional goals didn't come, but with 85 minutes gone United hadn't broken through either. Many felt that Neill had sent on substitute Steve Walford in place of midfield worker David Price in order to give him experience of a final, although Neill insisted, 'David was fading fast', an observation Brian Clough shared in ITV's commentary box as Price left the field.

The stage was set for 'The Five-Minute Final'. United centre-back Gordon McQueen swung his left boot at the ball and made it 2-1 after Arsenal failed to clear a free kick. A minute or so later, Sammy McIlroy chased Steve Coppell's pass into the penalty area. 'And McIlroy's through,' John Motson told BBC viewers, his voice rising in excitement as O'Leary failed to halt his progress. 'McIlroy's through,' he repeated as Walford was left standing. 'And McIlroy, has done it,' he exclaimed as a left-footed shot slid beyond the grasp of Jennings and squeezed inside the post.

'There are some things no coach can plan for,' Brady is able to laugh these days. But at the time he had an 'awful feeling that we had lost the game' and wanted to 'scream my head off at our collective stupidity'. He quickly got the ball, put his head down and ran at the defence; out of a desire to ensure that Arsenal at least made it to extra time by keeping the ball in the United half. Evading a sliding tackle by Mickey Thomas, he slipped the ball to his left into the path of Rix, who clipped it across the box just before two defenders could close him down. As it dipped beyond the far post, Sunderland stuck out a leg to score Arsenal's winner.

When the cameras turned towards the Arsenal bench, Howe was the one man sitting down, looking as impassive as someone who'd expected nothing else. But when the final whistle sounded a few seconds later, the large sigh that was picked up on television betrayed the extent of his relief.

Such scenes were able to be enjoyed at their leisure by some Arsenal fans, thanks to the resourcefulness of Street and club shop manager

Jack Kelsey, the former Gunners and Wales goalkeeper. 'I had recorded it at home on my tape deck,' Street explains, 'and over the next two or three days Jack got people ringing the Arsenal shop asking if it was going to be available on tape. I said to Jack I could run off some copies. He said, "That's good we can sell them," but it was BBC copyright so first he wrote to them. They said we could do what we liked. Can you imagine that today? So I ran a load of copies and Jack charged 40 quid in the shop, including a tenner to me for making the tapes. He would keep calling me up and saying, "I need 10 more." They weren't great copies but they had all the interviews before and after. I told Jack to keep that letter from the BBC in the safe in case someone came looking for some money.'

* * *

Going into 1979/80, it was becoming apparent that Arsenal were destined to lose the services of Brady the following summer to his ambition of playing overseas. 'My contract was coming to an end and I wanted to go abroad,' he says. 'Terry and Don knew I had made my mind up.' As well as following the trail blazed by Kevin Keegan when he left Liverpool for Hamburg in 1977, Brady made the same decision as the Anfield icon in declaring his intentions in advance. While some Liverpool fans turned against their former hero, the response from most Arsenal followers was regret. The largest part of any anger they felt was directed towards an Arsenal management team unable to convince him to remain at Highbury and a board apparently lacking ambition. The £75,000 summer signing of 33-year-old former Chelsea and Queens Park Rangers midfielder John Hollins would prove a valuable addition to the squad, but was barely even a footnote in a transfer market that had exploded with the £1 million move of Trevor Francis from Birmingham City to Nottingham Forest and would shortly see Steve Daley and Andy Gray signed for roughly half as much again by Manchester City and Wolverhampton Wanderers respectively.

Yet the campaign would be an historic one as Arsenal entered the new decade fighting on three fronts: to retain the FA Cup, achieve further success in Europe and finish high enough in the table to ensure continental competition. It was not quite the epic treble quest that Leeds United had embarked upon exactly ten years earlier – when they finished as runners-up in the League and FA Cup and semi-finalists in the European Cup – but the Gunners' total of 70 matches was seven more than Don Revie's team had been forced to play and the outcome no less heartbreaking. Two epic semi-finals would go down in the annals of the club, yet both were followed by anticlimax.

In the European Cup Winners' Cup, Arsenal were paired in the last four with Juventus, Italian champions five times in the 1970s. Yet their preparation for the first leg at Highbury was virtually non-existent, having squeezed in the small matter of a 2-1 win in the north London derby at Tottenham on the Monday, two days before their first European semi-final for ten years. Normally preparation for a big European game would have involved the first team taking on a group of players adopting the style and tactics of their upcoming opponents. 'Once Don and I had analysed the opposition,' says Neill, 'if there was something specific they did I was young enough to play the role of a particular opposition player. I would play the role to the best of my ability to familiarise our team.'

Yet by this time, training had ceased to be part of the Gunners' week, as Neill explains. 'With a squad of 15 or 16 players and all the games we played it was Don's idea that we didn't train from the Easter period on. He felt we had to give the players a bit of free time. We asked them not to go traipsing round the supermarket, and we would just bring a couple in every now and again for a rub down and a little loosening up to keep them ticking over. That, really, was Don's wisdom.'

Juventus took an early lead at Highbury when Antonio Cabrini scored from the rebound after Jennings had saved his penalty, but they were reduced to ten men when Marco Tardelli added another entry on his long ledger of infamy by taking out Brady and being sent off. O'Leary's night also finished early when he had his shin sliced open by Roberto Bettega, who was the victim of karma when he turned the ball into his own net with five minutes remaining. The 1-1 draw kept Arsenal in the tie, but the fact that no English visitors had beaten Juventus at Turin's Stadio Comunale in 11 previous attempts demonstrated the size of their task.

Arsenal stretched the much-vaunted home defence by getting full-backs Pat Rice and John Devine forward as much as possible, but after 88 goalless minutes Juventus's away goal in the first leg looked like being decisive. Then Paul Vaessen, an 18-year-old substitute introduced as a last throw of the dice with quarter of an hour left, made the intervention that would define his brief Arsenal career. As he had at Wembley a year earlier, Rix got behind the defence on the left and crossed to set up the winning goal, the unguarded Vaessen nodding in at the far post. 'It has got to be one of the best European results ever,' said Neill.

Howe had made a significant contribution to Vaessen's development by assigning Macdonald to work with him after training, as he had done previously with Stapleton. 'Don saw the potential in Paul and would work one-on-one with him,' Macdonald explains. 'But he felt he'd hit a dead end so asked if I would help him. Don just sat back and watched, and he was picking up all the stuff I was passing on. In his head he probably sifted the good, bad and indifferent and worked with Paul on the good stuff. That was Don; always happy to use somebody else's expertise for the good of the side.'

In the FA Cup semi-final, a dull 0-0 draw against Liverpool at Hillsborough gave little indication of the twists and turns that lay in store. Goals by David Fairclough and Sunderland cancelled each other out in the replay at Villa Park, but Arsenal's European commitments meant it was almost two weeks before they tried again at the same venue. It took less than 15 seconds for Sunderland to force his way into the Liverpool penalty area to give the Gunners the lead, and it was almost the same amount of time before the final whistle when the ball dropped to Kenny Dalglish to snatch an equaliser. Three days later, the scene shifted to Coventry City's Highfield Road. Arsenal old boy Ray Kennedy stumbled over a clearance and Stapleton centred from the right for Talbot to head his team into a 12th-minute lead. O'Leary and Young proceeded to protect their area like guard dogs and the Gunners were back at Wembley, the first team to qualify for three successive FA Cup finals since Blackburn Rovers between 1884 and 1886, and the first at the home of English football.

Having drawn 1-1 at Anfield in the League in the midst of their Cup marathon, Arsenal had played Liverpool, soon to clinch back-to-back titles, five times in three weeks without being beaten and while conceding only three goals. Not for the last time in his career, Howe had found a way to combat and overcome the mighty Anfield machine.

In his preview of the final against Second Division West Ham United, Norman Fox of *The Times* accurately characterised the team that Howe had built:

> Arsenal's practical outlook has not endeared them to everyone. They are a product of the times, designed by one of the most gifted coaches of the decade in Don Howe, who today achieves the remarkable record of having taken Arsenal teams to seven different finals. Yet they have lustrous talents in Brady, Stapleton, Rix and O'Leary, more than enough to form the basis of future champions. Collectively they can raise their game to a high level of attractiveness, but only after winning control at the back and in midfield. They are not a team to risk much for the sake of pretty patterns.

West Ham might have boasted the artistry of Trevor Brooking and the dash of Alan Devonshire in their midfield, but the biggest danger to Arsenal threatened to be fatigue. In the build-up to the final they'd at last had four days without a game after playing 13 in 34 days. Neill felt it was 'inhuman to expect footballers to fulfil such a taxing programme, but we accepted the task without complaints reminding ourselves that only successful sides have these demands'.

Brady remembers, 'It all caught up with us by the time the finals came around. Don and Terry were trying to balance the team and there was some rotation going on so that we could get through the season. But when it came to the finals, we were disappointing against West Ham and very unlucky against Valencia because we attacked them all through the game.'

In its subsequent Wembley match report, the *Sunday Times* talked about 'a Cup final in which logic, League status and the bookmakers made West Ham so much the underdog that there was a danger of somebody calling in the RSPCA.' Yet West Ham took the lead after 13 minutes when Brooking stooped to score an unlikely headed goal, and Arsenal, looking increasingly tired as the warm afternoon progressed, were unable to respond. At half-time, Howe ordered, 'Get yourselves under the showers. For God's sake wake yourselves up.' It made some difference, but not much.

Another controversial Wembley selection had left Arsenal without much game-changing ability off the bench. Sammy Nelson had not been fit enough to start at left-back, but Neill had named him as substitute. O'Leary would recall, 'I thought making a full-back substitute was a mistake.' And on Nelson's introduction for Devine in the second half, he added, 'It was full-back for full-back. Utterly pointless.'

Now Arsenal had to pick themselves up to face Spanish club Valencia at the Heysel Stadium in Brussels on Wednesday night. 'Defeat at Wembley, especially for such clear favourites, usually requires a summer's healing time,' noted *The Times*. 'Arsenal have been given four days.' During that time they had to assure themselves of the fitness of Talbot, who had collapsed from exhaustion on the team bus leaving Wembley, and of O'Leary, whose calf strain would make him a doubt almost up until kick-off. The *Daily Mirror* went as far as suggesting, 'Anyone with any affection for football wants [Arsenal] to beat Valencia.' It was a sentiment that recalled the support for Liverpool when they lifted the European Cup for the first time three years earlier after losing against Manchester United at Wembley, but it might have exaggerated the place this Arsenal team occupied in the nation's hearts. As it turned out, events in Brussels meant that maybe only supporters from across the north London divide remained unmoved.

O'Leary was fit enough to play and good enough to snuff out the threat of Mario Kempes, the swashbuckling hero of Argentina's World Cup triumph two years earlier. Without their long-haired musketeer firing, Valencia appeared to have little ambition beyond taking the game to penalties. And although Stapleton's header forced a goal-line clearance and Sunderland's quick reaction to a wayward Rix shot brought a brilliant point-blank save from goalkeeper Carlos Pereira, Arsenal again failed to break through. In 210 minutes of football across two finals, they had not found the net.

The shoot-out began with the two most-vaunted players on view, Kempes and Brady, having their penalties saved. Then came a series of successes, with Stapleton, Sunderland, Talbot and Hollins on target for Arsenal. Their sixth attempt fell to Rix, needing to score to extend the drama. His act of pretending to catch the keeper off guard as he moved up to place the ball betrayed nerves rather than nonchalance and, after a three-pace run-up, he struck his penalty at a saveable height as Pereira dived to his left. For the second time in a week, Arsenal bore their yellow shirts wearily from the field as their opponents celebrated with the trophy.

Somehow they managed to win at Wolves two days later, but still needed victory at Middlesbrough the following Monday to achieve third place and a berth in the UEFA Cup. It was a game too far. They lost 5-0. 'We were just dead,' Brady explained. 'It was a heartbreaking memory, especially as it was my last Arsenal match.'

Neill looks back at that three-year period with a mixture of pride and regret. 'We had fantastic players; it was as simple as that,' he says. 'Over those three seasons we could not have asked for any more from the players. We just ran out of steam. It was tragic, but they were only human beings. It is sad because, with all respect to Ipswich and West Ham, we could have swept the board.'

9

YOUR COUNTRY NEEDS YOU

Under Ron Greenwood, things were a little slack.
It got much better when Don was brought in.

England striker Tony Woodcock

RON GREENWOOD had been stagnating in the three years since giving up the manager's role at West Ham United in 1974, a decision that ended a reign that had brought the FA Cup and European Cup Winners' Cup to Upton Park in the mid-1960s but only frustration since. In handing over the reins to his coach, John Lyall, and moving into a purely administrative role, he had not foreseen the loss of self-esteem that would haunt his days.

Part of the new wave of coaches who had learnt the game at the feet of Walter Winterbottom in the aftermath of Hungary's visit to English shores, he had found neither peace nor contentment when freed of the pressures of day-to-day management. Once considered one of the most forward-thinking minds in the game, he was now a 55-year-old who had lost his love of football once denied the opportunity to put his ideas and methods to the test.

Then, in the weeks after Don Revie cut short his management of the England team to follow a lucrative path to the Middle East, the Football Association approached him about returning to the training ground. Greenwood offered them the safe option they needed to help repair the position's shattered reputation after Revie, fearing that his England days were numbered, negotiated a reported four-year £240,000 deal, plus a £100,000 bonus, to manage the United Arab Emirates. For Greenwood's part, having been accused of carrying an idealistic approach into the harder and harsher environment of football in the 1970s, here was a chance to prove he still had something to offer. 'I had a hope,' he said, 'that my ideas might be better suited to international football.'

Greenwood brought some interesting theories to the role. For his first game, a goalless draw against Switzerland, he decided to build his team around the successful Liverpool side, selecting Ray Clemence, Phil Neal, Emlyn Hughes, Terry McDermott, Ray Kennedy and Ian Callaghan, who had last played for his country during the 1966 World Cup, as well as the recently departed Kevin Keegan. A similar approach brought only a 2-0 win against Luxembourg, after which he admitted that 'simplicity was our best bet – we needed to fall back on a basic pattern that was immediately understandable'.

For the visit of Italy, the last game of a World Cup qualifying campaign that had been derailed by defeat in Rome a year earlier, wingers Steve Coppell and Peter Barnes were given their international debuts in a forward line that also included new cap Bob Latchford at centre-forward alongside Keegan. Some national pride was restored with a 2-0 win. The result secured Greenwood's position beyond a three-game trial, even though the FA went through the formality of an interview process to which they invited Bobby Robson, Lawrie McMenemy and self-styled 'people's choice' Brian Clough.

His long-term confirmation in the job gave Greenwood the chance to put in place another of his notions; that England's various teams should be the responsibility of the country's leading managers and coaches. Hence, in January 1978, Don Howe was named as Bobby Robson's assistant on the B team, which was being reinstated for the first time since 1957. Terry Venables was to help Dave Sexton with the Under-21s; and, most intriguingly, Clough and his Nottingham Forest sidekick Peter Taylor would help out with the youth team. Unsurprisingly, the latter arrangement quickly fell apart.

Helping out with the senior team were Scotsman Bill Taylor, the Manchester City and ex-Fulham coach who had been part of Revie's staff; and Greenwood's old West Ham student, Geoff Hurst, who would soon be combining England duties with the job of Chelsea manager. But Howe was clearly already in Greenwood's mind for a bigger role. Instead of being sent to Malaysia, New Zealand and Singapore on the B team's summer tour, he was asked by Greenwood to go as part of his entourage to the World Cup finals in Argentina.

Having failed to secure an invitation to that particular party, England earned their place as one of eight teams in the 1980 European Championship finals in Italy by romping home with seven wins and a draw in their eight qualifying games. The Republic of Ireland were the only team to take a point from England, whose 22 goals were the most in the qualifying tournament. It was a convincing enough way to end a ten-year absence from major finals, having missed two World Cups and two European Championships since the Mexico 70 tournament. The weeks leading up to the competition in Italy saw England achieve encouraging wins in Spain and at home against world champions Argentina, although there was also a 4-1 defeat against Wales.

'I was certainly happy with the quality and depth of our squad before the European finals and I was equally pleased with the success of the squad system itself,' said Greenwood. 'I introduced players to the squad before they were likely to be picked to make them familiar with the accommodation, training methods, atmosphere and the set-up in general. I wanted newcomers to get used to shouting at men like Keegan and Brooking and to receiving advice from coaches like Don Howe and Geoff Hurst. The system also helps create a club spirit.'

England's final 22 included European Cup winners from Liverpool and Nottingham Forest but only one player to have been part of a major international tournament – although Wolverhampton Wanderers and former Liverpool captain Emlyn Hughes had not got on the field as part of Sir Alf Ramsey's 1970 squad. Greenwood chose to take most of his support coaches to Italy, with Howe and Robson – who had both played in the World Cup finals – part of a team that also included

Sexton, Venables, Howard Wilkinson, John Cartwright and Eddie Baily. The latter three would watch the games in Group 1, while Howe and others would scout England's opponents in Group 2. Conscious of accusations that Revie had attempted to fill players' heads with too much written information, Greenwood explained, 'There will be no weighty dossiers. I want them to come back, mix with the lads and talk generally about what they have seen.'

It was an approach that would later be ridiculed by Liverpool midfielder Ray Kennedy, who admittedly had something of a grudge to bear after being dropped during the tournament. 'Did ever an international team take so many [coaches] on tour?' he asked early in 1981 after retiring disillusioned from international football. 'For me, that was a fiasco. I'm sure Greenwood had difficulty finding enough jobs for them all to do. One took us for shooting, another for defending, another for four-a-side, another for heading and so on,' – which one might argue represented foresight more than fiasco. But Kennedy concluded, 'I heard so many different things about the opposition that it became comical. I wanted a psychiatrist to clear my head when they were finished.'

England began against Belgium in Turin, where Howe had enjoyed a momentous victory in front of a packed crowd two months earlier, but where the stands and terraces now stood mostly empty – even though the attendance of 15,186 was the highest in the tournament for a game that didn't include Italy or wasn't the final. Those that were there made their presence felt, however, when Jan Ceulemans equalised a brilliant chipped goal by Ray Wilkins three minutes earlier.

The evening before the game had seen a running battle between English and Italian fans on the city streets, resulting in 36 arrests. And when the Italians cheered Belgium's equaliser, fighting broke out in the crowd. The police response was to fire tear gas, with clouds of it drifting across the pitch, temporarily blinding England goalkeeper Ray Clemence and causing a delay in the action.

No more goals meant that England's hopes of topping the group and qualifying for the final required them to beat Italy in the same stadium three days later. With Forest's Garry Birtles thrown in for only his second cap and Peter Shilton taking his turn in goal as Greenwood continued his system of alternating goalkeepers, England lost 1-0 to a goal after 79 minutes by Marco Tardelli. There was still a shot at a place in the third-place qualifying game to play for when they took on Spain, but even a 2-1 win could only secure third in the group behind Belgium, who took top spot on goals scored ahead of Italy, whose strike against England was the only time they found the net.

* * *

By the time England were planning another shot at tournament football two years later, Howe was playing a bigger, more formalised role in Greenwood's set-up, a development that began to unfold in November 1981 as England prepared for a must-win World Cup qualifier at Wembley against Hungary.

England's performances in the previous summer reflected the volatility of a nation that was erupting in violence in cities up and down the country – even if the fortunes of Greenwood's men were insignificant when set against the racial tension and social unrest that sparked night after night of unrest. A 2-1 defeat in Switzerland at the end of May meant hopes were low when England went to Budapest a week later to face Hungary, considered their main rivals in the qualifying group. Yet, inspired by Brooking, scorer of two goals, and Keegan, who also found the net, they resurrected their hopes of returning to the world stage with a 3-1 win.

And then Greenwood told his players and coaches that he was resigning.

The result in Basle, which intensified the criticism of his management, had brought him to the conclusion that it was time to withdraw from the firing line. 'A humbling and shaming match,' the Press Association had called a night that featured further crowd trouble instigated by England's travelling fans. Greenwood shared his intentions with Dick Wragg, head of the FA's international committee, but revealed, 'We agreed not to tell anyone else for the time being and I did not even ring [wife] Lucy or mention it to Don Howe, Fred Street or any other member of our inner circle.'

In the meantime, he was determined to go out with a victory that would leave his successor with realistic hopes of qualification. 'We got right down to detail. We concentrated on such basics as movement of the ball, our service into the area and general passing. Not a second or word was wasted.' He called the subsequent victory 'one of the great moments of my life'.

But it had not changed his mind. As England's chartered Boeing 737 headed towards Luton Airport, Greenwood left his seat next to Howe, pulled the cabin curtains so that he and his players had some privacy and told his men, 'I'd just like to thank you all. It's been great working with you and I've enjoyed every minute of it. I think we've more or less sealed our place in the World Cup finals now but I have decided that the moment is right for me to retire. There are no problems. There's been no pressure. It's my own decision.'

After a shocked silence, the players surrounded him like Don Revie's Leeds men hounding the referee. 'As far as we were concerned, he was going nowhere,' Kenny Sansom said. 'We loved him. The press could slaughter him all they liked but we were firmly in his camp, totally convinced he was the best man for the job.'

'I felt really screwed up inside,' Greenwood remembered, 'unbelievably touched that they cared in this way.' So he promptly changed his mind.

But things were about to get even worse. In the early weeks of the new season, England travelled to Oslo and were beaten by Norway for the first time in their history. The reaction of local radio commentator Bjørge Lillelien has gone down in broadcasting history: 'We've beaten England! England, birthplace of giants – Lord Nelson, Lord Beaverbrook, Sir Winston Churchill, Sir Anthony Eden, Clement Attlee, Henry Cooper, Lady Diana! We've beaten them all! Maggie Thatcher, can you hear me? Maggie Thatcher, I have a message for you: We have knocked England out of the World Cup in football. Maggie Thatcher, as they say in your language in the boxing bars round Madison Square Garden in New York: Your boys took a hell of a beating!'

In among the voices calling for blood, the *Daily Mirror*'s Frank McGhee could not remember 'a more inept England performance in 30 years', while Clough called for all the team's coaches to be fired, with the exception of Howe. Subsequent results in the group meant England had a last chance to qualify if they could beat Hungary, a game for which Howe was required to take a leading coaching role when Bill Taylor was reported to have been laid low by a stomach bug.

An emotional night in front of 92,000 at Wembley lay ahead, prompting unavoidable memories of eight years earlier when England failed to beat Poland and were condemned to the World Cup wilderness. Paul Mariner banished many of those thoughts by redirecting an off-target attempt by Brooking into the net after 14 minutes. At half-time, Howe could be seen racing to the dressing room in order to be waiting for the players, to pass on further instruction. He could not find the words to produce another goal, however, as England missed almost as many chances as they had on that infamous night in 1973. This time, though, they didn't get caught on the break and a 1-0 win was enough to return them to the World Cup finals.

In the BBC studio, Howe's old Arsenal team-mate, Bob Wilson, was finding it 'ironic' that England had clinched qualification without the 'naturally gifted' Trevor Francis and Glenn Hoddle on the field. But Lawrie McMenemy, who'd had his own ambitions about leading his country's World Cup campaign, recognised the pragmatism of Howe in England's approach. 'We won tonight playing the English-style game,' he said. 'We've closed people down and we've muscled them.' Gesturing towards Wilson, he added, 'He's been going on about Glenn Hoddle, but here's a lesson that, for all his natural ability, if he gets a little bit of that other stuff…'

Hoddle recalls, 'People were looking for players to get forward and track back. That was English football at that time. You had to do everything. If you were a creative player like I was it was sometimes difficult. You were fighting against the tide.'

But he believes he was already learning about the 'other stuff' that McMenemy spoke of, courtesy of Don Howe. 'A good lesson that stuck with me was when Don gave me the biggest rollicking I have ever had in football,' Hoddle recalls. 'It was an Under-21 game in Bulgaria [in 1979] and he ran off the bench to the side of the pitch after I let somebody run into our penalty area. Fortunately the lad didn't score, but Don was up screaming at me. We didn't fall out over it. It was the right thing. Don saw what happened and I was a young man trying to learn the game. That was Don. He would call it if it needed to be called.'

Howe had also seen that Hoddle needed a tougher edge to his game. 'We had a chat about what it meant when you are a player that the opposition are trying to stop,' the future England manager continues. 'He put a seed in my mind and it stayed with me.'

'Sometimes, Glenn, you have to meet fire with fire,' Howe told him. 'These players are trying to put you out the game. They have been told to mark you man-for-man and to try and hurt you sometimes.'

Hoddle continues, 'It made a lot of sense to me. I didn't go out to do things, but I realised I had to protect myself a bit more and be a bit stronger. I needed to make players realise that if they tackled me it was not going to make me fear playing my normal game. I had to stamp my authority on them – not the other way around. I had that in my mind.' Hoddle would remember it being a particularly valuable lesson after he was transferred in 1987 to French club Monaco, where the style of game featured more man-marking than in England. But even before that, he can cite an example of putting Howe's advice into action in Tottenham's 1982 FA Cup Final against Queens Park Rangers.

'Gary Waddock was told to man-mark me,' he remembers. 'He was following me everywhere. Late in the game the ball comes free in the middle of the pitch and Gary gets onto the ball and I go in with a tackle that would definitely be two-footed nowadays. I smashed the ball and it went out to Graham Roberts and he cuts the ball back into me and I score from the edge of the box. That is a prime example of what I think I picked up from Don.'

Less than two weeks after England's World Cup qualification came the tragic news that Taylor had died, aged 42, from a brain tumour, meaning that Howe was formally appointed as the England team's chief coach in early January. 'I think Ron and I will be a good team,' he stated. 'I am a little more abrasive than he is. You need a fatherly figure like him and a shouter like me. I want the England players to know that when they join up for internationals they are going to have to work.' Addressing the commitment he still had as Arsenal's first-team coach, he argued, 'There is a hell of a busy period coming up because of the backlog of fixtures, but unless Arsenal play on exactly the same night as England there must be room for compromise.'

Without overstating the impact of Howe, it is interesting to look at the results of the England team with him working directly next to Greenwood. After beating Hungary, they reeled off four more wins without conceding a goal, including a clean sweep against the home nations and a 2-0 Wembley win against Holland.

According to Tony Woodcock, 'Before Don came in things were far too relaxed. I approve of a bit of freedom, but it went too far.' Noting that Greenwood appeared to be indulgent of Brooking and Keegan's desires when it came to practice routines, Woodcock continued, 'When Don was brought in, that sort of thing changed, particularly in training. We used to have five-a-sides and … they were a joke. You have 21 players playing on a small pitch, running around, laughing and joking. You could have a bit of fun, but I hated playing them. Don got things organised. You could still have fun with Ray Clemence playing as a striker, but it was everyone really trying in a serious, competitive game, which can be equally enjoyable.

'Don had a reputation as being a good coach and the players liked him and got on well with him. He was tough when there were physical days and the old saying about being no gain without pain would come out early. You knew you were going to be in for a hard session. But he was always perky and cheerful and up for having a joke.'

Hoddle felt Howe was 'difficult to get to know' but describes him as 'a very organised coach'. He continues, 'Don was very intense. It was through his love and passion for the game. You could see it when he was talking in team meetings or about set plays. Kenny Sansom used to say, "Wait till the jugular comes up." He wanted the players to do what he was telling them and you could see his enthusiasm to get the job done, get the information across that would make us a better team. It was funny at times when we would talk about looking out for the jugular.'

Brooking would admit of himself and Keegan, 'If Ron and Don Howe were both taking a training session we tended to drift towards Ron. Eventually the group would be split in two and those selected to work with Don seemed to do twice as much running as those working with Ron.'

Keegan described Howe as 'an outstanding defensive coach and a great believer in hard work', which he said could sometimes create problems for Brooking, who was 'a little more laid-back in his approach'. Keegan also recalled Howe upsetting his friend with a slip of the tongue that he 'had to take back because the lads were in uproar'. He explained, 'Describing an opposition player, Don said, "This one is a bit like Trevor – he cheats." What he meant was that, like Glenn Hoddle later or Paul Gascoigne, he didn't go chasing back. Don realised he had dropped a clanger, but it showed how his mind worked. We wouldn't have wanted Trevor back defending in our penalty area, where he might have been more of a liability than a help, but obviously Don felt otherwise.'

Greenwood recalled in his 1984 autobiography, 'Don was quiet to begin with, but then he began to express himself, showing what an outstanding technician he is. He is a hard worker and a formidable driver; he makes training an interesting challenge and because he has always kept up with the game abroad he is full of ideas and variations. He is a student of football; never satisfied, always learning.'

Ipswich centre-back Terry Butcher, who had played only four England games before becoming a first-choice selection during the 1982 World Cup finals, would retain good memories of preparation leading into the summer. 'Training was short and sharp and I felt a marked improvement in my game from playing with such good teammates. Don Howe and Ron Greenwood had done their homework.

We knew there would be a lot of movement from opposing forwards, hoping to drag our central defenders apart and we worked hard on countering this in training with plenty of possession play. Don drilled it into us that we had to keep talking to each other and telling teammates what was going on.'

Playing in Howe's old right-back position, Viv Anderson enjoyed special attention. 'He used to help me out in many respects,' he explains. 'Positions to get into and certain things like that. He was very proactive. He would say when there were times to go forward and when to stop and he helped a lot, especially when I was new into the England squad.'

According to Peter Shilton, who would eventually become Greenwood's preferred goalkeeper, the manager was 'quietly strong' but, 'His masterstroke was his appointment of Don Howe as his assistant. As manager of West Ham, Ron had advocated purist football, but often to the detriment of a well-organised defence. Don Howe brought organisation to the England defence and proved the perfect foil for Ron.'

Hoddle continues, 'Don put on really good sessions and training was really interesting. His enthusiasm was second to none of people I have worked with. You could see his love of the game. Ron let Don do most of the training and would just take a session now and again. If there was any defensive organisation to be done then Don would take that and he would talk to the team about the set-up of the midfield and whatever we were trying to do. Don made us all aware of how important set plays were, both attacking and defending. Back then there wasn't anyone who concentrated or worked as much on defending as Don did. With most teams it was a little bit off-the-cuff.'

In his first match as No.2 in his own right, a 4-0 win against Northern Ireland, Howe pulled Wilkins back into a more withdrawn role, playing as a midfield sweeper – the 'quarterback' position, as it would become known in the 21st century. Bryan Robson's quick-fire strike after 44 seconds was also a foretaste of events to come. After a Trevor Francis goal secured a 1-0 win against Wales in Cardiff, Howe defended a generally disappointing performance by highlighting their good passing, although even Greenwood admitted 'it was far from a classic'.

In making his selections for the summer, Greenwood, according to his successor Bobby Robson, rejected a piece of advice from Howe that might conceivably made a difference late in England's campaign as they sought to unlock stubborn defences. 'Don is an advocate of attacking football and when he and Ron Greenwood were discussing the squad for the World Cup finals in Spain, it was Don who was in favour of taking a winger like Peter Barnes or Tony Morley and Ron who decided against it.'[8]

Meanwhile, Howe's Highbury colleague, Fred Street, had been focused on ensuring that the players would not get bored at their base in Bilbao. 'I recorded about 50 Betamax tapes of BBC and ITV shows – comedies, plays etc. We took them with us, along with two British televisions and video decks because the Spanish ones weren't compatible. We had a big TV room where players would go and watch shows like *Parkinson* and *Morecambe and Wise.* We took books galore and had a games room with Space Invaders. I had to organise games afternoons like a holiday camp. You couldn't let the players go walking down the street because of security issues. Kidnapping was also a possibility, especially as we were in the part of Spain where there were problems with ETA.[9] Taking a player could have achieved publicity for their cause. You had to be overprotective.'

Security concerns had been heightened by events involving British military forces in the South Atlantic. As England got ready for kick-off in their final pre-tournament friendly against Finland in Helsinki, troops had advanced to within seven miles of Port Stanley, two months after Prime Minister Margaret Thatcher had dispatched a 'Task

---

8 Villa winger Morley's, ahem, consolation was having been part of the recording session as the squad trilled out, 'We're on our way; we are Ron's 22,' as the opening line to 'This Time (We'll Get It Right)', England's first World Cup release since 'Back Home' made it to No.1 in 1970. He also made the squad picture on the sleeve of the single.

9 Euskadi Ta Askatasuna was a paramilitary group campaigning for independence for the Basque country in northern Spain and southwestern France. Bilbao was the largest Spanish city in the region.

Force' to take back the Falkland Islands for Britain after invasion by Argentinian troops. Thatcher, who was offering Argentina's leader, General Leopoldo Galtieri, a final opportunity to withdraw his men from the capital of the Falklands before battle commenced, had expressed serious concerns about England, Scotland and Northern Ireland participating in the World Cup while British troops were at war, especially given the prospect of running into their rival on the field. The conflict, which would claim almost 1,000 lives across the two sides, overshadowed England's re-entry to world football's biggest playground. On the third night of the tournament, BBC interrupted its coverage of Brazil's victory over the Soviet Union to bring live updates as Port Stanley was retaken by the British, leading to Argentinian surrender. Greenwood would describe the conflict as 'something which had never been out of our hearts and minds'.

Politics and war aside, 'the mood in the camp was good,' according to Bryan Robson. 'Everything about the set-up put the players in a positive frame of mind. We thought we were good enough to have a long run in the tournament.'

But weighing heavy on the mind of the England management team was the fitness of the squad's two most influential players, Brooking, who had been battling with a groin injury, and Keegan, who suffered a flare-up of an old back problem the day before the opening match. 'I knew I was in deep trouble,' the England captain recalled.

Street explains, 'In England games that were one-offs you didn't have any injured players with you. If they weren't fit for selection, you sent them back to their clubs. In a World Cup it is different. You have got three games to prepare for and hopefully another three, so if you have got a player who might not be able to play in the first three games but might play in the fourth you keep them around. It is more of a club feeling. And a player wants to go to the World Cup and take part. It is a once in a lifetime. We hoped Kevin's back was going to get better, so we stuck with him, but even if he had done it before the World Cup squad was named I think we would have taken him because it was Kevin Keegan's team. He was a charismatic character and thrived in that arena.'

Greenwood was forced to announce that both star players were out of the line-up to play France in Bilbao. Graham Rix and Trevor Francis would take their places, with Greenwood reminding everyone that 'this is a squad game'. In north London, much would be made of Howe's Arsenal player, Rix, being selected throughout the tournament, while Hoddle was given limited opportunities. Hoddle, however, neither bears a grudge nor harbours suspicion of a Gunners bias. 'That would never have come into it,' he says confidently, 'even though Don had a big influence on the manager. That wasn't the position for me anyway because I played for England mostly on the right or maybe in the centre. And in those days it was very rigid 4-4-2; we didn't come away from that and we never played the diamond. So it never came into my mind at all. Don was very professional and he and Ron would do what was right for England.'

Regardless of the identity of their replacements, anyone who had witnessed the combination Keegan and Brooking had established over the previous five years could not help but fear for England's chances against France. Without them, England's red shirts, numbered according to alphabetical order of names, would read: Shilton – Mills (captain), Thompson, Butcher, Sansom – Coppell, Robson, Wilkins, Rix – Francis, Mariner.

What they needed was to get off to a good start to ease the nerves. To that end, their final training session before their first World Cup finals match for 12 years was significant. Howe had introduced a set-piece routine where Sansom would take a long throw from the left; Butcher or Mariner would help the ball on; and Robson would arrive late in the box to get on the end of it. As training wrapped up, Manchester United winger Coppell put down his drink and, referring to Sansom's role, called to Howe, 'I can do that, you know.'

After a brief thought, Howe decided, 'We're not going to put the lads in again because we've done enough. Just show me how far you can throw it.' Coppell hurled the ball into the penalty area and Howe nodded. 'That's fine. You take them from the other side.'

Greenwood's autobiography recalls things slightly differently, saying that he suggested the move after Howe had gone through England's set pieces in the dressing room before kick-off. Whatever the truth, nobody would have expected England to win a throw down their right wing after only 15 seconds. Coppell's delivery was nodded towards the far post by Butcher and Robson ran in to hook the ball home. One-nil after 27 seconds. England had been pegged back by half-time, at which point the players were doused in cold towels – a tactic Howe would reproduce at Wembley six years later – and they grew stronger as the game progressed. Robson, the only man picked by Greenwood in all eight qualifiers, scored again when he headed in Francis's cross and Mariner completed an impressive 3-1 win.

The most difficult test of the opening group behind them, England beat Czechoslovakia 2-0 and Kuwait 1-0 to take their place in a tough second-round group with West Germany and hosts Spain, the winner of which would advance to the last four.

The Germans, who had been upset by Algeria in the earlier group but were unbeaten against European opposition for four years, rarely worried an England team who secured a goalless draw and received mixed reviews. 'Advantage Greenwood' said *The Times*, basing its calculation on the fact that Germany would face Spain in the next match, meaning England would know exactly what was required when they played a week later, and would also have more time to get Brooking and Keegan fit. Yet reporter Stuart Jones called the game 'ponderous', with both teams scared of the damage that defeat would inflict. 'We've done all right,' said Greenwood, who felt the Germans were 'a bit scared of us' and admitted, 'We have probably missed a bit of a chance to grab two [points] instead of one.'

It was that latter aspect that angered many critics; none more vocal that ITV panellist John Bond, the Manchester City manager, who had no doubt where to lay the blame. Once more, a coaching achievement by Howe – getting a previously unfancied England team to the brink of the World Cup semi-finals – was in danger of being undermined by its manner. 'I watched that game tonight and I can't relate that to Ron Greenwood at all,' Bond ventured. 'Don Howe, you know, he's taken an awful lot of credit for what's happened since he's been with England, but I'm just wondering if there's a lack of adventure now.' Fellow analyst Mick Channon, the former England forward, chipped in, 'The England team's becoming Arsenal. I think Don Howe is beginning to pick the team. That's the way it looks to me and I was very disappointed in the performance.'

And then Bond continued, 'I played under Ron Greenwood for six years and his style, his attitude to the game, was to make things happen – to get forward, to get bodies forward – and that wasn't there tonight. If Don Howe is having that sort of influence, that's all right over a league programme, but that's not going to win cup games.'

ITV wasn't finished with the topic, dispatching World Cup winner Jack Charlton to confront Greenwood and Howe as they sat by their hotel pool in groin-hugging shorts typical of the 1980s. It produced a fascinating piece of television, with frank views being exchanged between football men; no 'outsiders' from the world of journalism involved. Howe offered the kind of counter-attack that critics felt was lacking against a German team that was there for the taking. 'It's funny how people never said that before the game; that the Germans were rubbish,' he said. 'You see, Jack,' he continued, pointing at his inquisitor to emphasise every point, 'they dictated to us by playing five in midfield. Now we are going to have to cope with that, like it or not, because we don't wanna lose the game, do we?'

Charlton replied, 'I wasn't meaning that, Don. I understand the point about the five. I thought you were overprotective of your back four yesterday. Robson and Wilkins didn't move and if they are anchoring the midfield the wide men had the responsibility to go and play, but neither Coppell or Rixy got up fast enough or often enough or quick enough.'

Greenwood chipped in, 'I think that's a fair criticism in the first half. They did more in the second half,' adding that Rix and left-back Sansom 'began to play like they do for the Arsenal, and rotated, and created a few problems'.

Howe conceded, 'Perhaps we overdid the long ball at times and if you overdo the long ball the midfield players can't arrive, can they? The ball's gone before they can get there. The build-up's got to be a bit shorter and then perhaps the ball's played into the corner of the pitch. The old, old story. You're dependent on the players' interpretation out there.'

When Charlton made a point about England not playing as he had witnessed in training, Greenwood chuckled, 'You're turning out to be a good TV man,' and turned to Howe for approval. Howe, squinting into the sun, looked like he'd been asked to laugh at a loved one's funeral. 'How do you think we played against France in the second half?' the affronted coach continued. 'Didn't we shut it down and then score goals? What do you say then? "Well done. Great talk at half-time. Adjusted great. Smashing." So you give us all the plaudits. Now we're using the same system, you are saying it's wrong, Jack. You can't have it that way. You cannot have it that way. The game is adaptable. There is no one system wins the game.'

On England's day of destiny in the Bernabéu Stadium, by which time the Germans' 2-1 win against Spain meant Greenwood's men needed a two-goal victory, *The Times* was more ready to acknowledge the positive aspect of Howe's influence. In his piece about Greenwood – 'the manager who has restored national pride' – Stuart Jones pointed out, 'Mr Greenwood belongs to the old, romantic school that encourages individualism, but he has bowed to his principles and, with the help of Don Howe, the master tactician, who has proved the perfect foil, threatens to achieve as notable a feat as Sir Alf Ramsey in 1966.'

Other notable journalists had previously defended Howe's contribution to a more secure-looking England team, with Jeff Powell of the *Daily Mail* responding to criticism of the coach's methods by asking, 'What else did England initially need after their pathetic failures against the Swiss, Norwegians and Romanians?' And the *Sunday Telegraph*'s Colin Malam had argued, 'Greenwood's idealism is counter-balanced by Howe's realism; Howe's innate caution is offset by Greenwood's predilection for bold, attacking football.'

Yet Brooking, one of Greenwood's most loyal disciples, felt that 'something was nagging away at me' as the decisive game approached; a sense that his long-time boss was about to be guided in the wrong direction. 'This was a match where we needed to go for the jugular,' he would remember. 'But some of the training had suggested a more cautious approach. Don was a very good coach and a strong disciplinarian. He was hands-on and liked a rigid team structure. You had to play the way he wanted. Ron was much happier to delegate some responsibility to the senior players. He used to say, "If it's not working, just change it. Don't wait for me to tell you." That wasn't the way Don worked. I don't think he was happy on the one or two occasions when Kevin or I changed things on the pitch.' Brooking concluded, 'For the Spain game we needed Ron's approach. It was a situation made for a positive team with an attacking strategy.'

It was Keegan and Brooking who once more dominated news reports coming out of the England camp. Greenwood chose to gamble on their fitness – although placing them among the five substitutes was an each-way punt rather than the bold on-the-nose stake both men craved. It was Woodcock, newly recruited by Howe's Arsenal from Cologne, who replaced Coppell, who was suffering from a swollen knee. 'Kevin felt that Don had pressurised Ron into picking Tony,' suggested Brooking. Greenwood and Howe delivered their pre-match instructions. 'It's not a race,' Howe advised. 'You've got 90 minutes. Be patient and take your time.' Brooking and Keegan craved more urgency.

The home fans in the crowd of 75,000 chanted 'Malvinas! Malvinas!' – the Spanish name for the Falklands – at the England team when they took the field. 'The atmosphere inside the stadium was poisonous,' Butcher recalled. The action on the pitch was somewhat less intense and after 63 minutes England were still unable to break down a team beaten by Northern Ireland earlier in the competition. The wounded duo were sent on. Brooking was immediately denied by goalkeeper Luis Arconada after manoeuvring himself some space in the box and Keegan, who had won his argument to be allowed to travel to Germany for treatment on his back during the tournament, headed wide of a gaping goal a few minutes later. 'I was definitely fit for the Spain game and so was Trevor,' Keegan would argue years later. 'Leaving us on the bench was Ron Greenwood's biggest mistake. We were his two best players, we were influential in the way England played and I do not believe any other country in the world would have made that decision, even if the team had done all right without us. I think that the decision was probably made after discussions with Don Howe, but if it was Ron's decision and his alone, it shows what a strong man he was.'

Despite almost being caught on the break on occasions, England continued to create chance after chance, with Wilkins and Butcher encouraged to fire shots from the edge of the box and Robson creating problems with his well-timed arrivals in the penalty area. But there was no breakthrough and, after five unbeaten games and only one goal conceded, England were denied a semi-final berth against France.

'There is nothing for them to be ashamed of because they have done everybody proud,' said Greenwood. Despite Brooking's pre-game misgivings, on this occasion there were few complaints about England's approach, although their lack of truly world-class talent was emphasised by events earlier in the day, when one of the most pulsating World Cup games of all-time had seen Italy overcome the magnificent Brazilians 3-2 in Barcelona. Greenwood reflected, 'I would have given anything for a pinch of Brazilian skill in our matches against West Germany and Spain and, who knows, Brazil might have been well served by a little of our organisation and application in their game against Italy.'

Butcher would describe the tournament as 'the one that got away. To be part of a team going through a World Cup finals undefeated and not even to reach the final was hard to take. I thought we were good enough to win it.' Defensive colleague Sansom thought similarly, saying that with a fit Keegan-Brooking partnership and 'that special ingredient of good luck' England could have been world champions. 'When you know you are part of a team that is as good as any other and better than most but have still failed to make it through to the end, it's a bitter pill to swallow.'

By the time Italy overcame West Germany in the final six days later, Greenwood was sitting at home in Brighton, thinking similar thoughts and starting to plan an autobiography of which David Miller of *The Times* would complain that there was 'no detailed discussion of Don Howe's influence on improved defensive qualities'. Watching the game in Madrid in his role as Greenwood's successor was Bobby Robson. 'I've learnt a lot from this World Cup,' said Howe when asked what the appointment of his old friend meant for his own England future, 'and I would love to continue as coach.'

10

HIGHBURY'S NUMBER ONE

At first glance this is almost a hazy dream; of baffling managerial decisions, unfathomable defeats and some faith-saving individuals and performances.

Jon Spurling, *All Guns Blazing: Arsenal in the 1980s*

SINCE THEIR disappointment on three fronts at the end of the endless 1979/80 season, Arsenal had embarked on a decade whose first half is accurately summarised in the words of the author above. It was a period that saw Don Howe attain the managerial job he wanted above all others, but ultimately led to his second unhappy and acrimonious exit from Highbury.

Liam Brady followed his ambitions of playing overseas by joining Juventus in the summer of 1980 for a tribunal-set fee of £600,000, and Frank Stapleton's departure would follow a year later. 'They were major blows,' Terry Neill explains, 'but they were free to go and you couldn't stop them.' The Gunners manager was resigned enough to the situation to help smooth Brady's path to Italy. 'Liam was a bit depressed at one stage that he hadn't heard from [Juventus manager] Giovanni Trapattoni, so I got him into the office at the training ground and got Trapattoni on the phone.'

Neill's response to the loss of Brady was to pay a reported £1.25 million for Queens Park Rangers' teenage goalscoring discovery, Clive Allen. But then he stunned everyone by effectively swapping him for Crystal Palace's England left-back, Kenny Sansom, before he had played a competitive match for the Gunners. One suggestion was that Allen had been Palace's target all along but QPR would not sell to them, meaning that Arsenal offered to be some kind of clearing house. Neill's explanation that his forward line 'didn't look right' after three pre-season friendlies did little to silence the conspiracy theorists.

Sansom's first impression of his new home was the gaping hole left by Brady. 'I can't emphasise enough how bad it had been for the club,' he said of the Irishman's departure. 'It was the one single thing that dampened my arrival at Arsenal. Brady was a huge loss. He was a Highbury legend and the fans as well as the players missed him badly. It was as if the North Bank were mourning a terrible death.'

Arsenal proved effective enough to finish the campaign with an eight-game unbeaten run that lifted them into a respectable third place. The final day of the season saw celebration reverberate from every corner of Highbury as Arsenal achieved the victory that assured them of European football, while their opponents, Aston Villa, became champions of the First Division thanks to Ipswich Town losing at Middlesbrough. After which Stapleton signed for Manchester United for £900,000.

According to Pat Jennings, 'The Mickey Mouse contract they offered Liam in 1980 was unacceptable and the club didn't learn from losing him … They should have tied down those young players with a decent contract. And then, of course, Frank left a year later. It just shouldn't have happened.'

Neill, who spent the rest of his time at Arsenal in an elusive search for the players who could replace the missing Irish magic, admits, 'With Liam and Frank gone I knew I was losing the heart of the team. I was scouting around Diego Maradona, Michel Platini, Frank Arnesen, Soren Lerby.' Neill says of Denmark midfielder Arnesen, 'At one time his children had more Arsenal kit than the club shop. I kept going over there to see him and going to their apartment.'

The 1981/82 campaign was forgettable: a fifth-place League finish and a disappointing UEFA Cup exit on away goals against little-fancied Belgian club Winterslag, a tie that ended with the most noticeable evidence so far of a 'Neill out' sentiment within the Highbury crowd.

The following season saw Neill and Howe unveil a new strike partnership: Tony Woodcock, signed on the eve of the World Cup finals, and Lee Chapman, the big blond with the looks of a male model and, in many eyes, the mobility of a mannequin. Before handing over £500,000 for Stoke City's top scorer in the previous two seasons, Neill was said to have been told by players such as Willie Young and Graham Rix that Coventry City's Garry Thompson would be a better purchase.[10] December 1982 saw Neill finally capture one of his international targets, the Yugoslavia international Vladimir Petrovic, although the former Red Star Belgrade midfielder was only a sporadic influence and was quickly informed that he would not be staying for a second season. 'I was in the reserves with Vladimir and saw how good he was,' says defender Colin Hill. 'If Arsenal had him coming into the team now he would do well. He was that good. But it didn't work at that time.'

Stewart Robson, who had risen through the youth system to become a forceful midfielder or versatile defender, remembers, 'That was the poorest season of them all. We had that on-off transfer of Petrovic, which never really came off until it was too late. He didn't start playing well until he was told he wasn't getting a new contract.'

Woodcock recalls that 'the first season went reasonably well for me', in that he scored 21 competitive goals, although in a revealing diary in which he wrote about 1983 he said in an April entry, 'I've been bad all year – in my general play that is.' Several decades later, he

---

10 In fairness to Chapman, while his much-ridiculed and injury-hit Arsenal career would feature only four goals in 23 League appearances, he proved an effective force at most other stops on his career, notably at Sheffield Wednesday and Leeds United, where he helped the club recapture the League title in 1991/92.

continues, 'Although we had some good players, you could tell there was something missing; something not quite right. You could have a good result and then a bad one. Without being down on Don and Terry, this is where management comes into it. There is nothing to say they did a bad job, but when you look at some of the players that were coming to the club it was a mystery why things didn't go better.'

Woodcock encountered a somewhat different Howe to the man he had become accustomed to in an international setting, suggesting that he was 'a bit overpowering for the young players, which I hadn't expected from how he is with England'. He also suggested that such a trait might have been because his livelihood didn't depend on an England result as it did at Arsenal. 'At the club he is so caught up in the game that he wants to play it for you, and I think that affects the young players.'

The season got off to an inauspicious start with two defeats in a pre-season tournament in Rotterdam, the second of which was a thrashing by Austria Vienna that resulted in one of the directors going to the dressing room to tell the players they had let the club down. Howe would normally have resented invasion of his domain, but this time he let the club official have his say and, once he had left, showed his own frustration by barking at his players, 'You are all c***s.' According to Sansom, 'Don never, ever swore like that so it just goes to show that this was probably one of his most miserable moments.' Sansom approached his coach and protested, 'It was poor and we let you down, but I'm not a c***; none of us are that.'

'Like a true gentleman, he apologised for using that word,' Sansom continued, admitting, 'I can see just how mortified he was with our play.'

According to Jon Spurling, 'If the previous season had been a straight-to-video-type year doomed to end up in the £2.99 bargain basement bin in Woolies, some of the grisly slaughters of '82/83 almost turned this season into a snuff movie – unsuitable viewing for all but the tough-minded or the mentally sick.' One Highbury contest on the way to a tenth-place finish in the First Division – a 0-0 draw against

Nottingham Forest – was so dire that Neill felt compelled to apologise to the fans for wasting their time and money. It was the kind of game that had observers fretting about the state of English football, especially considering that the 21,698 at Highbury was one of only three League crowds in excess of 20,000 that Saturday. Woodcock's diary, published in book form as *Inside Soccer*, called it 'probably the worst game I've ever been in'.

Beaten by Manchester United in both legs of their League Cup semi-final, the Gunners qualified for a last-four rematch in the FA Cup with a victory over Aston Villa; a game that provided the highlight of the season. 'Something strange seems to happen to Arsenal whenever they put their lips to the FA Cup,' wrote Clive White in *The Times*. 'The usual dullness and impotence of their character is replaced by something much sharper.' It was Petrovic who illuminated the afternoon, providing the Highbury fans with something to remember him by and justifying his reinstatement to the team ahead of the more workmanlike Brian Talbot. That decision had been the topic of conversation during a ten-mile training run that Neill and Howe shared in preparation for the third staging of the London Marathon the following month.

Arsenal were already leading via Woodcock's sharp finish when Petrovic took the ball in stride as he arrived purposely in the box and fired an angled shot inside the far post. The 2-0 half-time lead was rarely threatened and the Gunners booked a semi-final date at Villa Park. Woodcock's diary, an honest and frank account that offers valuable insight for anyone writing about Arsenal in that period, reveals his concerns going into that game. 'At the moment I don't know what is going on,' he wrote. 'Some weeks they tell us to come for it to be played to feet. Other times they say we come too short too quickly and want too much played to our feet ... we don't know what we are aiming for; we haven't got anything you can say is typically Arsenal.'

It didn't help that two weeks before facing United in the game that would define their season, Arsenal had crashed 5-0 at Tottenham, a day that ended with Howe accusing Woodcock and Sansom of not wanting to play and blaming the former for being offside too often. Woodcock, who couldn't understand why blame was being apportioned to him after the defence let in five, claimed, 'Don never seems to be in the wrong. You can't explain anything to him.'

The semi-final, played the day before Howe, Neill and Fred Street took to the pavements and roads of the capital, had its turning point shortly before half-time. The influential Robson, whose goal-bound prod had been finished off by Woodcock to give Arsenal the lead, went down with an ankle injury after a challenge with Arthur Albiston. 'Terry took me off on his shoulders,' he remembers. 'They tried to ice it at half-time and said I might be able to carry on, but when they said "jump" I just couldn't. I'd ruptured the ligaments.' As the second half kicked off, the television cameras caught Howe with his chin in his hands looking as though he feared the worst. His demeanour was justified. Without Robson's presence in midfield, Arsenal were pegged back within five minutes of the restart, Bryan Robson making a typical surge into the box to convert an Ashley Grimes delivery. The goal was particularly painful for Howe as it came after centre-back Chris Whyte had tried one short pass too many, contrary to the coach's pre-game instructions that no more than one square ball should be played before it went forward. A further goal by 17-year-old Norman Whiteside rewarded United for their domination of the second half and left Arsenal short of Wembley once more.

Howe was at the centre of a row when Arsenal and United met for the fifth and final time of the season; a 3-0 Easter Monday win at Highbury in which United midfielder Remi Moses was sent off for headbutting Peter Nicholas. United manager Ron Atkinson accused Howe of provoking referee Eric Read into his course of action. 'Howe had already been screaming out for Moses to be sent off,' he claimed. 'That sort of thing really appals me. I never felt so angry about anything since I came into the business.'

Howe responded by pointing out that Gordon McQueen had been urging the United bench to remove Moses before he got himself sent off and suspended for the final. He said of Atkinson, 'For him to accuse our players and bench the way he did is completely out of order. United beat us in three cup semi-final matches. Each time we shook hands and walked away. It's a pity they couldn't do the same this time.'

Arsenal and United, who went on to beat Brighton and Hove Albion in a replayed final, had not done with their battles. The next one would pit them against each other in the biggest transfer saga of the summer as the Gunners went after the kind of headline-grabbing acquisition being demanded by the 8,000 fans who had signed an anti-management document organised by the newly formed Action Group. 'We are not stupid,' was Howe's response to the petition. 'We have been in the game long enough to know what the public likes to see, but the sort of players they want to see are hard to get. We have tried to run this club sensibly and the directors have ensured Arsenal are solvent at a time when some clubs are in danger of going under.'

Howe's comments prompted Arsenal fans to write to the *Daily Mirror*, with one suggesting, 'He clearly does not know. Why else would he allow Vladimir Petrovic to go?' Another said that 'if they can release a Rolls-Royce and keep some horse-and-cart players, my place on the terraces next season will be vacant'.

The solution, it seemed, was to be found north of the border in the shape of Charlie Nicholas, a mullet-haired showman who had just scored 48 goals in a season for Celtic and was considered the most exciting talent to be produced by Scotland since Kenny Dalglish. He was exactly the kind of vibrant talent that the North Bank craved; and would represent the sort of flashy move that had not been seen at the club since Neill signed Malcolm Macdonald.

Howe had been sent to Glasgow to watch Nicholas several times, but such a talent attracted other suitors, notably champions Liverpool and Cup holders United. 'At first United were my original choice,' Nicholas said in 1999, 'but I wasn't too impressed with Big Ron's long-term plans.' The sales pitch that secured the Gunners their man for £750,000 might have been more convincing, but it would end up seeming somewhat hollow. 'Arsenal's plan sounded really promising.

Don Howe said Arsenal were going to bring Brady back from Italy and also try and get Ray Wilkins to join,' Nicholas continued. 'I just felt Arsenal were maybe going to go big and go for the title.'

On the pursuit of Manchester United and England midfielder Wilkins, Howe admitted, 'Ray's the man we need, I would love him here.' Yet Wilkins remained at Old Trafford for a further season before heading to Italy to play for AC Milan. Woodcock felt Arsenal were guilty of not making a bid when Wilkins was out of the team at the start of the season and United might have been ready to cash in.

According to newspaper reports, Howe had been contemplating his future options, which included an unidentified overseas job or a full-time role as England No.2 under Bobby Robson. It was a state of affairs that the always prickly Alan Sunderland exploited to retaliate against Howe when he accused his players of having the wrong attitude. 'What about yours, Don?' Sunderland fired back. 'Are you finally going to move down from Wolverhampton? Are you signing with England? Are you staying with Arsenal? We don't know. Does that mean your attitude isn't 100 per cent?'

According to Howe's son, Rob, his father never wanted a full-time role on the coaching England staff. 'He was very proud to be involved with England and at one point he was close to getting the manager's job and he would absolutely have loved that,' he says. 'But I don't know that my dad would have done that [been a permanent coach] because he liked working with the players and obviously a full-time England coach is not working with the players very much. He would have spent a lot of time going around the country looking at the coaching set-up and I don't think that would have suited him.'

Howe put the question to bed by signing a new three-year Arsenal contract and beginning the process of moving to Hertfordshire. It meant he was still in Highbury's glass dugout when Nicholas was afforded an American-style solo entrance for his debut against Luton Town, an honour which embarrassed the player. Arsenal began the season with a 2-1 victory and Nicholas netted his first two Gunners goals when they repeated the score at Wolves two days later. But it was more than two months until he found the net again, in a 2-1 League Cup victory at Tottenham.

By that time Arsenal were struggling below halfway in the table, despite a spectacular 6-2 win at Aston Villa that allowed Howe to state, 'It's nice to show people how wrong they are about Arsenal and the way we play.' Yet Woodcock, who scored five goals at Villa Park, had noted in his diary, 'The real problem is that we just don't play with much confidence. We're not sure enough about our jobs to push a back-four player into midfield so a midfield player can push up and make an extra forward. We seem to … keep it tight and wait for someone to produce a bit of magic.'

Hill recalls, 'It was a period of transition. There was a changing of the guard. We'd sold great players like Brady and Stapleton and there was only David O'Leary from that group of homegrown players left. There was a lack of confidence and we had some big players who were struggling with their form.'

Once more, Arsenal looked to the cup competitions to salvage their season. A home tie against Third Division Walsall in the League Cup was expected to pose few problems, even if they were going into it on the back of a 3-0 defeat at Leicester City that had Howe stating, 'It was probably the lowest point of the season for me. I did my nut in the dressing room afterwards.'

Howe had been angry that his words before the game appeared to have fallen on deaf ears. In an impassioned pre-match talk he had challenged the players to show greater desire and said, 'It's not about having a nice car or a nice house. It's about what you do inside the game; it's about winning medals; about playing as well as you can play.' Using American tennis star John McEnroe as an example of someone who counted his victories more than his money, he concluded, 'He has got this winner's streak in him. You have got to have that.'

According to Woodcock, 'It was a brilliant talk, but he might as well have saved his breath because it just made the performance even more unforgivable.' Robson, meanwhile, remembers that game as symptomatic of Arsenal's problems at the time. 'For all Don's making us get stuck in, we were quite a weak team. Manchester United in those cup games knew that they could roll us over by getting stuck in and being aggressive. Some of the away games, teams quite enjoyed playing against us. I remember at Leicester, Gary Lineker, Alan Smith and Steven Lynex ran all over us. When you are a big club and not being successful and there's whingeing and moaning, and he doesn't like him and they don't like them, then you could see why we weren't successful.'

Such deficiencies – lack of team spirit perhaps – were painfully evident against Walsall as Arsenal lost a first-half lead and suffered the indignity of a 2-1 defeat after being outplayed for much of the game. 'It was a real kick in the teeth,' says Hill.

The result intensified the dissatisfaction of a large section of Arsenal supporters, but Howe remained willing to front up to the criticism. 'There had been demonstrations calling for Terry Neill to be sacked,' recalls long-time Gunners fan Chris Hudson. 'At around 11pm that night a friend and I were walking past the main entrance and bumped into Don Howe. We said, "Excuse me, Mr Howe, what is going on here?" He stopped and for the next 60 minutes opened up on why things were going wrong, naming players who were letting us down and saying how he regretted leaving in 1971. I could have earned a fortune if I had rung up the media, but I felt it would be letting him down, so I have not told anyone before now.'

Woodcock was forced to admit in his diary, 'Obviously Don and Terry are on the line now … but they can only work with the players they've got.' He also felt compelled to offer a defence of Howe. 'You can't judge Don by looking at Arsenal's record this season and dismiss him as a failure, as some people are doing. The way to judge him as a coach is to find out how he is regarded. If you ask Liam Brady, Frank Stapleton, Alan Ball or people like me and Graham Rix, top players who have worked with him, we all respect him. That's the basis on which he should be judged. When Arsenal won the Double he had great players to work with and good characters; people who wanted to win even if they weren't the most skilful players.'

The England forward had already chronicled his belief that Howe had been back to his energetic best during the season so far. 'Several of the lads have remarked that Don has really got his enthusiasm back,' he'd written in August. A few weeks later, it was, 'I had my complaints about him, but this year he is really on the ball. He is a good coach. Training is ever so interesting – he never lets you get bored.'

Hill retains similar memories. 'Don was an unbelievable coach. I had gone there as a young kid and he was the authority at the club, even though Terry was the manager. He was the one you were out there to impress and the one you worked hard for. His sessions were brilliant; it was never boring. With footballers, the important thing is keeping them entertained because their attention span is very short. He had a dour image and you had to be a strong character to deal with people like Willie Young and Alan Sunderland, but he was not a schoolteacher and he was full of jokes and anecdotes. Mind you, he had the most unbelievable whistle without using anything but his lips. I was recently with Simon Barker, who played under Don at QPR, we were talking about that haunting whistle. If Don gave you that whistle you thought, "Oh no, he's going to have a go at me now."'

But it would have taken more than the power of Howe's lips to silence the protesting crowds on Avenell Road. Neill shut out the sound of the crowd and soldiered on, completing the £600,000 signing of Manchester City centre-back Tommy Caton. He would make his debut in the next match in partnership with 17-year-old Tony Adams after Whyte was dropped and O'Leary ruled out by injury. Meanwhile, Peter Hill-Wood, who had succeeded his father as club chairman, declared that 'the players have let the club down' and new director David Dein, whose increasing influence would soon see him holding the position of vice-chairman, even told the squad, 'I am proud to wear an Arsenal tie; you should be proud to wear an Arsenal shirt.'

Hill-Wood was called upon to give further support to the management team the following Saturday after a 1-0 home defeat against West Brom. There were plenty of cautionary notes within Hill-

Wood's words, however. '[Terry] is not perfect, but nobody is,' he said. 'I'm going to support him until I am certain he is wrong.'

The Arsenal players were fully aware of the feelings of the fans, but, as Woodcock explains, 'All you can do is go out there and give everything. It is difficult and at times you have got to battle through. If there are fan protests or criticism, you have got to go out there every week and give 100 per cent. I can remember we played at West Ham next and I had one of the best reports I have ever had as a player, saying that there was an England centre-forward giving his all trying to save his manager's job.'

As it turned out, the moment when Hill-Wood's support ran out arrived after that game at Upton Park, where Arsenal went down 3-1 to fall to 16th in the table. Hill-Wood called the sacking of Neill 'a horrible decision to make. It hurt me to do it.' According to Neill, 'I spoke with Peter and he was in tears and he said he hadn't slept. I told him not to worry and that he should keep the continuity with Don; that was what I would recommend.'

The chairman said that the pressure Neill had been under had affected his decision-making, which – more than Neill's recommendation – might explain Arsenal retaining Howe and making him caretaker-manager. 'It was a surprise,' Woodcock explains, 'because Don ran day-to-day training and had a lot of influence. Don wasn't just pumping up the balls and putting the cones out; he had an influence on how the team was playing. You think that everyone goes if there is a clear-out. If the people coaching don't have any influence, why are they there? And if you have got influence then you are involved in the whole thing.'

Robson adds, 'I said to my family that nothing is going to change as Don runs the football side of it anyway. Terry will come and watch but he is not having an influence. He is taking the stick for the results and Don's really got away with it.' But Hill offers a different perspective. 'Historically, Arsenal are a club who do things their own way,' he says. 'Look where they got Bertie Mee from. And they don't just sack people for the sake of it. So it was a surprise to us, but maybe it shouldn't have been. Don knew the players inside out.'

While Queens Park Rangers' Terry Venables, Luton Town's David Pleat and Southampton's Lawrie McMenemy were being mentioned among the long-term candidates for the role, Howe saw Raphael Meade score a hat-trick in a 3-1 win over Watford in his first game in charge. The gist of his team talk had been, 'Now I'm in charge. Anyone who doesn't do it is out.' Then came a 4-2 win at Spurs, where Nicholas and Meade scored two each. Howe's reintroduction of Meade to play alongside Woodcock allowed Nicholas to play 'in the hole' behind the front two as the search continued to find the position in which the club's big-money signing would be most effective.

Woodcock offers an interesting perspective on that conundrum. 'I think Charlie's big problem was whether he was an out-and-out striker or a midfielder? Where is he going to be most useful for the team? I had no problems with Charlie, he was obviously a talented footballer. But when people talk about him playing in the hole I have to go back to Brian Clough when I was a young player with Nottingham Forest. I knocked on his door and I said, "I don't like playing on the left-hand side, I need to be playing inside somewhere." He asked where and I said behind the front two and in front of the midfield. I said, "I am quick, I score a few goals, and I think that is the best place for me and the team." He looked at me and his voice was getting louder and he said, "That tells me, one, that you are too lazy to play in midfield and, two, you are not brave enough to play up front. Get out." With the great Brian Clough there was no such position as playing in the hole.'

Robson suggests, 'Charlie obviously had a lot of talent and we all expected him to do wonderful things, but it didn't quite pan out that way. I don't think he was Don's cup of tea anyway. If Don was honest, Charlie would have made him pull his hair out most of the time if he'd any because he couldn't quite fit him into the side. In the end we played with that diamond formation, with Charlie at the top of the diamond.'

Arsenal put together a seven-game unbeaten League run to begin Howe's reign, prompting suggestions from some journalists that the 'dithering' board were waiting for him to fail before giving the vacant position to someone else. 'I hope now that Don gets the job,' read

Woodcock's diary entry for 31 December. 'Everyone has noticed the change in Don. He's doing really well and everyone is behind him. He doesn't go on about opponents now. It is much more, "C'mon, let's get out there and do it," before the games. And he is more relaxed. But he is still hard.'

Club captain Graham Rix said ahead of a third-round FA Cup tie at Middlesbrough, 'We are all behind Don and I think it shows. The spirit is fantastic.' Far from being the fall that some felt the directors had been awaiting, a 3-2 defeat at Ayresome Park was followed by a board meeting that assured Howe there would be no changes until the end of the season. 'I shall carry on doing the thing at which I consider I am best – working with the players,' he said, admitting that he had 'expected to get the bullet' when Neill was fired.

England World Cup centre-forward Paul Mariner arrived from Ipswich for £150,000, contributing to a sequence of nine games without defeat that lifted the Gunners to a final finish of sixth. The improvement proved enough to land Howe the permanent job of Arsenal manager, an appointment confirmed a couple of weeks before the campaign ended. A third win of the season over local rivals Tottenham – Nicholas providing a clever finish during a 3-2 success – was the match that appeared to make up the directors' minds, although, once again, Hill-Wood was reserved in his support. 'Don has been an outstanding coach here, but was a disaster as manager of West Bromwich Albion,' he reminded people. 'Like everyone, he has good points and weaknesses. We wanted to see how he handled both sides of the job. It is my personal view that he has done very well.' Hill-Wood also made it clear that he saw Howe's overriding responsibility as continuing his coaching duties. 'You do not want the manager to concern himself with contracts, building stands and the marble in the halls.'

Observers of events at Highbury also expressed reservations. Writing in *The Times*, David Miller said that the months since taking over from Neill had given Howe 'the opportunity to prove he was more than a predictable hammer in the hands of an unimaginative blacksmith; that free of the control of the Terry Wogan of tactical thinking he could perhaps contribute positively to the Arsenal revival.' Yet his conclusion was, 'To a point he has done so.'

Accepting a two-year contract, Howe said, 'The days are gone at the really big clubs when the manager is the be-all and end-all.' He was reflecting a reality that has become commonplace in the 21st century, but which would have been unthinkable to the likes of Matt Busby and Bill Shankly. 'I would go along with the directors if they came to me and said they want to sign a leading player,' he added. 'It would be my job to fit him in.'

For Howe's first full season in charge, another England man, former Nottingham Forest right-back Viv Anderson, arrived at Highbury after the manager's furtive visit to the player's home. Having refused to say what he wanted to see Anderson about, Howe turned up on his doorstep, checking over his shoulder for unseen danger before slipping inside. 'I want you with me at Arsenal and I'm ready to talk terms,' he said, all the while checking the doors and windows. 'I was excited about working with Don,' Anderson recalls. 'He had big plans and was going to make Arsenal a force in the First Division again. And there were a lot of England internationals there that I knew. A lot of people were leaving Forest and I think I was the last of that European Cup-winning team to go.'

Anderson immediately recognised 'the atmosphere of tradition and success' that permeated Highbury. 'You were always in the shadow of the Double-winning team,' he explains. It was the circle of Highbury life. Howe's squad laboured under the burden of his 1971 team's achievements, just as those players had sought to live up to the teams of the 1930s and early 1950s. At Forest, Anderson and his team-mates had no such history to measure up to; nor did they have to endure an intense training regime; a point of difference that had always fascinated Howe.

Woodcock recalls, 'When I was with England in the early days he would pull me and Viv aside and say, "Tell me about Clough. What do you do?" I said we didn't do a lot; we might go for a walk along the Trent. It was completely alien to Don. How can this team be winning when they are not doing anything that he thought of as real coaching? Clough focused on player selection and telling you what he wanted you to do. He wouldn't be training different patterns of play or anything like that. Don couldn't get his head round it.'

Anderson is able to ponder what working under a Clough-Howe partnership might have been like. 'When it came to matchdays, Cloughie was always the boss, but he needed someone to put on the training sessions. When he came down to the training ground and said he was taking the session, we would just say, "Let Jimmy Gordon do it." Cloughie needed people like Don to coach; to tell you where you need to be at certain times, who you should be marking at corners – all the fundamental things he didn't have time for.'

Anderson had to get used to an unfamiliar regime of hard runs, weight training and strict monitoring of players' condition. Sent on a five-mile run on his first day of training, Anderson was surprised when Howe caught him up near the end, despite having given his players a big head start. 'I heard this puffing and panting behind me and remember thinking, "Who is that?" It was only Don! I had to sprint to the line so that he didn't beat me.'

As Fred Street observes, 'If Don had nothing else when he was manager at Highbury, he had discipline. He was a hard worker and you wouldn't get away with an easy morning. When he left, people at Arsenal started saying that they needed more discipline.'

A fitter-than-ever Anderson scored his first Arsenal goal in a 2-0 win over Newcastle, sending his new club into a meeting with League and European champions Liverpool in confident mood. 'We believe we can achieve the big breakthrough,' said Sansom before he led out the team at Highbury. After Talbot converted a first-half free kick, it was two typically dynamic surges down the right by Anderson that set up further goals for Woodcock and Talbot, clinching a 3-1 win that sent Arsenal to the top of the table. Yet, according to Anderson, 'We were hopeless in the League. With the good players we had, we should have been challenging for the League every year but we were always inconsistent.'

Even though Arsenal occupied first place for many of the autumn weeks, it is a sign of the general frustration of the period that Woodcock laughs, 'I am glad you reminded me about that. I had forgotten. My memory is that the intensity that you need, the pressure, didn't seem to be there. That intensity of, "Can we win it? Do we want to win it? Are we geared to win it?" I am not sure if that was present.'

A greater memory of that period, regrettably for a club that prided itself on its reputation for correctness, was the prevalence of players appearing in court for drink-related offences. In 1982, Sunderland had been fined and banned from driving for a year for having excess alcohol in his system after being involved in a late-night accident in which two people were killed – although Sunderland's driving was not to blame for the fatalities.

As the 1984/85 season was beginning, Woodcock appeared in court on drink-driving charges and in November it was the turn of Meade to be banned for a year. Meade had previously been fined £50 for obstructing police in the course of making an arrest in 1982 – his original 14-day jail term being overruled on appeal. That same November saw Nicholas banned from driving for the second time in two years – this time for three years – after being over the limit in Glasgow in May. In August 1985, Rix was fined £1,000 by the club and stripped of the captaincy after his conviction for drink-driving. Meanwhile, Sansom might not have found himself in court, but had already owned up to a serious gambling problem. He would drive around bookmakers in the Epsom area after training, placing bets, before stopping at the pub to play the fruit machines on his way home. He called the routine his 'pocket of escapism'.

Sansom's suggestion that 'Don was a coach rather than a manager of men' is supported by Robson, who adds, 'For all the discipline on the training ground, which Don was excellent at, I don't know that he knew what was going on after training. I would be the first player to turn up for training and [coach] John Cartwright used to say to me, "They were all out in the Orange Tree again last night – most of them are coming here almost straight from their night out." Don never did anything about it. There was a big drinking culture at the time, and it was no wonder that the players were never quite consistent enough. Don had full control of the dressing room and the training ground but I'm not sure he had full control of what was going on outside of that environment. Or he didn't want to confront it. He didn't want to be talking to players about what they were doing on a Thursday night. He was a football man.'

A forgiving Anderson adds, 'To stamp your authority was always difficult when results weren't going well. He was more worried about the next training session: "How am I going to freshen things up and get my point across?" He had his moments when he would shout and scream after a defeat, but he was very good on Monday morning analysing what had gone wrong and how to change it. So he was very good in that respect. A lot of managers are still screaming on Monday or Tuesday. I think he liked the senior players to do the discipline of the younger players away from the field, but it is very difficult when they are spread all over London.'

One of those younger players, Tony Adams, has a somewhat different memory of Howe, saying 'he could be ruthless in his own way' and admitting that he feared him away from the training ground. When still only 16, he went out one Saturday night after missing a game injured, only for Howe to check his whereabouts with his parents. 'I had to go in for treatment on the Sunday morning and Don was waiting to give me both barrels,' he wrote. "'You are nothing but a little boy who thinks he's back at school." He shouted, "In nightclubs? Not good enough. What's going on with you?" I nearly cried but it was part of the toughening up process.'

After the Rix incident, and with Arsenal embarking on their centenary season, Howe would feel compelled to tell his senior players that enough was enough.

He said that Arsenal's rule book had 'always been thick, but players rarely took any notice'. Now, he said, 'I've looked at it myself and added a few points, as well as those from the players' union and the Football League. I told everyone at the end of last season that it would be an important year for the club and everyone must accept their responsibility.'

Howe's authority on the training pitch had never been in doubt. When Sansom tested his manager's resolve by walking out on a training session where the players were made to run as punishment for poor performance, he was fined £1,000. 'I tried to talk Don out of such a harsh session, but anyone who knows Don knows it's like talking to him while he's wearing earmuffs,' said Sansom, who had mistakenly expected other players to follow his lead as he marched to the car park and drove off.

Arsenal's spell at the top of the table in 1984/85 had been ended by defeat at Manchester United, another club whose star players, typically of the period, were not averse to enjoying themselves off the field. Frank Stapleton would even go as far as arguing that they could have won the League titles of 1984 and 1986 had they curbed the excesses of their leisure time. Arsenal never cracked the top two again and finished seventh. Having gone out of the League Cup against eventual Second Division champions Oxford United, they suffered a shock 1-0 defeat at the icy home of Third Division York City in the fourth round of the FA Cup. The only goal was scored from the penalty spot by Keith Houchen, a future Cup-final scorer for Coventry City, after he had been hauled down by Steve Williams, the midfielder Howe had signed from Southampton for £550,000 a few weeks earlier. Howe, wearing a blue cap and flanked by national newspaper reporters whose overspill press area placed them next to the Gunners' bench, could only look at the floor in despair. Since Arsenal's dual semi-final defeats against Manchester United two seasons earlier they had now been knocked out of four cup competitions by lower division opposition.

On the day that national newspapers were blaming union leader Arthur Scargill for having bungled the miners' strike and cost them a chance of victory, match reports of the York game found Houchen blaming the Gunners' defeat on high-priced players such as Williams and Nicholas, who 'would struggle to get into a good Third Division side'. Of Williams, he claimed, 'All he did was moan all the time.' In the space of a couple of months Arsenal had gone from top spot to becoming targets for the barbs of less-exalted fellow professionals.

Before the season was over, rumours were once again circulating about Howe's uncertain future, especially when Hill-Wood said after the final home game that he was not happy and that 'we simply have not been playing well enough'.

The 1985/86 campaign was prefaced by Howe facing criticism in the Sunday newspapers by Williams, who said he was 'daft' for leaving him out of some games, forcing Howe to respond, 'I could have done without it. Everyone knows Steve's a winner, but he's also undisciplined.'

Robson – keen to stress that his assessment of a man he liked and admired is an attempt at honest appraisal rather than a stream of criticism – believes that, for all of Howe's qualities on the training ground, Arsenal's players were taking the field too frequently without a clear strategy; a judgement that echoes those comments by Woodcock before the 1983 FA Cup semi-final. 'I always say Don was the best session coach I worked with; the one that would get maximum effort out of all the players. I loved turning up for training when Don was in charge and when we went on the training field I knew we were going to work hard, no one was going to mess around and you were going to get the benefits from it. He had an imposing manner and if anyone was shirking he would pull them up and make players jump – and that was the senior players as well.

'But the sad thing is that when someone asks me about Don's philosophy on football, or his game-plan, I couldn't tell you one. I've played under other managers – some not as good as coaches – where I could tell you exactly what their game-plan was. Don put on good sessions but I'm not sure that always translated to Saturday. We never really did tactical work on the game itself. He would give us pointers on how we were going to play against, say, Alan Devonshire: "We are going to block him off and you are going to do this." But I went into some of my early games at right-back, having never played there before, not really knowing what my job was. When George Graham came in his sessions weren't as good but we worked on the tactical side of the game.'

These were issues that never seemed to afflict the Double team, perhaps because so many of those players developed together in a system that became instinctive and did not need reinforcement on a weekly basis. Or maybe because Howe was operating with a clearer head and greater focus without the distractions of being Arsenal manager and England coach.

Howe, it appears, was aware of his shortcomings, conceding that the challenge of combining management of the club with oversight of everything relating to training and tactics was becoming too great. Introducing former England youth-team coach John Cartwright as his new right-hand man, he said, 'I've been shouting at the players for nine years now. It's time for a new voice. You can get set in your ways.'

He added, 'I'd like John to do for me what I did for Bertie Mee.' Which was all well and good, but ignored the fact that Howe was not the organisational expert that Mee had been, and that trying to become one would take him away from his core skill of coaching. The job of running Arsenal might well have been a two-man job, but there was a danger that Howe was now sitting in the wrong chair. Robson suggests, 'Maybe he was under pressure from the board to do more stuff in the office. I really don't know why he went away from the training field.'

Howe felt his players were ready for some new ideas and that Cartwright, who had developed his coaching skills with Malcolm Allison and Terry Venables at Crystal Palace and was returning from three years of coaching in Kuwait, could provide them. But the new first-team coach's comment that 'I believe the game should be played simply and directly' proved unpopular with some.

'John was a very good coach,' says Robson, 'but he changed his philosophy from when I knew him with the England youth team, when he was playing out of the back. He was more direct and he wanted to hit balls in behind the forwards and they would spin and play from that. Our forwards couldn't do it really. Charlie couldn't do it. Woodcock could do it but didn't really want to run down there. Mariner was probably past his best, which is why they brought in Niall Quinn. The players kept saying, "You just want to kick it long," and John said we were going to be more like Liverpool. If you watched them for the first 20 minutes or so they were just sticking balls down the side. He said, "They don't play out from the goalkeeper, they play up from the half-way line and play the game in the opposition half. When we get that first bit right then we can move on to the second."'

Players such as Rix, Williams and Woodcock were resistant to the change, as Anderson confirms, adding, 'Chasing balls in the channel wasn't really Charlie's forte. He wanted the ball at his feet and to work around the box.'

If Arsenal were to rely more on the long ball, they were reflecting a trend that had been developing in the wider English game during the 1980s; characterised most vividly by the rise of Watford from the lower reaches of the League to runners-up behind Liverpool in 1982/83 and a place in the 1984 FA Cup Final under the management of Graham Taylor. Meanwhile, Dave Bassett had employed a route-one approach to leading Wimbledon from the Fourth Division to the Second and was embarking on a season that would see them achieve promotion to the top flight.

The Football Association had also become enamoured of such an approach, which was generally attributed to the influence of Charles Reep, an RAF wing commander who began watching games and recording moves in a notebook in 1950 and was soon preaching that most goals were scored as a result of moves of three passes or less. 'Passing for the sake of passing can be disastrous,' was his conclusion.

Charles Hughes, a committed disciple of Reep's thinking – even though the two men were said not to have got on personally – was the man appointed by the FA as its director of coaching and author of the coaching manual, *The Winning Formula*. Yet, according to critics, what was ignored was the truism that the majority of all moves in English football at that time consisted of three moves or less, given the frequent changes of possession. This was, after all, still many years before Premier League teams were routinely knocking around 20-odd passes in the manner of the modern global game.

Meanwhile, two of Heep's analysts, Simon Hartley and Neil Lanham, had begun working with Watford and Wimbledon respectively, the influence obvious in the clubs' respective success using big target men such as Ross Jenkins and John Fashanu. 'All they do is help the ball forwards,' remarked Tottenham Hotspur manager Keith Burkinshaw after a home defeat against Watford. 'For us to play that way we may as well get rid of Glenn Hoddle, Ricky Villa and Micky Hazard because you don't need any sophistication in midfield.'

Taylor, who had employed Bertie Mee to work with him and club chairman Elton John, was unapologetic about his team's direct and physical methods, arguing, 'Getting into the other team is the only way to play.' A player such as the prodigiously talented John Barnes had to acknowledge its effectiveness and learn to live with it – even if it was, as he described it, 'anathema to my personal view of the need for patience in football … the football was too direct, too one-dimensional'.

And as for Wimbledon, well, more of them later.

That Howe's team at Highbury should elect to follow the direct route is described by some as not being 'the Arsenal way'. It may be an accurate comment when events are viewed through the lens of football under Arsène Wenger. But it should be no great surprise that Howe and Cartwright proposed such an approach.

Besides, Woodcock had recorded in his diary at the start of the 1983/84 season, 'Virtually from our first day back [Don has] been stressing that, whenever it's on, the ball must be played forward quickly. It's the Watford method, but Don wants us to be a bit more sophisticated than that, to do it a bit more like Liverpool because he thinks they have got good players. He says they don't just toss it forward like Watford, but play it forward.'

This was, after all, the basic tenet upon which the 1970/71 Double had been won; and it was the manner in which Howe had tried to make West Brom play when he was manager at The Hawthorns. The Brady-inspired passing game of the Arsenal team Howe had guided under

Terry Neill actually represents something of an outlier on his coaching résumé. Besides, as Cartwright was keen to point out to his players now and as Howe had done two years earlier, the dominant team of the period could be as blunt in their approach as anyone. In analysing Watford's matches, Hartley observed that Liverpool matched Taylor's team long ball for long ball when they played them.

Woodcock suggests, 'John wanted to do different things and we just needed to get results. It wasn't a nice atmosphere.' That atmosphere became even more toxic when Arsenal lost 6-1 at Everton on the first Saturday in November. 'We were walloped,' admitted Howe, who had his players report for an hour-long meeting at Highbury the next morning. 'I am very disturbed, but I like to keep things private,' he said when asked what had been said. Over the course of the next two games, winger Martin Hayes and centre-back Martin Keown were given their first-team debuts, following young midfielder David Rocastle into the side and preceding by a month the introduction of gangly centre-forward Quinn, who instantly scored in a 2-0 victory over Liverpool. 'The star system is gone now,' Howe had said. 'I just can't deny these lads any more. If I held them back it would be wrong.'

It turned out that the introduction of a group of players who would form the foundation of George Graham's success as Arsenal manager was the final, and perhaps most important, contribution of Howe's own reign at the club. A clock that many already thought was ticking was wound up to full speed during a three-game battle with Luton Town in the FA Cup. The new calendar year had begun with an article in *Shoot!* under the headline 'DON HOWE ON TRIAL', in which Howe bemoaned the run of injuries to Mariner, the loss of form of Woodcock and Rix's insistence in trying to play like Liam Brady instead of settling for being 'one of the best one- or two-touch players in the country'. Saying he had been 'around too long' to worry about job security, he insisted that 'Arsenal are within an ace of having a very good team'.

A decent FA Cup run might have justified his faith, yet with a goalless replay at Highbury reaching the midpoint of extra time, chairman Hill-Wood agreed to a toss of a coin to determine the site of a third match. His defeat in that contest sent Arsenal back to Luton's hated artificial surface at Kenilworth Road. An angry Howe confronted his boss and told him that his choice would have been to play at a neutral venue. Inevitably, Arsenal lost the second replay 3-0. Robson, who missed the game injured, remembers, 'David Dein came in the dressing room and started saying to the players that it was not good enough. Don said, "Get out. This is nothing to do with you," and almost threw him out.'

The team's response was to win a quartet of League games. After the fourth, a 3-0 victory over Coventry City that kept them on the fringe of the title race, Howe was summoned to see Hill-Wood and told that his contract, and that of Cartwright, would not be renewed at the end of the season, but that they were invited to stay for the remaining 11 games. The directors, it emerged, had already sounded out Terry Venables about the possibility of leaving his position with Barcelona, where he had won La Liga in his first season as manager and was now directing them towards a place in the European Cup Final.

Howe flew to Tbilisi on England duty the next day. He was hurt at the manner in which Arsenal had conducted themselves and felt his history with the club merited greater respect and consideration. He had decided to leave rather than wait to be pushed out. 'Everyone was after the latest developments,' England manager Bobby Robson recalled of the situation at the airport. 'Don had handled an awkward situation well with his usual dry humour and I even thanked him for taking the spotlight off me. I couldn't help feeling that Arsenal would regret the move in the end far more than Don.'

Journalist Bob Harris remembered that 'the media mob were satisfied' at the scoop that had fallen into their notebooks. 'To hell with fitness tests and a game against a team with one of the best home records in world football. They had their story.'

On the morning of Thursday, 28 March, having returned from England's victory against the Soviet Union, Howe met Hill-Wood again and confirmed that he was resigning – a result of what *The Times* described as 'the shabby way' in which he and Cartwright had been treated. Venables, who would end up spending another year in Spain, said that he had been under the impression that Howe was aware of the conversations taking place. 'Don was a proud man,' says Stewart Robson. 'He wasn't going to stand for that.'

Rob Howe recalls, 'My mum always said he got really frustrated when the Arsenal sacked him. It was the way they approached Terry Venables that really upset him more than anything else. He felt they were doing quite well and they obviously didn't feel he was the right person for the job. He built a wall at the back of our house and my mum calls it the wall of frustration because he just didn't know what else to do with himself at that point.'

In 1996, Howe would tell the *Highbury High* magazine, 'I had had a few differences of opinion with Peter Hill-Wood. I felt from experience that the club was looking for a change and I'd heard that he'd been talking to Terry Venables. I then discovered that they'd approached Terry behind my back and I felt I had to make a stand at that. I didn't object to them approaching Terry, but I felt I deserved more honesty from the club.'

Woodcock admits that, however it might have been handled, Howe's departure was not exactly a shock. 'It's a results-based business,' he says. 'If things are not going right, you have got to do something.' Adams recalled, 'I was personally very sad when Don went,' and concluded, 'I think he found it difficult to deal with such maverick characters as Steve Williams and Charlie Nicholas.'

With Cartwright declining the offer of managing the team for the rest of the season, chief scout Steve Burtenshaw reluctantly took temporary charge before George Graham had little hesitation in accepting the opportunity to move from his job as manager of Millwall in the summer. The next chapter in Arsenal's history was about to be written, but there was still a further page to be filled by Don Howe.

11

THE ROAD TO MEXICO

One word sums up Bobby Robson's relationship with Don Howe. Brothers. They were rock solid.

Journalist and author Bob Harris

BOBBY ROBSON, like Sir Alf Ramsey two decades before him, earned the job of England manager on the back of achievements at unfashionable Ipswich Town. While Ramsey had shocked English football by leading his club to the First Division title in 1961/62, their first season after promotion, Robson might have performed even greater wonders in East Anglia. Taking a club that had been going nowhere in the early 1970s, he made them consistent title contenders for the best part of ten years, FA Cup winners in 1978, producers of a steady stream of England internationals, and conquerors of Europe when they lifted the UEFA Cup in 1981. For all Brian Clough's claims to be the popular choice as manager of the national team, there was no other realistic contender to inherit Ron Greenwood's position after the 1982 World Cup finals.

Given their long friendship and Don Howe's international experience, nor was there much debate when Robson chose to keep the Arsenal coach in his position as right-hand man to the national team boss. 'His experience is invaluable,' Robson would record. 'It is common knowledge that I would have liked Don with me full-time but the Football Association's budget would not stretch to it. Few know the game as well as he does and he is an inventive and thinking coach who retains the players' interest even when warming them up. There is always a new routine which is punctuated by Don's shrill whistle.'

Bob Harris, one of Robson's closest friends in the game and author of various books with and about the England manager, recalls, 'Don was the natural choice and Bobby desperately wanted him to be a full-time employee of the FA so they could work together seven days a week. He thought it would make his job easier and help make England a better side. The FA wouldn't give him the money for Don's salary. That was a joke when you think of money going into the FA and when you think of the set-up they have now.' Howe would remain at Robson's shoulder throughout his eight-year reign, but never would the FA change its stance on offering to make him a full-time staff member.

Harris lived for a while in a cottage opposite England's training base at Bisham Abbey in Buckinghamshire and spent many evenings in the company of Robson and Howe. 'We talked about people in the game and vented our spleen on referees and officials,' he explains. 'The only diversion from football was cricket, which we all loved. If there was cricket on – and quite often there was because a lot of our time together was in the summer – we would have the Test matches on and talk about them.'

Harris's observation of the former clubmates is illuminating. 'The two of them were very different; not dramatically, but enough to cause debate and discussion and at times a row. It was a very healthy relationship. Don was not the type to kowtow to anybody or to say, "Yes, you are right," if he thought you were wrong. I covered Arsenal a lot when he was there early on and I am amazed he survived with Bertie Mee. Bobby liked to be right in the end, but he loved the debate, to argue the finer points of tactics. Football was his life and equally it was Don's life. It was never a problem for them to sit on tour and talk for hours on end. Quite often they were close in their views and Bobby might sway towards Don's idea, but there was no blame game either way. Don never said that Bobby got it wrong.'

England's campaign to reach the 1984 European Championship finals in France began with a 2-2 home draw against Denmark, a game most notable for Robson's decision to leave out Kevin Keegan, who was now playing in the Second Division for Newcastle United. Yet it was not Keegan's step down from the top flight after his transfer from Southampton that had made up Robson's mind.

Robson would note in the diary he published after the 1986 World Cup that he'd taken 'the toughest decision I have ever made' because he had heard stories – presumably including those from Howe – that 'because of his back injury, he was being a little difficult and had lost some of his huge popularity with his team-mates' during the 1982 finals. 'I gathered that he liked to take over and yet I knew that it was vital that I should be in control from the first match.'

After losing a friendly against West Germany, England achieved their first win under Robson and their first success in five matches when they dispatched Greece 3-0 at Wembley, with two goals by Tony Woodcock, before a nine-goal romp against Luxembourg. Watford's Luther Blissett marked his first international start with a hat-trick. Wales were beaten 2-1 at Wembley in the British Championship – a tournament no longer condensed into one week at the end of the season – before a goalless European qualifier against Greece at Wembley brought Arsenal colleagues Howe and Woodcock into conflict.

'The emphasis was on the lads at the back hitting long balls up to us as quickly as possible,' Woodcock recalled. 'Trevor [Francis] and I looked at each other at that. It's not really what we want.' Having felt uninvolved in the game, Woodcock remembered, 'Don said afterwards I should have moved around more, maybe moved back into midfield for a bit.' But his conclusion was, 'Tossing balls in from the back is futile with Trevor and me up front. If they are going to do that they should play Peter Withe and Paul Mariner up there.'

Yet Howe's influence on those tactics was unclear, especially when Woodcock and Howe discussed it on their return to Highbury. Howe said he could not understand the approach. 'That really surprised me because I thought he had more of a say in things than that,' Woodcock recorded in his diary. 'As coach I thought he would have a fairly big say, but from what he was saying he thought much the same as I do about it, which suggests he doesn't have much influence on what tactics we play, contrary to what people think.'

Perhaps Howe was backtracking; perhaps Woodcock's insight was accurate. The tactics were hardly alien to Howe's approach at club level, although later in the year he would articulate some concern about their deployment in international football.

England followed the Greek stalemate with a notable 2-0 Wembley win against Hungary, a game in which Howe had an important input on the shape of the side. 'Mind if I tell you something?' he asked Robson on the Sunday before the midweek match. 'When we needed to beat them in the World Cup we played one in the hole, with Brooking placed behind Keegan and Mariner, and they did not know how to cope with it.' Feeling that he didn't have a high-quality winger to call upon, Robson followed the advice and fielded Blissett behind Withe and Francis, the two goalscorers.

Yet England's European qualification hopes were to be undermined five months later when they went down at home to Denmark. Robson called it the 'worst moment I had experienced at any level of football' and added, 'The walk back to the dressing room afterwards, the abuse of the crowd, the feeling of total confusion, all contributed to the desolate feelings.'

It was then that Howe made his observation about the unsuitability of domestic tactics at international level. 'At our clubs, everyone is talking about winning the second ball, the knock-downs to the front men,' he said. 'We concentrate on doing that every Saturday, but on the Continent they care more about not losing the first ball. They don't give it away. We follow our method because that's what the fans want. The gates may be going down but if English crowds had to watch the kind of possession game that is played abroad, they wouldn't go at all. Yet we saw tonight how effective it can be.'

It sounded very much like the comment Bill Shankly had offered after Liverpool had been beaten in the 1973/74 European Cup by

Red Star Belgrade. While the Anfield boss had growled, 'Would our public watch the sort of football they play on the Continent?', he and assistant Bob Paisley also filed away some important lessons that would lead to ball players like Phil Thompson and Emlyn Hughes occupying central defensive positions instead of the big stopper, Larry Lloyd, as Liverpool moved towards their position of dominance at home and in Europe. Howe continued, 'Liverpool have done it over here, but they are accepted because they are successful. They are adaptable too. We ought to have international players who can adjust, but they can't change their club habits, particularly with so little preparation, and I am not sure we can ever hope to get the balance right. It's all so frustrating.'

It is a sign of the quality and versatility of the Liverpool side of the 1970s and 1980s that Howe was praising them for their ability to play a continental style in one breath yet ended up, along with his Arsenal coach John Cartwright, using them as an example of the efficacy of playing a direct game when needs arose.

A few weeks later, with the pressure growing on him and Terry Neill at Highbury, Howe felt compelled to react to suggestions that he was earning as much as £20,000 per year for his England role and the implication that it was diverting attention from his day job. 'After tax I take home £80 a game,' he pointed out, a sum Robson described as 'little more than pin money'. Howe continued, 'I am hurt and disgusted at the idea that I am making money out of the FA. It's destroyed my credibility with our supporters. I love my country and I'm proud to work for England … I'm sure fans believe what they read and because I'm linked with so much cash they assume I put Arsenal second. I can tell you my loyalty is to Arsenal.'

It was not the final time that Howe was accused of being compromised by working for England while employed by Arsenal. In February 1986, Brian Clough would declare himself 'fascinated' when four Gunners players were named in Robson's squad for a game against Egypt. 'I cannot imagine who could have so much influence on the England manager to get that many players from one club,' the Nottingham Forest manager sniped. 'I might give Don Howe a ring and ask if he knows who the fellow is.' Howe, by then manager at Highbury, scoffed, 'There is no way I would use my position to influence Bobby. In fact it is the other way around. I am very critical of my players.' While Viv Anderson, Kenny Sansom, Tony Woodcock and Stewart Robson had been selected on this occasion, Howe said he had agreed with Clough's assertion that Forest forward Peter Davenport should have been included, but he had been overruled.

As England's 1983/84 programme continued, convincing wins in Hungary and Luxembourg were not enough to lift them above second place in their qualifying group, finishing a point behind Denmark. It meant that while France were winning a thrilling Euro 84 tournament in front of their home fans, England had to content themselves with summer friendlies. After winning only one game in the last staging of the British Championship, England lost 2-0 to the Soviet Union in front of only 38,125 at Wembley before flying, without much wind beneath their wings, to South America. A game against Brazil in the Maracanã Stadium seemed as futile and intimidating as the task facing England's cricketers back home in that same week as they embarked on a series against the mighty West Indies that would become the infamous 5-0 'blackwash'.

Brazil were missing many of the names who had captivated viewers with their glorious failure in the World Cup two years earlier. But even without Zico, Falcão, Socrates, Eder and others, there were few giving England much chance, even with only 56,126 in attendance rather than the crowd of twice that number which previous visiting teams had had to endure. Most observers feared for an English team anchored in defence by a partnership of Norwich City's Dave Watson, on his international debut, and QPR's Terry Fenwick, playing only his fourth game, and led in attack by a Second Division striker, Portsmouth's Mark Hateley.

Robson, who'd had to endure *The Sun*'s stunt of offering 'Robson Out, Clough In' badges to its readers, had decided he might as well gamble on having two wingers in his line-up, picking Watford's John

Barnes and Stoke City's Mark Chamberlain and leaving skipper Bryan Robson and Wilkins to fill the expanses of the midfield. 'I wanted some imagination, I wanted England to attack, be exciting and to brighten things up generally and to get rid of some of that gloom and despondency which surrounded all of us,' was his explanation.

With half-time approaching, Hateley, who had already had a header tipped over the bar by goalkeeper Roberto Costa, swung the ball out to the left. Barnes controlled with his chest, set a diagonal course for the penalty area and burst between two defenders to get there. On the bench, Robson and Howe screamed at him to pass the ball. But with no apparent thought of letting up and the ball switching effortlessly from foot to foot, Barnes evaded two more yellow shirts and then steered the ball past the keeper with his right boot as another pair of opponents tried to close him down. He had maintained full stride throughout the entire movement.

'We discussed how we wanted to play, really worked hard at it,' Howe would recall. 'John Barnes was given a tucking-in job, more than going forward, but he picked up this ball and went on a mazy dribble. We were all doing handstands, you can imagine. All the subs, all the squad were jumping around.' While England fans were still marvelling at this piece of South American-style artistry, their team added a second goal 20 minutes into the second half; this one straight from the old English playbook as Barnes got to the byline and Hateley rose at the far post to head in the cross.

England's 2-0 victory and the Barnes goal – destined to go down as one of his country's greatest – would survive in the memory for decades longer than the tour's subsequent 2-0 defeat in Uruguay and 0-0 draw in Chile. By the time England next played, beating East Germany in a Wembley friendly in September, Wilkins, on the basis of a decade of achievement in English club football, and Hateley, apparently on the strength of one header, had been signed by AC Milan.

Now came the important business of World Cup qualification, a task in which Robson could not afford to fail if he had any ambition of retaining the England job. He and Howe set about their task, under the close eye of Harris. 'Don's joy in football was being with the lads on the training ground,' he says. 'He loved the games and being sat on the bench, but he was in his element when he was coaching. Back then you would have a good coach and he would often stay in the background, but Don was larger than life and successful and had great ideas, so he did come to the fore. Watching training sessions can be incredibly boring because they are so repetitive, but it was never like that with Don. He and Bobby got them at it.'

Howe would explain the approach to coaching at international level. 'There is not a minute to be wasted when you are working with your players,' he said. 'You don't get them for very long so everything has to be in place to make the most of your time together. They all have different ways of doing things at their clubs.'

As had been the case in the finals in Spain, England's performances in qualification for the 1986 finals were characterised by how difficult they were to beat. While winning only four of their eight games, they went through their group undefeated and conceded only two goals. They began at a gallop, thumping Finland 5-0 at home and Turkey 8-0 away, but cantered their way to Mexico and had eased up by the time they played out a goalless Wembley draw against Northern Ireland in their final match. The result not only made England the only unbeaten team in the whole of the European qualifying competition but also ensured their opponents reached their second successive finals.

Even before England had secured their return to Mexico – where their reign as world champions had ended in 1970 – Robson had taken his squad there on a 1985 summer tour. Once again they had flown west with the manager under pressure. 'Robson Must Go – time for him to resign', was the headline in the *News of the World* after the defeat to Scotland that preceded their trip.

For all the affection that now accompanies the memory of Bobby Robson and the general acknowledgement of what he achieved as England manager, his eight years in the role were punctuated by regular tabloid campaigns to get him removed from his job and damaging stories about his personal and professional conduct. It was a time of shifting relationships between the media and the country's biggest sporting figures, with the landscape changing vastly throughout the 1980s. Even England cricketers, who once used to share drinks, japes and female companions with journalists under the unspoken agreement that 'what happens on tour stays on tour', now had to contend with news reporters and photographers lurking in bushes outside hotels.

Harris explains, 'Back in those days there had been a pretty good relationship between the media and football managers. We were a lot closer and when we went on trips there were never as many journalists. It was a small coterie of reporters chatting with the management and the coaching team and players. You would make friends. The problems that arose were strictly down to the red-top war.' As the likes of *The Sun*, the *Daily Mirror* and the *Daily Star* fought over exclusives, bingo games and sensational headlines, and the *Daily Mail* and *Daily Express* were joined by *Today* in the fight for the middle market, Harris recalls, 'It really fractured relationships between people in football and people outside football. It was really sad.'

It was when the headlines reached maximum levels of spite that Robson was most grateful for the friendship of Howe. Robson would recall in later years that it was 'quite ridiculous, obscene and outrageous what happened to me', especially when he was accused of being a 'traitor' prior to the 1990 World Cup for looking at potential future employment. 'I remember Don when we had to explain to the players what had happened, Don said, "Well you don't have to explain anything. The players are going to carry on next year. They might get transferred after the World Cup or before the World Cup or during the World Cup and you'll do the same." That was very sensible and very intelligent. And he was very supportive of me.'

Harris continues, 'Don was there at Bobby's shoulder. Nothing like this had ever happened in football before. Remember when they tried to pin that blonde-headed girl on Bobby? That one caused ructions in his private life and public life everywhere. That was real nasty.'

Before England played their first summer match against Italy in Mexico City, Robson had more far-reaching issues than his own employment status to contend with after events at the Heysel Stadium in Brussels. Switching on their hotel television sets, the England party were confused about why the kick-off of the European Cup Final between Liverpool and Juventus had been delayed. When it became known that a number of mostly Juventus fans (eventually rising to 39) had died when a wall collapsed during a charge of Liverpool supporters, the forthcoming England-Italy contest assumed a different personality. Eventually, discussions between the two governments and football associations agreed that cancelling the game – scheduled for a week after Heysel – might create an irreparable rift. Also, the relatively remote geography of the match offered the ideal opportunity for football relationships to continue without the incendiary atmosphere that would have surrounded the game if played in one of the two countries.

Defeat against Italy and then Mexico did little to advance the cause of World Cup optimism, although for the second straight summer one notable victory highlighted England's trip. On the same day that Prime Minister Margaret Thatcher was announcing her intention to make all fans carry identity cards in order to access grounds – a response to the recent escalation in hooliganism[11] – Robson's men helped to add a layer of gloss to English football's tarnished image with a 3-0 victory over West Germany in the Azteca Stadium. Chelsea's Kerry Dixon marked his first start for his country by scoring two goals and setting up another, while Glenn Hoddle enjoyed a free role in midfield against a German side who looked predictably tired after arriving in Mexico only two days earlier. Robson admitted that the opponents' travel itinerary had given his team 'a terrific advantage' but the fact that England exploited it ruthlessly sent them happily on to Los Angeles to thump the Americans 5-0.

—

11 Thatcher made little effort to hide her impatience with the Football Association and Football League's apparent inability to deal with the sport's most pressing problem. Things had come to a head with the televised rioting of Millwall fans during an FA Cup tie at Luton Town and the tragic events of the European Cup Final. UEFA responded to the latter by banning all English clubs indefinitely from European competition, two days after the FA, prompted by the Prime Minister, had voluntarily withdrawn them for the following season.

Held in December 1985, the draw for the World Cup finals saw England given the city of Monterrey as their base – which Robson described as 'the short straw' – but Portugal, Morocco and Poland did not appear to offer the most testing opposition. 'It's all about getting it right before we play our first game against Portugal,' said Howe, 'and I am sure that Bobby Robson will have it right. The biggest problem is going to be the heat and ensuring that the players are able to pace themselves and knowing they are capable of doing it over a full 90 minutes. We must not underestimate the quality of the opposition for there are unlikely to be any easy games in Mexico.'

By the time it came to think about packing his suitcases, Howe was no longer splitting duties between club and country. Not that Robson – as much as he wanted Howe as a full-time colleague – had ever been concerned that his friend's club commitments diminished his value to England. 'That's because he trusted him,' says Harris. 'That trust in football is a rare thing. They had a special relationship.'

However, Glenn Hoddle believes that Howe became 'more relaxed' and therefore more effective. 'There must have been a lot of pressure on him with the Arsenal stuff,' he suggests. 'It wasn't a question of one extreme to the other, but he was a lot calmer.'

Robson's team flew to their pre-World Cup training camp in Colorado Springs on the back of a 2-1 win over Scotland, although the date of their departure had disappointed Robson, who'd hoped that the English clubs' ban from European competition would allow for a slightly condensed season and longer preparation time before Mexico. Instead, new competitions – the Screensport Super Cup and Full Members Cup – were added as a way of filling gaps in the fixture list and generating extra revenue. 'I could not believe it after all the complaints of overcrowding,' said Robson. 'I thought both ideas ludicrous … a golden opportunity was thrown away.'

Hoddle cites the domestic fixture list as a reason why 'under both Ron Greenwood and Bobby we didn't do that much tactical work'. He continues, 'Looking back, we should have done, but there were maybe only four or five sessions over nearly ten years where we ended up having an 11 versus 11 and trying to work out what we were going to do with the ball. It was very different to what I was used to, but at international level it was justified. By the time we finished League games on Saturday you were shattered and you were still stiff on Monday or had a couple of knocks. Then you had a game again on Wednesday, so there wasn't much time to prepare for games. We didn't make it easy for ourselves back then.'

At least there were no complaints about the facilities England had the use of at the American Air Force training base, down the road from luxurious, if ominously named, Broadmoor Hotel. Looking at a roofed stadium, Howe commented, 'You walk in there and you see this green synthetic pitch surrounded by a bright blue running track and you just stop. The sheer size of it just takes your breath away.'

The facilities on site showed that nothing had been left to chance. 'Vernon Edwards, the team doctor, made a science of preparing our hotels,' explains physiotherapist Fred Street. 'He used to measure things and check the size of showers. If [6ft 4in goalkeeper] Joe Corrigan was in the squad he would get a special long bed. And he looked at things like security at the training centres.

'The doctor would control most of the diet and menu. You have got to try to make it reasonably interesting without being silly. It is not a holiday, but they are away in a hot, sunny climate and sometimes they felt they were under restrictions and you can get low morale. You would let them off the leash every now and again to go out to a restaurant, but the doctor would monitor their intake. English players didn't need much encouragement to get a few beers inside them and if they were out boozing every night then it would be detrimental to their training and fitness, but it was all right if it was done sensibly and the players were being guided – or bullied or whatever you want to call it. With it being hot weather you would weigh them every day. In Mexico, we took blood every few days. A few had a little problem with the altitude, but mostly it was in their head. It wasn't a real problem.'

The altitude of 7,500 feet offered Robson and Howe a chance to get their players used to the conditions they would encounter in Mexico, with Peter Shilton recalling, 'The training was probably the toughest I had ever known – two hours a day in temperatures that were in the high 90s.'

According to Hoddle, 'We were shocked when we first got there. Because of the altitude we thought we would be nursed into it. I don't know if they were taking medical advice, but they threw us in at the deep end and it was quite intense and hard work. The boys were moaning about it after a long season.'

But no amount of planning and altitude training could guarantee against injuries. Just as skipper Kevin Keegan's back had dominated the England camp in 1982, so the current captain's health was a major talking point four years later. Bryan Robson had first dislocated his right shoulder in a fall at Old Trafford in January 1985 and did it again at West Ham with the World Cup only three months away. An immediate operation would have fixed the problem and probably seen him fully fit for Mexico but would have ruled him out of United's title challenge. He played on; the threat of a further dislocation hanging over every challenge, every tumble. Aged 29 and at the peak of his powers, Robson was – his England manager believed – worth the risk. But in the warm-up friendly against Mexico in Los Angeles, the inevitable happened. Street's deftness popped the joint back in place without the crowd or the press corps being aware of what had happened – for now.

Two weeks later, Robson took his place in England's team for their opening World Cup game in Monterrey, although team doctor Edwards had left camp in the meantime after suffering a heart attack. With such distractions on his mind, Bobby Robson admitted to 'praying everything would go right' against Portugal. It didn't. Skipper Robson threatened with his trademark arrivals in the box – prompting much holding of breath when he landed heavily after one header and again following an overhead kick – but it was Portugal who scored after 75 minutes when Carlos Manuel was presented with an easy tap-in. 'It was as unbelievable as it was shattering,' the manager said of the 1-0 defeat.

England faced the group's outsiders, Morocco, with an unchanged team. With half-time approaching in a goalless game, Bryan Robson was foraging in the opponents' area again when he went down on the hard surface on his right side. This time there was no bouncing back up, nor was there any opportunity to hide what had happened. Street helped Robson trudge towards the dressing room, his arm in a sling. 'I was keen to take Bryan down to Mexico but in hindsight it was the wrong decision,' Street admits. 'It was an emotional decision in some ways, but it was the wrong one because he broke down. If we had lost that match we would have gone home.'

The prospect of a shock defeat loomed even larger a couple of minutes later when Wilkins, frustrated at being ruled offside, threw the ball towards the feet of the Paraguayan referee and was shown the red card. At half-time, Howe and Robson delivered a damage limitation message: that the point that would keep them alive in the tournament was achievable and imperative, and with a bit of luck and a few heroics they could even win the game. There was a brief discussion of maintaining two up front, but discretion won out and the fear of Morocco dominating possession forced a reshuffle to keep midfield numbers at full strength. In the end, a 0-0 draw meant they needed to beat Poland five days later to advance to the last 16.

Steve Hodge and Peter Reid came into midfield to replace Robson and Wilkins, with Trevor Steven given the wide role in place of Chris Waddle. Meanwhile, Hoddle stayed in the central position he'd occupied after the dismissal of Wilkins. 'I thought that was my best position and I felt that it showed against Morocco when we had to play with ten men,' he says. Hoddle also remembers that the build-up to the make-or-break game against Poland featured a rare lengthy tactical discussion.

'We were under pressure at the time. The crowd had turned on us and we were right under the cosh for the Poland game. We went to this beautiful monastery and we sat on a hill at about midday and started talking about how we were going to approach this game. We discussed how we were going to play and we had a little bit of a back and forth with Bobby and Don. The players were saying that they were trying to get us to play the English way and press from the front, but at that altitude we couldn't do that. We had this open chat – the first time we'd ever had that. I remember Don taking it all on board. As players we gave our opinion and we sorted it out. We stayed behind the ball a little bit so that when we went and pressed we weren't so high that we were stretched out. That was probably the longest and most intense sort of thing we ever had in terms of meetings. But we were there for an hour and a half in the roasting heat and what we didn't realise was that we're all getting sunburnt.'

The mobile Peter Beardsley replaced Hateley up front. Not only did he offer greater fluidity in attack, but he was more suited to Howe's desire to have his forwards putting defenders under pressure in possession. New set pieces and new responsibilities were worked on. There would be no second chances.

This time, things could not have gone better. Shilton reckoned that moving from Monterrey's smaller Stadio Tecnológico after the first two games into the larger Stadio Universitario 'gave us a mental boost' and made them feel like their World Cup had truly begun. And after some early defensive scares, Lineker – now one of four Everton men in the starting line-up – was able to raise the bandaged wrist he had broken before the tournament three times in celebration before half-time. The first two goals came from flowing passing movements that demonstrated the new-found cohesion in England's performance, and the third resulted from goalkeeper error. Lineker's ability to find space and get ahead of defenders in the box was a contributory factor, of course. 'It's just movement basically,' he would explain later. 'You make one run for the defender and one run for yourself. Don Howe used to say that and he was exactly right. It's about checking to one way and then just moving back.'

Now that England were through to the knockout stages and heading to the capital city, Howe and Street called upon their former Arsenal boss, Terry Neill, to help Bobby Robson relax. Neill, in Mexico as a FIFA technical observer, recalls visiting the England dressing room and being pulled to one side by his old colleagues. 'We're going down to Mexico City,' they began. 'You couldn't do us a favour, could you?

Bobby is a bit uptight because of Bryan Robson's injury and things like that. You couldn't take him out on the piss, could you?'

Neill replied that he would be helping to stage an evening event for legendary players, including Stanley Matthews, Ferenc Puskas, Just Fontaine and Francisco Gento. 'I had my own driver so I said I would pick Bobby up,' Neill remembers. 'We took Bobby out and went round to this penthouse suite. There were about 25 or 30 of us there, nice and casual and informal, and I got Bobby pissed and got him back to the hotel and put him to bed. I made sure he got to the right room. I went to the training ground the next day and the first two people I bumped into were Don and Fred and they gave me the thumbs up and said, "Great job. He was arseholed."'

Sleep was not always so easy to come by. Howe had been one of several members of the England party who reported a disturbed night as traffic raced relentlessly past the Vallé de Mexico Hotel, located close to a major highway, prompting Robson to insist upon a move to the quieter Holiday Inn. England certainly appeared relaxed and rested as they dispatched Paraguay 3-0, with two more goals for Lineker.

The quarter-finals brought England up against Argentina for the first time since the 1982 Falklands conflict. Events in the South Atlantic were a distant-enough memory for the form of Diego Maradona to be of greater concern than any diplomatic hangover, although Peter Reid recalled 'an edge that couldn't be ignored' and Robson made reference to the conflict in his final team talk and informed his players that they'd received good-luck telegrams from the Queen and Prime Minister Margaret Thatcher. And it undoubtedly added another layer to the strong pro-Argentina sentiment among the 114,000 crowd in the Azteca Stadium.

After a cagey, scoreless opening 45 minutes, the moment that would go down in football folklore occurred a few minutes into the second half. Maradona cut in from the left, drove towards the penalty area and laid the ball to his right, where Hodge, attempting an interception, succeeded in lofting the ball back towards Shilton. As the goalkeeper came out to collect, Maradona continued his run and, to the remote view offered to commentators and TV viewers, appeared to beat the England keeper to the ball to head it into the net. Noting the England protests, it was not until the second action replay that the BBC's Barry Davies asked, 'At what point was he offside? Or was it use of the hand the England players are complaining about?' The gestures of Shilton, Fenwick, Butcher and others made it clear that they were indeed enraged about a handball that had been clearly visible to those at pitch level – except for Tunisian referee Ben Naceur.

While Maradona would famously credit 'the hand of God' for coming to his aid, it was his own heavenly footwork that created his second goal a few minutes later, a pirouette in his own half setting him off on a run that left defenders floundering and ended with a calm finish from a narrow angle. 'You have to say that is magnificent,' exclaimed Davies, calling it 'pure footballing genius'. England looked like a different team in the game's latter stages after Waddle and the previously unused Barnes were sent into the action. With nine minutes remaining, Barnes skipped behind the Argentina defence to cross for Lineker to head in, and with full time approaching the pair almost repeated the trick. Yet the tournament's leading scorer was inches away from making proper contact and England were out. That Argentina would go on to be crowned world champions was small consolation. As was the fact that, for the second World Cup running, it was easy for the England squad to go home with justifiable thoughts of what might have been. Kenny Sansom was certainly not alone in thinking it was a competition 'we could easily have gone on to win – that should have been our year'.

Robson described England's team bus as it left the stadium being 'more like a hearse' and looked with gratitude at the man by his side, where he had been for four years. 'Don Howe is another true professional,' he said. 'What an unselfish man. He was going back to look for a job, having put aside all concern about his future to give everything he had to England's cause. We were closer than ever after he had shared the problems and worries and he had provided great moral support.'

Howe would end up finding an old friend able to offer some support of his own.

12

CRAZY AFTER ALL THESE YEARS

We played for Don. With my hand on heart, we played for Don.

Wimbledon midfielder Vinnie Jones

DON HOWE returned from England's World Cup adventure to find himself unemployed. His England work continued to be part-time only and when the 1986/87 kicked off – and when it ended – Howe was nowhere to be found on the benches of Football League grounds. Yet one year further on, he would be skipping round Wembley after what might have been the greatest feat of his coaching career.

As teams up and down the country began pre-season training, Howe satisfied his urge to pass on his knowledge of the game by agreeing to do some coaching in Saudi Arabia and visiting various centres around the south of England to tutor eight to 14-year-olds as part of the FA's 'Fun Weeks' programme. 'Their enthusiasm rubbed off on me,' he reported. 'When you are involved at a club, as I was at the Arsenal for nine-and-a-half years, you get so engrossed in your own problems that you never get out and about. It was pleasant to travel round; to get the broader view.'

For a while he welcomed the downtime and an opportunity to take a more detached view of the game he'd been working in for more than three decades. 'I have always been busy,' he said. 'At the end of a season, instead of taking three weeks off to play golf in Marbella, I usually shoved off with the England team. I do love it, but it doesn't give you time to sit back and relax. Now I can see the things that are wrong with our game. It is a nice change anyway to be on the outside. I am one of the most criticised coaches and now I can take a back seat and see who else is taking the criticism.'

But as the season moved through the autumn months, Howe admitted, 'I feel hungry and the sooner I get back in a full-time role the better.' The sacking of Graham Turner at Aston Villa the day after a 6-0 defeat at Nottingham Forest brought speculation about Howe's return. Bottom of the First Division and perceived to be lacking organisation and strategy, Villa soon found out that Howe would not be sending his résumé to chairman Doug Ellis. 'I shall not be applying,' he declared. 'I don't believe in it. Even when clubs advertise they generally know who they want.' The man Villa wanted turned out to be Manchester City's Billy McNeill, although future events at the club were to have a significant, and ultimately glorious, impact on the course of Howe's career.

Again, a full-time position with England was discussed. 'The FA chairman, Bert Millichip, intimated to me that Bobby should have a full-time assistant and that I should be the one,' he said. But then the international committee, with Dick Wragg as its chairman, said there was no prospect of such a development. Howe would have to continue as a £200-per-game part-timer rather than being put on a £25,000 salary.

The development prompted speculation, fuelled by Howe himself, that he might reconsider the position of Saudi Arabian national team manager, which was worth a rumoured £100,000 per year. It had been floated while he was in that country earlier in the year. 'I have never been offered a full-time job by the FA but I was offered one of the biggest jobs in football and turned it down, something I regret doing now in view of Mr Wragg's remarks,' he said. While making it clear that he wanted dearly to continue working with England, he added, 'It has reached the stage where I have to consider my own future very carefully.'

And then a familiar voice came on the telephone. Ask Bobby Gould when his relationship with Howe moved from player and coach to that of friends and he states unequivocally, 'The 14th of December 1972, when he transferred me to Bristol City. That was another £3,250 in my pension.' Gould continued his well-travelled Football League playing career with further stops at West Ham United, Wolverhampton Wanderers (for a second time), Bristol Rovers and Hereford United. Since then, he'd coached with Geoff Hurst at Chelsea; managed two of his former clubs, Bristol Rovers and Coventry City; and had now returned to Rovers for a second stint.

'You know when you get a good feeling about something?' he says, recalling events of January 1987. 'Don had been sacked by Arsenal so I phoned him up and said, "Do you fancy coming to help me?" He said he was getting a bit bored and peed off, so he would come and do two weeks with us.' Gould announced Howe's agreement by saying, 'It's rather like finding Miss World is free and asking her for a date.' It was a development that pleased Robson, who was becoming increasingly worried about losing Howe to a foreign team.

In March, Howe was at White Hart Lane to see George Graham's Arsenal mark their new manager's first season in charge by beating Tottenham Hotspur to reach the final of the League Cup. Howe was sitting next to his former Highbury captain Frank McLintock as they watched many of the players he had introduced to the first team win their replayed semi-final. 'I couldn't help feeling sorry for Don,' McLintock revealed. 'George has quite rightly taken all the credit and done a smashing job, but Don encouraged a lot of this success and it's all been forgotten.'[12] Howe was not a bitter man, but there was no disguising his regret when he commented, 'I don't want to take anything away from George Graham but I look at players like Adams, Davis, Robson and Rocastle and remember that I was bringing them through a year ago.'

—

12 Arsenal would go on to beat Liverpool 2-1 in the final on the greatest day of Charlie Nicholas's career at the club. He scored both goals as Arsenal came from behind to win.

While his old club went to Wembley, Howe was offered an opportunity to pitch up at Roots Hall to help out a Southend United side heading for promotion from the Fourth Division, but now lacking a manager after David Webb resigned, citing interference from the board. Howe declined when asked if he would help out by coaching two days a week, telling club officials that he was too busy.

In June came an opportunity to find a permanent football home, albeit in Turkey. Besiktas, who had just finished as runners-up behind Howe's old club, Galatasaray, declared excitedly that he had agreed in principle to join the club, but Howe made no secret that the ability to continue in his England role would have to be part of the deal. That, however, would depend on Robson and the FA. 'I would not be in a bad position out there,' Howe said. 'Turkey is only three hours away and has terrific media coverage of English football. I would not be losing contact with the game at home. It is Bobby's decision but I want to remain with England.' When Howe admitted that he felt he would be unable to participate in England's upcoming European Championship qualifier against Turkey in October, it was clear that the two roles were not compatible.

Once again, Gould was ready to intervene. Aston Villa's appointment of former Celtic legend McNeill had not gone well; fired after overseeing the club's relegation. The man chosen to replace him was Watford's Graham Taylor, who in turn was succeeded at Vicarage Road by Dave Bassett, who had guided Wimbledon's rise from the Fourth Division to an impressive sixth place in their first season in the top flight. Bassett had played in non-League Wimbledon's heroic draw at League champions Leeds United in 1974/75 and become manager in 1981 during the club's fourth campaign as a Football League team. Having been promoted and relegated at the end of his first two seasons in charge, Bassett then led the club to three promotions in four years to reach the First Division.

But now he was gone and the club whose unruly and chaotic – yet effective – approach to the game had seen them christened 'The Crazy Gang' needed a manager. Club owner Sam Hammam, a Lebanese businessman who had bought the club on a whim a decade earlier, decided on Gould, who had just finished 19th in Division Three at Bristol Rovers but had top-flight managerial experience at Coventry. Gould's memory of a typical day at Wimbledon would be that 'if they weren't letting each other's tyres down in the car park they were burning a team-mate's dodgy gear or smearing black shoe polish over the private parts of some poor soul whose birthday it happened to be' but that the owner 'seemed to thrive on the organised chaos and obviously thought I was cut out to join him'.

Gould knew he would need help. 'It was automatic to ask Don to join me,' he explains. 'He was still out of work and Dave Bassett had taken most of the staff to Watford. When I introduced him to the lads at Wimbledon they clustered round and were so keen to learn from him. I just stepped back and admired the selection I had made. They wanted to be better players. It was fantastic.'

Initially, Howe agreed to help out in pre-season, accompanying the Dons on a tour of Sweden, where, according to Gould, 'Don and I learnt plenty about the squad.' The players also discovered that Gould was intent on raising standards. 'It was a two-star hotel and Don and I looked at each other and said it wasn't good enough. We went to the chap organising the trip and said we would get on a plane and go home unless it was four-star. The players had accepted it back in the day because that was the financial situation, but now they were lording it in a four-star.'

Howe was offered a lesson in the Wimbledon way when, at the first team meeting, his discussion of tactics on a pair of flip charts was halted by midfielder Lawrie Sanchez and goalkeeper Dave Beasant. 'They told us to sit in the front row while they told us how they had succeeded,' says Gould. The players outlined the effectiveness of Bassett's method of sending the ball into the attacking third of the field as quickly as possible, delivering the required numbers of crosses per game, and made it clear that they saw no reason to change.

Far from being scared off by what many in the game had seen as a primitive approach, or by the team's growing reputation for rough play, Howe enjoyed the tour enough to commit himself to the club indefinitely. Clive Goodyear, a defender signed by Gould from Plymouth Argyle, recalls his own positive experience of the trip. 'There were quite a few new signings and it was a new beginning for everyone. It was something different for Don after where he had come from, but the club had assembled a group of players who wanted to work hard and he saw that on the pre-season tour.'

Speedy left-back Terry Phelan was signed from Swansea City for £100,000 and stopper Eric Young from Brighton and Hove Albion for £70,000, but Gould was able to announce perhaps his most important personnel move on 12 August, three days before the new Barclays Bank-sponsored Football League season kicked off. 'It's a two-man job,' he said as he revealed Howe's decision to remain at Plough Lane. 'Don Howe has no long-term contract, but he has assured me he will give ample notice if he wishes to move elsewhere.'

The culture shock Howe must have experienced as he surveyed Wimbledon's sparse training facilities close to the A3 in Roehampton and the tiny, homespun stadium at Plough Lane was soon being felt by another new arrival, striker Terry Gibson, who'd endured an unhappy 18 months at Manchester United after spells at Tottenham Hotspur and Coventry City.

'It was totally different to what I had known before; the training ground and the lack of facilities, Plough Lane itself,' he remembers. 'I guess the same applied to Don. But the thing that stood out quickly for me – and I know for a fact it would have done for Don as well – was the attitude and the work ethic of the people at Wimbledon. How everybody was pulling in the same direction. They had a style, not just in the way they played, but the way they approached life in the top division and it really was refreshing. I didn't mind that the training ground wasn't as good as United or Tottenham or Coventry; it was just about playing first-team football in the top flight and winning games for a team punching above their weight. That was something I embraced and I know Don did as well.'

Gould offers an example of the basic nature of Wimbledon life. 'We travelled to Everton and we hadn't arranged to train anywhere, so we went down to the local park by the hotel. Don was brilliant with them and Dennis Wise was practising corners and dead balls. Big Eric Young goes to head the ball and all of a sudden there is dog shit all over it. The ball hits the crossbar and then hits Dave Beasant smack in the face. So there is dog shit here and there and all of a sudden there is a riot, and Don and I are just standing in the middle of it laughing.'

Howe's reaction is indicative of the ease with which he had settled in his humble surroundings. 'Don started to unwind,' Gould explains. 'He was a different person. I could always hear his steps coming up the stairs to my office. He was so enthusiastic. This was a different challenge, and there was no responsibility. All he had to do was put on his coaching sessions and the lads responded. As a manager you put people together and I loved seeing that.'

Gibson continues, 'It did come across that Don enjoyed himself and it was great for us to share the current England coach. That was a thrill. I had some trepidation because of his image and what you had read in the media, but it couldn't have been further from the truth. He was an outstanding coach, probably the best I ever had in senior professional football.

'Don said it was less pressure because he was there only to coach. He didn't have to go scouting; that was Bob's job. A lot of the players there give Don more credit than Bob, but I look upon it that every good decision Don made was because Bob made that one decision to put his ego to one side and bring in his old manager to work under him. As a young manager, there is the danger that by appointing someone older and more experienced he could easily get your job if things don't go according to plan. But their relationship meant that Don could be trusted and he enjoyed going off and doing England and coming back and working with the Bash Street Kids.'

Gould and Howe quickly came to realise the extent of the unruliness that had earned Wimbledon such nicknames. A 1-1 draw at Chelsea at the end of November saw two Wimbledon players, Carlton Fairweather and Brian Gayle, sent off and the yellow card brandished five times. 'These players were never taught the professional ethics of the game,' said an exasperated Gould, who recalls, 'I pinned them when they stepped out of line, and Don backed me.'

On that occasion Gould announced the introduction of a code of conduct, but any fears that Wimbledon would lose their competitive edge if subjected to behavioural rules disappeared as the team responded with six consecutive victories. Besides, the players were prepared to go only so far to clean up their act.

'One or two things happened that Bob and Don wanted to clamp down on in terms of discipline,' Gibson recalls. 'There was a meeting of the players and the management at which some of the more experienced players told Bob and Don how it had to be. It was quite shocking to be honest. The message was, "We are not changing. This has seen us go through the divisions. We are not going to stop making challenges because that is what we do. Our game is built on being physical, aggressive and intimidating teams. We are not as good as the teams we are playing against so we have to be in their face, we have to be aggressive in our rubbish little stadium and make it uncomfortable for every team that comes to Plough Lane." It was a kind of ultimatum. I'm not saying that Don and Bob buckled but there was an agreement that they would have to embrace it.'

Victory over Arsenal, which Howe said 'shows how much we've learnt', was reported in *The Times* with the note that the Dons committed 'a mere 15 fouls'. And as 1988 dawned, Gould was able to describe the progress they were making under Howe's tactical guidance. 'People have realised what the Wimbledon game is and now pack their defences with bodies,' he said. 'We needed more refinement in the final third of the field and Don has helped to give us that. We've kept 75 per cent of the old Wimbledon and improved the other 25 per cent.' Their style of play was still direct – and Howe's career had proved that he had no issues with that – but it now had greater purpose. Gould might have been describing the Arsenal team of the late 1960s and early 1970s when he said that the aim now was to 'fade the ball into the channels instead of whacking it'. He concluded, 'I would like to believe that this season the players have released themselves from Dave Bassett's shackles

… Don and I would like to believe they are now getting credit for being bloody good players.'

They were also prepared to work hard to execute Howe's desire to keep pressure on the opposition high up the field. 'It has been proved that the more times you win the ball back in the opponents' half, the more goalscoring chances you will create,' was his philosophy. 'The correct mental attitude and fitness standards are of the utmost importance. Without these qualities, pressuring will fail.' Again, it was an approach that even the Double-winning Arsenal players had bought into, as Bob McNab recalls, 'In the old days, the better team won. When you had the ball, you played – and when they had the ball they played. There was no pressuring. But Arsenal were pressuring, hustling, knocking people down all over the field like ice hockey.' Clearly, Howe and Wimbledon were not such an unlikely liaison.

As well as a focus on fitness, Goodyear recalls that Howe's training sessions were 'very detailed and very precise and you knew what you had to do, what he expected of you and it was something different nearly every day'. He explains, 'We had a style of play that was a little different to most teams, but he adapted to that and coached it very well. He took on board what had happened in the past and added to it and improved it. With the long-ball system you had areas to hit as a full-back; you had to hit the channel and the training sessions and practice were all about that, as well as your defensive line and positioning. I had been a centre-back so, moving to full-back, he was the best person for me to have as a coach. It was mostly about positional play.

'Don put his foot down when he had to and he didn't take any nonsense. I remember him telling someone, "If you don't want to be here and work hard, then I don't want you in the session." You had to be concentrating for the whole time at training.'

Wally Downes, a veteran whose days at the club were approaching their end before he embarked on a long coaching career, recalled, 'The only thing that kept me interested in training every day was Don Howe … Don's sessions were terrific and inspired me to want to coach. His enthusiasm was terrific and his sessions ran like clockwork.'

They even left a mark on 12-year-old Simon Bassey, who would one day be first-team coach at what would by then be a newly formed AFC Wimbledon.[13] 'I used to go to the training ground on my BMX in the school holidays to see Don work,' he recalls. 'He looked like an old man to me, but his voice was constant and loud. I learnt more about him when I was 16 and my coach was John Cartwright, who was with him at Arsenal and always spoke with great fondness about him. Don is still the best I have seen.'

Yet the varied nature of training sessions that two generations of Arsenal players speak of so fondly was not, Howe realised, what was required in his latest role. 'It wasn't the case at Wimbledon,' says Gibson, 'because we were repetitive. Our game was based on doing the same thing, so we had to do the same thing every day. Where other teams had variations and would play different styles, with us it was like a book with laws in it that you had to adhere to: no square passes; full-backs hitting the channels; one striker chasing in the channels and one cutting off the goalkeeper. It was tough going and not a lot of fun sometimes when you were told it's another 11 versus 11 and both teams are playing like Wimbledon. It took the thinking out of my game. Don couldn't come in and do different styles of play because the whole thing would break down, so the coaching couldn't be varied. So you knew exactly where the ball was going to go and where you played it, and you knew we were going to spend hours on set pieces, defending and attacking.

'You didn't have to make too many decisions. You didn't have to think whether to drop off to get the ball to your feet in open space because it was not going to be played there. I remember Dennis Wise saying to me, "Gibbo, just stick with the fucking program." It was Don's job to ensure that we adhered to that. Everybody did their own job and everybody knew everyone else's job so it worked out that we had 11 coaches on the field. If the full-back got the ball and didn't hit

13 The original Wimbledon FC moved to Milton Keynes to become the MK Dons in 2004.

the channel as quickly as he could then everybody else would have a go at him. If it went down the channel and Fash chased and I didn't cut off the backpass to the goalkeeper then everybody knew I was at fault. If Vinnie had two or three touches in midfield and got caught in possession everybody knew he was at fault. If Alan Cork didn't attack the cross at the far post everybody knew he was at fault. So it was all straightforward and Don's job was to make sure that the fitness side was good. I found it really tough. I used to wake up on Saturday for the games knackered because we were working so hard during the week. But if you are training as long and hard as we were then a 90-minute game of football was a walk in the park.'

The willingness to work hard for Howe came partly from the way he interacted with his players. Gibson explains, 'He was quite blunt at times and he treated everybody in that manner if you didn't do that job. At my other clubs it was quite common that certain players didn't get dug out if they weren't doing their job. At Wimbledon, it didn't matter to him. He had managed higher profile players than he had at Wimbledon and if one or two of the big hitters were out of line then Don was the one to put them back in line.'

The contrast of working with the cream of England's footballers and the undeniably less-gifted men of Wimbledon was not lost on Howe. Yet far from seeing it as a problem, he saw only an opportunity to satisfy a desire to learn that is identified by so many of those who worked with him. 'I describe myself as a student of the game,' he explained. 'I want to learn about every way of playing and being at Wimbledon gives me the chance to increase my own knowledge and to understand how to combat the system should I need to in the future.

'There was no point in telling them to forget everything they know because their style has been ingrained in them for years. What they have done with it has been phenomenal. Bobby and I might change things as we go along, but not now. The players have taught me a lot and I have grown to respect and admire them. They are very strong and positive characters and I haven't come across sharper footballing brains. People overlook that and tend to think they are just crash, bang, wallop.' He warned, 'To underestimate them is wrong. People don't realise there are not a lot of players in England who can hit a long, accurate ball.'

Asked to compare the work he did with Wimbledon to that at Bisham Abbey with England, he concluded, 'The technical stuff will be similar but the functional tasks are completely the opposite. Wimbledon will practise one pass, whereas England will do four, five or six.'

As well as the ability to adjust his coaching sessions to accommodate both groups of players, Howe was also able to recognise the character strengths of those in his charge. 'There are no stars,' he said of the Dons squad. 'When they go out, they go out together. The spirit is magnificent.'

Midfielder Vinnie Jones credits Howe with preserving the essence of Wimbledon with his support for their established style of play. 'I remember Don Howe coming in and telling us to keep things going,' Jones said in his contribution to Downes and Bassett's book, *The Crazy Gang*. 'I think Gouldie on his own would have fucked it up, that's the truth. He did not like anything at the club that still had anything to do with Bassett. He wanted it to be his team and he wanted his players to play.'

No one better epitomised the Dons' spirit or offered a sharper reflection of how the football public perceived Wimbledon than 23-year-old Jones, who had come through non-League football at Wealdstone and whose former employment as a hod carrier offered an ideal analogy for the critics of his physical style of football. The frustration that Howe eventually came to feel over Jones's ability to get into trouble could not disguise his admiration for the job he could do on the field when properly focused. 'People talk of Nobby Stiles and Ron Harris being great man-to-man markers and Vinnie Jones does a similar job and is criticised for it,' he said. 'Vinnie does it well and he will develop his game more.'

Jones entered folklore on 6 February 1988 when he was photographed by the *Daily Mirror*'s Monte Fresco reaching back to grab a yelping Paul Gascoigne's testicles during a First Division game at Plough Lane. The 20-year-old Newcastle midfielder was being hailed as England's most precocious talent for years and Jones was happy to grasp at any method of reducing his effectiveness. 'Vinnie, they've got that lad Gazza,' Howe had said, echoing the kind of conversation he'd had many times with Peter Storey. 'You are going to stop him playing. They're really going to miss him; we won't miss you so much.' Howe warned Jones that the game would be lost unless he did as instructed, telling him to prepare for the match by 'thinking quietly about marking one man'. Legend has it that at one point in the game Jones had to take a throw-in and, pointing at Gascoigne, barked, 'Oi. Fat boy. Stay there and don't move. I'll be back.'

Jones, who said, 'We absolutely adored Don Howe – we had so much respect for him,' would discuss that day, and Howe in general, years later alongside Wise on Sky Sports. When Wise pointed out that 'you needed a strong personality to control those personalities in the dressing room', Jones added, 'We were a bit scared of him to be fair.'

Wise continued, 'You don't mess about with Don. Don would put you in your place. He knew if you were not doing what you were supposed to do … you never want to be on the end of Don at half-time.'

'He organised everything,' Jones went on. 'When I marked Gazza, when I grabbed Gazza that time, he actually pulled me after the game and said, "Don't listen to all the headlines and everything. That's one of the best man-to-man marking jobs that's been done."' Jones would also write, 'What was heartbreaking for me was Don Howe's appraisal of my performance being wiped from history. He was somebody the football world would listen to.'

To the delight of the tabloids who were now casting Jones in the role of the game's anti-hero, he was up against Gascoigne again two weeks later at St James' Park in the fifth round of the FA Cup. 'Wimbledon have trusted Vinnie Jones for what will be a test of his professionalism,' said ITV's Martin Tyler in the introduction to his commentary. Booed loudly when he touched the ball, Jones almost silenced the home fans with a 20-yard blast that was well saved by Gary Kelly. By then Wimbledon were already leading after the unlikely 5ft 5in figure of

Gibson glanced in a sixth-minute header from a Wise free kick. It was another dead-ball delivery from the left by the winger that Gayle headed in to make it 2-0 in the second half. And after Neil McDonald's header gave Newcastle hope, another classic Wimbledon execution gave them a decisive third, Beasant's long boot forward dropping for John Fashanu to score with a deft lob-volley.

In the end, Vinnie-Gazza II had not materialised. In fact, it had been Newcastle's Brazilian forward Mirandinha who had almost sparked fisticuffs by taking a frustrated kick at Beasant as the teams left the field. Gould admitted to concerns about how Jones would respond to the occasion and said he had spent more time with his player in the previous two weeks than with his wife. 'I deliberated over my selection,' he said. 'Don Howe and I discussed it and we went with him and I thought he was quite outstanding.'

For the second year running, Wimbledon were in the last eight. 'That was a great result at Newcastle,' Goodyear recalls. 'Coming back, there was a great atmosphere and a feeling we could go all the way to the final.'

Gibson concurs, going as far as saying, 'There had been some settling-in issues. Bob struggled at the start because Dave Bassett had been so popular, and a few players had replaced others' mates. So travelling back from Newcastle in our own carriage, with everybody together as one group, I thought, "This is better, everybody is getting on. We are all one now."'

Watford, who had fired Bassett after their poor start to the season, arrived at Plough Lane for the quarter-final. It was a day to forget for Dons centre-back Gayle, whose mistake let in Malcolm Allen to score the first goal of the game and who was sent off before half-time for swinging a left fist into Allen's throat. Gould couldn't bring himself to look at his player as he ran past him towards the dressing room.

During the interval, Howe asked the Dons players, 'Why are you not playing like you have in the past? You are not doing the things that have got you here.' And then he went to work. According to Gould, 'Don was magnificent in sorting us out at half-time. He said we were sending Eric Young on as a substitute and switching it to one up front and I just stood there nodding my head in agreement. He had everything down to a tee – or almost everything. Amid the haste of telling all the players what their roles now were, he omitted to mention that someone had to be taken off.'

According to Gibson, being a man short created no sense of panic. 'It never bothered us. We knew that even with ten we had enough to be competitive. We were desperate to continue the Cup run and, to be honest, we had plenty of practice at playing with ten men. What Gayle did in that game was silly – that was the type of aggression that put us in trouble. But we dug ourselves out of it.'

Within three minutes, Wimbledon had equalised. Another free kick on the left; another sweetly placed cross by Wise – and Young headed in. In the days before assists were recorded routinely in English football, Howe reckoned Wise was responsible for 75 per cent of the Wimbledon goals. 'We've worked hard on improving his crossing,' he said. 'We get him to screw it across as best and as soon as he can. You wouldn't believe the number of goals we've had from his delivery and crosses.' Along with the set pieces, Howe said, 'We've worked hard in getting him to come into positions where he can collect the ball himself. We've got him more involved and he has few restrictions placed on him.' Wimbledon won the game when Fashanu charged down a clearance and scored on the run from a narrow angle after 73 minutes.

By the time the Dons faced Luton in the semi-final at White Hart Lane, Jones was back in the headlines for the wrong reasons, sent off at Everton for kicking Peter Reid as he lay on the ground. Dropped by Gould as punishment before the FA handed down a suspension, he was told by his manager that he was 'at a crossroads' in his career. 'It was the personality of the team,' says Goodyear, 'but I am sure there were times when Bobby and Don got frustrated. But they were a good management team and were able to handle it and always come up with a solution.'

For Gould, management of Wimbledon included driving half the team to White Hart Lane for their semi-final in a minibus, which he admitted was 'a bit Sunday morning-ish'. He had also decided that Jones was too integral a part of the Dons not to take his place against a Luton team destined to go on to beat Arsenal in the League Cup Final a few weeks later.[14]

When Mick Harford gave Luton the lead two minutes after the interval, another Wembley appearance beckoned, but, as noted by Clive White in *The Times*, 'The point at which normal humans crack up, Wimbledon become stronger.' Sure enough, Andy Dibble – the goalkeeper who would be a penalty-saving hero for Luton against the Gunners – hauled down Gibson after 55 minutes and Fashanu calmly brought his side level from the spot.

With ten minutes remaining, Cork, the man who had come up with the club all the way from the Fourth Division, hooked a cross towards the far post and Wise slid in two-footed to force the ball in before racing to the Wimbledon dugout to celebrate. In the middle of the melee Gould could be seen to be trying to calm his players, and as they took their positions for kick-off. Howe, sporting the trilby that was becoming a regular part of his touchline uniform, joined in the signals for them to settle down for the final ten minutes. The message got through and Wimbledon, who had won the 1963 FA Amateur Cup at Wembley, were back there, in the final of the big boys' competition.

League champions Liverpool were the opponents and there was little doubt about the expectations – or the sentiment – of most media observers. In *The Times*, chief football correspondent Stuart Jones said that not only should Kenny Dalglish's side win, but 'they must. Otherwise many more viewers, particularly impressionable youngsters, might be persuaded to believe in a fairy story that is far from romantic.' Grudgingly acknowledging that the Dons deserved some credit for their rise, he added, 'Their simple and unsophisticated style is at best rugged and physical. At worst, it is wild and brutal. Trained like commandos, they chase the ball that is launched persistently into the

---

14 Luton had also played at Wembley in that season's Full Members Cup Final, losing 4-1 to Reading.

stratosphere and intimidate any opponent who happens to be standing in the landing area.'

Noting that Liverpool rejected such an approach after failure in the European Cup early in the 1970s, he concluded, 'This season they have elevated themselves to heights regarded as unprecedented,' and called some of their performances 'mesmeric'. Meanwhile, Wimbledon, with five red cards and 51 cautions during the season, were 'bull mastiffs rather than underdogs'.

Howe had suffered enough similar criticisms, even when winning the Double with Arsenal, not to be diverted from his pragmatic approach. 'People may not like it,' he said of Wimbledon's style, 'but they don't like playing against it. Opponents know that if they have a weakness, be it in the air or a hesitancy in releasing the ball, they will soon be found out.' The occasion made Howe even less inclined to entertain romantic notions of winning with beautiful football. 'The FA Cup makes demands on a team that are significantly different to those made in chasing the League title,' he said later. 'In the FA Cup the first requirement for me is simply not to lose. You can lose on a Saturday afternoon in the League and compensate for that the following Saturday.' He concluded that 'good defenders are essential to any team hoping to have a successful run … when you only get one chance you can't afford to lose'.

The problem was that Liverpool appeared to be a team without weakness. Of all the great sides coming out of Anfield over the previous three decades, this one – inspired by the creative partnership of John Barnes and Peter Beardsley – was thought by many to be the best of all. Unbeaten in the first 29 League games of the season, they finished nine points ahead of Manchester United. In beating Nottingham Forest 5-0 at Anfield in April they gave what was hailed as their finest performance since the title-winning team of 1978/79 had put seven past Tottenham Hotspur.

Gibson remembers, 'We went in the next morning and we're saying, "Fucking hell, did you see that last night?" But we had a meeting and went through that video and Don and Bob said, "Nottingham

Forest are everything we are not." They were right. They were the most opposite team to us in the League. Forest didn't close them down up front, they didn't get aggressive in midfield, and they couldn't defend when Houghton and Barnes and Aldridge and Beardsley were let loose. Straightaway that eased our fears that we were going to get smacked 10-0 in front of millions. For the next few weeks we kept dipping into how we were going to play Liverpool and it was a long-term plan that went into action.'

Yet the finishing touch was not added to Wimbledon's preparations until the day before the final. Howe had suggested that they train in the afternoon to replicate the late spring heat they would have to contend with the next day – and proceeded to go off to a lunch. 'It was about four o'clock and we were about halfway through the session,' Gould recalls, 'and Don comes to me for a chat and says, "I am not happy. They have got John Barnes playing out of his skin on the left and we have got Alan Cork wide right and Dennis Wise out left. We have got to change it. If Dennis goes in front of Barnes and Clive Goodyear stays behind they can't get the ball to him and that is what they live on." So, all of a sudden, he has come back on a Friday afternoon after lunch and come up with a plan.'

Working on the new shape took the training session into the early evening and even Howe had to admit, 'I've never known anything like this on the Friday afternoon before the FA Cup Final.'

As Gibson says, 'A three-hour training session on Friday night before the final? In boiling hot weather, with nothing to drink? That summed up Wimbledon, but no one moaned. And we were prepared to stick there and listen to Don and make sure that everything was ready for the next day.'

Goodyear remembers, 'Liverpool were absolutely ripping teams apart down the left with Barnes and Beardsley interchanging positions. Don's plan was just filling that gap. I had to keep Wisey in front of me to kill that space and stop them having so much room. We worked on it for a few hours in training. That was when Don came into his own.'

Gibson continues, 'Don's experience of big games helped because he knew the amount of excitement that would come with playing in a Cup final. He reminded us that if we didn't do what we had planned we were going to get embarrassed by Liverpool. He focused our minds on enjoying the occasion, but at the same time being professional and doing our job.'

The day of the final began with Howe making front-page headlines. This one, though, was Foreign Secretary Geoffrey Howe, who was backing the idea of the UK joining the European Monetary System, against the wishes of Prime Minister Margaret Thatcher. There was no such discord in the Wimbledon camp; just the usual high spirits to contend with, especially after the eve-of-game dinner at the five-star Cannizaro House Hotel in Wimbledon had become a bread-roll throwing contest. Sensing the players' need to let off steam, Gould had told Howe, 'We've got to get them out for a while,' and gave Beasant £50 to take them to a local pub. Shortly before midnight, Gould and Howe, drinking in the hotel bar, were informed by Jones that Fashanu had put his fist through the shower door. Just a typical Friday night with the Crazy Gang.

The temperature on the Wembley pitch as kick-off approached was measured at 80 degrees Fahrenheit. In ITV's glass-fronted presentation booth, the casually dressed Jimmy Greaves looked as though he'd just stepped out of a sauna but insisted that the players would welcome such conditions for a day that was still, at that time, the undoubted showpiece of the English season. Greaves warned that Wimbledon 'mustn't kid themselves that because they are at Wembley they have got to play football'. He continued, 'They get the ball, they leather it up and they leather it across and they get stuck in. If they do it any other way they have got no chance.'

Meanwhile, down in the dressing room, Howe was resurrecting an old trick. When his Arsenal team had faced Liverpool at a sunny Wembley in 1971, he and Bertie Mee refused to let their players join their opponents in the heat of the tunnel leading to the pitch until the match officials had been forced to summon them for a third time. This time Howe went one step further, instructing the entire Dons staff to synchronise watches and turn them back two minutes, before doing the same with the clock on the wall. According to Gould, 'We might as well have ripped up the protocol booklet the FA had sent us several days earlier because the idea was that we were going to be late at every juncture. Liverpool's players were looking daggers at us when we finally made it out into the tunnel. They seemed irritated.'

An estimated audience of more than 400 million people in 64 countries saw Princess Diana – sensibly attired for the heat in a flowing peach dress – introduced to the teams. Inside the stadium the last of the giant Cup Final crowds had gathered, with the forthcoming conversion of the upper tiers behind the goals into seats due to take 10,000 off the 98,000 capacity. BBC commentator John Motson noted that Liverpool had only two players in their matchday 13 who had never played in a major final and referee Brian Hill signalled for the action to begin.

Motson and analyst Jimmy Hill quickly spotted Wise playing out of his usual position, but Hill suggested it was in order to exploit the relative inexperience of Liverpool left-back Gary Ablett. Barnes had enough space for a fifth-minute cross, but the threat he offered was to be as sporadic as Howe had planned. 'Barnes had a couple of runs against me, especially in the first half,' says Goodyear, 'but their lack of quality on the day was really down to our tactics and the way we played.'

Meanwhile, Jones had hatched his own plan to subdue Steve McMahon, the driving force of Liverpool's central midfield. When the England international received a square pass in the tenth minute, Jones arrived at the same time as the ball and scythed his opponent to the ground in the coldest of blood. He wasn't even booked. 'The boys knew I was going to smash him because I'd told them that if I could early enough the referee wasn't going to send me off in front of about 100,000 people,' Jones would recall. 'When the ball came into him I started running. I was about 30 yards away and I kept thinking, "Just open up," and he did and I thought, "Merry Christmas." Boom!'

The greatest Liverpool threat was being posed by Beardsley, who set up a scramble from which both Aldridge and Barnes came close to scoring and had the ball in the net himself after 34 minutes, only to find that Hill had already awarded him a free kick. Two minutes later, Wimbledon earned a free kick on their left wing when Steve Nicol pulled back Phelan. Wise delivered with his right foot and Sanchez stepped in front of Ablett on the edge of the six-yard box to head the ball inside the far post. Liverpool 0 Wimbledon 1 at half-time. The champions had managed 13 attempts at goal compared to the Dons' seven but were far from being in charge. They had been frustrated in their efforts to discover their usual fluency, and subsequent analysis of the match would show that they ended up playing 35 long balls to Wimbledon's 32.

When the Wimbledon players reached the dressing room they discovered that Howe had been planning ahead. Kitman Joe Dillon had been ordered by Howe to go back early to soak towels in a cold bath, an idea he had brought back from previous World Cups. 'We thought we had walked into a scene from *Lawrence of Arabia*,' said Gould. 'All the lads had ice-cold towels wrapped around their heads. What we couldn't comprehend was how Kenny Dalglish could bear being in his red and grey anorak all afternoon.'

Gibson recalls, 'None of us had seen that before, but those little things really helped. We probably thought, "Well, Liverpool are not doing this so we have got one up on them already." I just wish someone had told us to drink something. All we had was hot tea at half-time and if you wanted water you had to get it out of the tap.'

Howe's calm approach was another important factor. 'Don would say, "This is what is going to happen,"' Gibson adds. 'He had an assertive authority that everyone respected. Not because he was England coach or because of what he had done before, but because of what he was doing at Wimbledon. We had something to hang onto and Don was the one who could instruct us on how we were going to get through the next half and win the FA Cup.'

Back in the sunshine, the second half was a quarter of an hour old when Beardsley pushed the ball through for Aldridge and the Liverpool man went down over the leg of Goodyear, who appeared to have played the ball first. 'I definitely won the ball,' says Goodyear. 'You can see it clearly. Aldridge has admitted it since.' Aldridge got up to take the penalty and Beasant became the first goalkeeper to save a Cup Final penalty at Wembley by diving to his left and pushing the ball away.[15] Gould was on his feet, pumping his fists and screaming with joy, only for Howe to grab him by the shirt and tell him, 'Sit down, you daft young bugger. There are still 25 minutes left.' Even so, a relieved Goodyear remembers, 'That's when we thought it was going to be our day.'

When John Scales replaced Gibson, whose variety of injuries had finally caught up with him, Wimbledon didn't feel the need to put the centre-back into his usual position to add extra protection. They preferred to keep the shape that was serving them so well and sent him up front. Meanwhile, McMahon continued to be dogged by the stalking figure of Jones, who ended the game as he had started, by flying into his opponent on the halfway line. Still he was not booked.

There were to be no blemishes on the Dons' day. Nicol was close with a header, but the whistle was soon sounding on one of Wembley's greatest upsets. 'The Crazy Gang have beaten the Culture Club,' were Motson's immortal words as Gould and Howe embraced. Arm in arm, the two friends then turned towards the stands, pointing and waving at their families.

Howe had a special hug for the Wimbledon stalwart, Cork, before Beasant climbed the steps to take the Cup from Princess Diana. 'It's a weird and wonderful world if you come from Wimbledon,' chirped Motson as Beasant raised the trophy. The cameras showed Gould and Howe apparently reminding their unpredictable players to keep their celebrations within the bounds of dignity. 'I needed eyes everywhere on that pitch even after the final whistle,' Gould chuckles. 'I was so grateful to Don for his advice. He was much more experienced in such

15 Ironically, the Football Association's official *FA Cup '88* magazine, published before the final, had run a feature over several pages highlighting that none of the seven Cup Final penalties at Wembley had been saved or missed.

protocol and was well ahead of me in recognising the danger signs and reminding the players how they should behave.'

And as Motson praised Gould's signings, he added, 'There are those who would say the best signing was Don Howe and I have a feeling that what he did behind the scenes this week had a lot to do with the way the match was played today.'

That was reflected in Howe being alongside Gould as the BBC's Tony Gubba grabbed his post-game interviews. After Gubba praised Wimbledon for not allowing Liverpool to play, Howe replied, 'We worked at that for virtually two hours yesterday afternoon. A lot of people wouldn't have done that, they'd have been saving their legs. But we worked at it for two hours. It filled their time in and they have carried it out superbly.' Gould said his team had believed in their ability to score from dead-ball situations and reiterated what 'the master next to me' had said about preparation. 'They were still out there working at ten to six last night,' he confirmed. 'I think – I know – that helped them through today.'

Howe was just warming up. 'For some unknown reason – and I really don't know – people look down their nose at certain people who want to work and graft, you know. And we're a terrific example; this club's a terrific example. There is room at the top. It shouldn't be Manchester United and Liverpool and all these teams every year. But to hear a lot of people talk, that is all they want. That's wrong, that's not how things should be. People from the bottom should be allowed to get to the top.'[16]

When Gubba suggested it was a 'grafting final', Gould had the last word. 'Tony, do you expect us to come here to please the media?' He signed off with, 'To the viewers at home, thanks for watching, and to the media … *[winking at the camera]* we did it.'

---

16 Those comments from Howe were shared widely on social media in April 2021 when 12 of Europe's leading clubs, including the six biggest from the Premier League, announced controversial – and short-lived – plans to form a closed-shop European Super League.

Howe departed for England's crack at the European Championship finals in West Germany, having achieved the most unlikely, and happiest, of club triumphs. 'You could see it meant a lot to him,' says Gibson, 'because he had done it in different circumstances, working with a club that had small wage budgets; a small band of people that worked around the club. It wasn't like Highbury – it was a little community, which made it even better. At the celebrations afterwards everybody who was involved full-time at the club was there and everybody knew everybody. That would have been different to Don. He played a huge part in what we did and I think it was fun for him.'

Asked to contribute his thoughts on the FA Cup to a souvenir magazine for the 1990 final, Howe recalled, 'That final gave me a lot of pleasure because few people expected us to get to Wembley. I never looked that far ahead – just to the next game. I'm just pleased if we can get through to the next round.' He also suggested that his history of success in the tournament meant he had been blessed. 'For most coaches, managers and players the FA Cup has a unique appeal,' he said. 'It's hard to explain and sometimes it's quite illogical. How is it for instance that a manager as successful and experienced as Brian Clough has never taken a team to the final?[17] It's peculiar how fate deals out the hands.'

Fate was about to offer Howe a darker experience. Only four days after England's early exit from Euro 88, he was taken into the intensive care unit at Watford General Hospital after a recurrence of chest pains that he had first felt during the tournament. At the age of 52, he required a triple heart bypass. 'I felt some chest pains and a few weeks later I felt the same pains, only more severe,' was his matter-of-fact account. 'The doctors discovered a couple of arteries had furred up and I was told I needed the by-pass operation.'

His son, Rob, suggests, 'I think it was an accumulation of living in hotels and the rich food associated with it. My dad didn't eat

---

17 Clough would lead Nottingham Forest to the final against Tottenham one year after this interview.

unhealthily, but when you live in a hotel a lot, as he did, it can be difficult. It was just blocked arteries basically. In his early days he used to shout a lot on the sideline and after that he was a lot calmer. I don't know if that was because he felt he should not be getting excited as much. But there was never any possibility of him stopping coaching.'

Howe's rehabilitation included four-mile jogs and long walks, where he was often joined by Goodyear, recovering from a knee operation. 'I was tapping into Don's knowledge of the game, getting some information,' Goodyear remembers. 'He loved to talk about football – he lived and breathed the game – but he was a fantastic guy and could talk about a lot of things. He was a very humble man and I loved working with Don. He was like your uncle, really. If he needed to he'd give you a rollicking, but he was always up for a beer afterwards.'

By the time the new season kicked off, Gould had seen Beasant leave for Chelsea, Thorn sold to Newcastle and Gayle to Manchester City, but he had Howe with him on the training pitch surprisingly quickly. 'Don's first session back was on a school field by the motorway when we were preparing for a League Cup game at Barnsley. He could easily have had more time off because there was nothing glamorous about that trip, but it was typical of him that he wanted to be back at work as soon as possible. He even became frustrated because the lads were struggling with their set pieces so he went to show them how it was done. To a man they shouted, "Don't run. Think of your heart." He just shook his head, smiled and realised how much he had missed the banter.'

But there were events on their way to test his resolve and patience. Jones had begun the season by earning a fine and a three-match suspension for elbowing a part-time player in a pre-season friendly on the Isle of Wight. In November, it was his reckless challenge at White Hart Lane that sent Spurs defender Gary Stevens to hospital with damaged knee ligaments, an incident – unpunished by the referee – that prompted home physiotherapist John Sheridan to clash with Howe in the tunnel. 'I had words with Don Howe,' Sheridan said. 'It was a heat of the moment thing. He just misunderstood something I said.'

In February it was Howe who struggled to retain control after Jones was sent off at Everton for pushing his head into that of Everton's Kevin Ratcliffe, having just committed a high tackle on Graeme Sharp. At the time an unnamed Dons player revealed that Howe was so angry that he told the dressing room that he was quitting, a story subsequently corroborated by Gould. 'What am I doing here with you thugs?' Howe yelled. 'You are barbarians.'

In the previous match against Aston Villa in the FA Cup, Young had been sent off for elbowing. That had forced Gould to announce, 'Certain things happened out there that I wasn't too pleased with. Professionals must learn what life is about and if that means hitting them in the pocket then that is what will happen and Don Howe and I will win.' Before the end of the season, Jones was in trouble again, fined £500 for making obscene gestures in a game against Queens Park Rangers. In June, Jones left Plough Lane for Leeds United, with Gould recalling, 'He was lucky to play for the right people and certainly couldn't have had a better tutor at Wimbledon than Don.'

Howe's own breaking point had also arrived and, in July 1989, the *Daily Mirror* splashed the headline, 'HOWE QUITS DIRTY DONS'. He was reported to be going to QPR to work with new manager Trevor Francis. Gould commented, 'Am I shocked? No, just grateful for his assistance. Don and I have a super partnership, personally and collectively. Wimbledon have done well by Don Howe. But Don Howe has done well by Wimbledon.'

Speaking on behalf of his client John Fashanu, agent Eric Hall added, 'Don Howe is the best coach in the country and Fash loved working with him. He will be very upset that Don is no longer the coach at Plough Lane. He got a buzz from working with him and Don did more than anyone to get him into the England team.'

Decades later, Gould, who tried to get Howe a pay rise to persuade him to stay at Wimbledon, remembers that his colleague's departure was not just a reflection of his concerns at the Dons' disciplinary issues, but a growing dissatisfaction – shared by Gould – about the manner in which the club was being run. For Howe, being crazy clearly came with a time limit.

13

SWEEPING AHEAD

Don Howe is convinced that the formation must be rearranged, and particularly at the back, if England are to be considered genuine contenders for the World Cup.

***The Times*, 1989**

DON HOWE had no intention of spending his unemployment in the autumn of 1986 doing the gardening or dozing in front of the horse racing on television. If his part-time role with England was, for now, the extent of his involvement in competitive football then he was going to dedicate as much time as possible to it, taking advantage of being unattached to a club for the first time in his working life.

'Bobby [Robson] used to ring me whenever an England squad player was playing against the Arsenal and asked me to judge their form,' he explained a few weeks into the new season. 'But I was so wrapped up in my own side and the game as a whole that I couldn't concentrate fully on specific opponents. It is amazing how much you miss. In the last few weeks I've seen players doing things for their clubs that they never do for England. They are picked because of the talent that they have shown in the League and Bobby wants them to take that into the international arena.

'The most noticeable aspect is the lack of technique,' he added, echoing an observation he'd made a decade earlier at a television show called *All in the Game*, in which teams from professional clubs competed in various disciplines, such as dribbling, shooting, heading and bending the ball. 'There were some excellent tests of skill and some of the players were furious they couldn't do them better,' he observed. The environment might have been light-hearted, but the seriousness of Howe's observation was hard to ignore.

Now, he continued, 'Too many players are not comfortable with the ball. When you see the calibre of the players in the World Cup, it gives you something to aim for. Players should be comfortable in all positions, more so now than ever before. We all have our renowned characteristics: running, enthusiasm and spirit. We have any number of what I call "fight players". The World Cup highlighted the fact that it is essential to be armed with individuals who have that touch, that control. That is what I will be practising with England.'

So were England a team that had been 'cheated' out of the 1986 World Cup by the eventual winners of the tournament, or were they as bad as they'd looked as they floundered against Portugal and Morocco?

The answers were presumably to be found in the European Championship of 1988, the seven qualifying teams for which would line up with host nation West Germany. Placed in a group with Yugoslavia, Northern Ireland and Turkey, England won five matches and drew the other, meaning they had now gone through two qualifying tournaments since losing a match. Howe's defensive contribution was again evident. The single goal conceded meant they had allowed only three goals in 14 qualification matches for the last two big tournaments, a record that no European side came close to matching. Without labouring the point, England's record in qualifying since missing out on Euro 84 now read: Played 14, Won 9, Drawn 5, Goals For 40, Goals Against 3.

The one strike against them in the latest campaign came ten minutes before the end of their final game, when they were already 4-0 up in Belgrade against Yugoslavia. It was a match that prompted *The Times* to rave, 'England yesterday sent a shudder down the spines of all the contenders for the European title … with a dazzling victory of extravagant ease and conviction.' Robson remembered that match as 'one of the best displays and results in my entire eight years [as England manager], but sadly it was underestimated by the critics who wrote off the Yugoslavs as a bad team'.

England's friendlies in that period – never the most reliable guide to a nation's true strength – included an impressive 4-2 win against Spain in Madrid, where Gary Lineker, now plying his trade in Barcelona under the management of Terry Venables, scored all four goals. They also drew against Brazil at Wembley. By the time they arrived at the European finals, the only defeat in their last 16 games had been a 3-1 loss in Düsseldorf against West Germany, whom they had been seeded to avoid in the first stage of the tournament.

All of which would count for nothing, of course, if they bombed out in a group that had thrown them together with the Republic of Ireland, the Netherlands and the Soviet Union. On duty for England would be largely the men who had gone to Mexico, the most notable addition being 21-year-old centre-back Tony Adams, introduced to First Division football by Howe at Arsenal.

England's opening game in Stuttgart against Ireland saw another newcomer, Nottingham Forest's Neil Webb, preferred to Glenn Hoddle in midfield, while injury to Terry Butcher found Adams partnering Derby County's Mark Wright at the back. Kenny Sansom's fluffed clearance led to Ray Houghton heading the Irish into a first-half lead and England had no way back, despite their dominance. Lineker, later revealed to have been suffering from hepatitis, couldn't get any of his several chances into the net as Packie Bonner had a blinder in the Irish goal.

Next up were Holland, whose defeat against the USSR meant that this was a do-or-die match for both teams. Lineker and the restored Hoddle both hit the post before Marco van Basten scored with a sweet finish shortly before half-time. Bryan Robson skipped into the box to level the scores but two more goals by Van Basten won the game. England's final match, against the Soviet Union in Frankfurt, began with an early goal for the opposition and, despite Adams heading in a Hoddle free kick, ended in another 3-1 defeat. 'England performed with the self-loathing absent-mindedness of a heartbroken man gazing at the pub spirits,' remembered *The Guardian*'s Rob Smyth two decades later.

In three games in Germany, England had conceded as many goals, seven, as they had in their previous 25 matches in major competitions, dating back to qualifying for the 1982 World Cup finals. The knives would now be out for Robson. Perhaps there was even something Freudian going on when BBC presenter Des Lynam showed the final group tables and said, 'Now we can go straight to Archie McPherson, who is talking with the England manager' – only for the screens to show the veteran Scottish reporter sitting across from Jack Charlton, who had been winning plaudits for his work with the Republic of Ireland.

'GO! In the name of God. GO!' was the headline that screamed from the pages of the *Daily Mirror*, causing Robson to confide in close friend Bob Harris that he expected to be fired and couldn't complain if he was. Yet FA chairman Bert Millichip brushed off such a suggestion and told the manager to begin planning the new World Cup campaign. Robson looked closely at the younger players who might be a force in Italy in four years' time; names including Paul Gascoigne, Paul Parker, Stuart Pearce, Gary Pallister, Nigel Clough and David Rocastle. 'I spoke at length to Don Howe and to Dave Sexton,' he said. 'Both were with me, both supported me, but at the end of the day I had to make the decisions and make whatever changes needed to be made.'

After beating Denmark in a friendly, England began their World Cup campaign with a 0-0 draw against Sweden at Wembley, a game that did nothing to placate the media mob. In November, England journeyed to Riyadh and were held 1-1 by a Saudi Arabia side who at that time had yet to qualify for a World Cup. The *Mirror* sports desk couldn't resist it: 'GO. In the name of Allah. GO!' was the headline this time. Never mind that eight of the 14 players fielded by Robson were playing either their first or second games for England. 'Robbo should be a train driver' was the brutal subheading on the back page.

When the team flight arrived back at Heathrow, Robson was shoved and hounded by reporters and cameramen to the extent that he almost lost his footing and was whisked away to a private room. It pained Howe, recovered from his heart operation, to see his old friend treated in such a manner. If he'd had to endure such treatment he would be tempted to quit, he told Robson. 'The media side of things can be a distraction if you are not careful,' Howe observed of the England job in later years. 'Reaction can be over the top at times when things do not go well. It can get personal. Bobby was slaughtered by some journalists but he retained his dignity.'

The campaign – in the press rather than for qualification – continued with a February friendly in Greece. The *Mirror*'s Nigel Clarke, interviewed during the journey to Athens, admitted, 'We are here to fry Bobby Robson.' When word of that got to the manager, he retained enough humour to turn to Howe when England went a goal down after one minute and ask, 'Where's the frying pan? Clarke will be boiling the fat ready for me.'

England came back to win in Greece and continued on an unbeaten path through the World Cup qualifiers. A 0-0 draw in Poland in the autumn made them one of the six best runners-up, enough to book a place in Italia 90 after winning three and drawing three games without conceding a goal. They were now unbeaten in 20 qualifying matches over three tournaments and Howe's well-organised defence had still been breached only three times. 'Bobby was fortunate in my opinion to have Don Howe as his right-hand man,' Adams recalled. 'Don was an exceptional coach at Arsenal and then with England, too. Although his playing era had been the '50s he never lost his enthusiasm and love for the game and kept learning, staying modern, all through the various changes of style over the years.'

Part of England's evolution since 1988 had been the establishment of Nottingham Forest left-back Pearce, a regular throughout the World Cup qualifiers. Noting that his club manager, Brian Clough, helped out with 'odd remarks and observations', it was under Howe that he really developed his game. 'I had respect for Don and once you have that you hang on to every word the coach has to say,' he said in the early stages of his own coaching career in 2000. 'I remember coaching sessions when he would be looking after the back four and he was so committed to what he was doing, almost dogmatic, that you could not help being sucked in. I find myself coaching some of the sessions the way he did. That I can remember them after 12 years shows what an impression he made.'

According to Pearce, 'Don was an out-and-out defender. He loved a clean sheet every bit as much as [Peter] Shilton. He would take the defenders away from the others and there would be a few moans and groans and we watched the rest go off for a five-a-side or crossing and shooting. We would be in the penalty area with Don. "Swivel your head," he'd shout. "Get your head round. Get your head on it. Go and win it." Rodders [Tony Adams], big Butch, me and the other central defenders would come off with headaches while all the others had been enjoying a jolly-up. But, when all was said and done, Don drummed it into every defender what it meant at this level. That was where I really started learning my trade, going from being a club player with potential to having Nottingham Forest and England after my name.'

According to media reports, the result in Poland – during which only a late shot against the England bar prevented them from elimination – had persuaded Howe that England needed a more modern approach if they were to compete with the best at the World Cup finals. He had been quoted offering that view, forcing Robson to argue that Howe's comments were taken out of context and 'exaggerated'. Robson said Howe had apologised and insisted there was no falling out between the two friends.

Yet Stuart Jones suggested in *The Times* that Robson's 'proposed inflexibility contrasts with the public thoughts which were uttered by his assistant'. Howe was becoming increasingly certain that there were times when England would be better served playing with three central defenders and two advanced full-backs, rather than the traditional 4-4-2. 'Though potentially hazardous, Howe's method could lead to greater progress,' Jones added. The need for a defensive overhaul could not be masked, Howe believed, by those impressive statistics in qualifying. The benefits of a more versatile, fluid system would be evident when England's back four was exposed to a higher quality of opposition in a more intense environment. As former England captain Emlyn Hughes trumpeted in one of his opinion-for-rent pieces in the *Daily Mirror*, 'Howe has seen enough of world football to understand we cannot persist in our old inflexible way.'

Yet even before the Poland game, another former England player, defender Terry Fenwick, had lumped Robson and Howe together for criticism in a book serialised in the national press. Fenwick, playing under Terry Venables at Tottenham after a transfer from QPR, wrote in *Earning My Spurs* – part autobiography, part diary of the 1988/89 season – that the England management wasted the limited time they had with their players and argued that training 'lacked inspiration and new ideas'.

Claiming that it was not a personal attack, nor sour grapes for having been out of the England team since February 1988, Fenwick said of Robson, 'There is nothing new in his coaching, the players are not stimulated or surprised at anything they do with England. And that is wrong because when you are called the best you should have that something extra to produce peak performances. Don Howe is Bobby's right-hand man but, let's face it, his ideas on football are boring.'

Fenwick concluded by saying Robson and Howe greeted any suggestions he had made in team meetings with 'Right, let's move on.' He claimed, 'It was as if they didn't want to listen. It went in one ear and out the other. I hope Bobby and Don prove me wrong, I really do. I'm not a person to criticise for the sake of it and repeat that this is not a personal thing.'

But it was impossible for such comments not to be taken personally. Robson recalled, 'The attack on Don was particularly unwarranted. I couldn't agree in any shape or form with the cruel things said about this extremely talented coach, who was not only very good but also well-liked by all of the players he worked with.'

While it was easy to view Fenwick's comments through the lens of a player no longer in the management's favour, his opinions were not far off those expressed by the eminent football writer, Brian Glanville, who said of the forthcoming World Cup, 'Under the deeply uninspiring, cautious and mediocre management of Bobby Robson and Don Howe I really don't give them a chance.'

One of the men who had kept Fenwick out of the England team was Mark Wright, the man who would prove key to the notion of defensive flexibility. The player deemed best able to fill the role of sweeper, he was reintroduced to the team in an April 1990 friendly against Czechoslovakia. Having missed the 1986 finals with a broken leg and been dropped after the European finals two years later, Wright was about to move ahead of Adams in the battle for selection for Italy because of his greater suitability for a new formation.

Much would be made during the tournament of the England players nagging Robson and Howe to make the switch, but Wright recalled Robson approaching him weeks before the tournament. According to Wright – speaking to author Henry Winter for *Fifty Years of Hurt* – Robson told him to make sure he recovered from a niggling thigh injury. 'Listen, son,' Robson said, 'I want you in the squad but we need you fit. The reason is we'll be changing to three at the back and I want you to play in the middle because you read it better, you can dictate to them.'

Wright's reinstatement allowed him to continue one of the most enjoyable elements of his long playing career. 'I loved every part of what Bobby Robson was about. He was a fantastic coach. Him and Don Howe together left no stone unturned in preparing a team. I loved playing for England and for those two more than anybody else. They were an absolutely fantastic pairing.' Wright described Howe 'ensuring the tactical and training ground work is right', while Robson 'bonds the team and makes players believe in themselves and in each other'.

England arrived at their Italian base on the island of Sardinia with news already having broken that Robson would be leaving his role after the tournament to take a job with PSV Eindhoven in the Netherlands, a move that prompted accusations of treachery from the more volatile sections of the media. Robson would insist that he'd had 'no intention of quitting a job I still loved' and had planned to go on to the European Championship in 1992, mentoring a successor in the meantime. Yet when stories emerged that he would be dismissed if England didn't win the World Cup and that Aston Villa's Graham Taylor had already been lined up as successor, Robson took the pragmatic view of listening to an approach from the Dutch champions, rather than running the risk of missing out by waiting until the summer. 'It seemed that everyone except me knew for sure that I would be leaving my job after the World Cup finals,' he argued. Given the FA's blessing to look for a new job, he regretted not being able to tell Howe and Dave Sexton what was afoot. 'They had no inkling that I was even considering my future, and as they were so involved it was crucial I should tell them before it all became public knowledge.'

The digging of journalists put paid to that. In a flurry of accusations about his private life and speculation over his professional future, Robson saw his plans out in the public before he had chance to confide in Howe. 'He is my best friend in football and he did not know anything about it until he read about it in the papers,' said Robson. 'I didn't like that. I wanted to use the next few days to tell him and all of my staff about the news.'

According to the *Daily Mirror* it was a case of 'Cup plans in chaos'. There was even a suggestion that 'Howe may be asked to take a more front-line role' because of fears over team morale, which was all nonsense.

Robson was relieved when 11 June arrived and the focus was fully on what happened on the field against the Republic of Ireland in Cagliari. Once again, there had been fitness concerns over England's World Cup captain, but Bryan Robson's injured Achilles tendon did not prevent him anchoring midfield in a 4-4-2 line-up. Alongside him was Gascoigne, who had blossomed since his encounter with Vinnie Jones and his transfer to Tottenham Hotspur. His place in the squad had been cemented by a virtuoso performance in the friendly against

Czechoslovakia in April, when he rounded off England's 4-2 win with a finish that had Bobby Robson turning to Howe on the bench and clearly saying, 'That's fantastic.'

Still only winning his 12th England cap, his unpredictable talent was seen as offering an X-factor ingredient that England's last two World Cup squads had lacked. Yet there was little opportunity for flamboyance in a contest that Robson described as 'an awful game to watch, all blood and guts and very little football'. Gary Lineker's early goal was cancelled out by Kevin Sheedy after substitute Steve McMahon was caught in possession on the edge of his penalty area.

With the delivery of newspapers banned from the England team hotel and players not talking to the media in the wake of another pasting in the press, a siege mentality persisted as another can't-lose game against Holland approached. It was time for Robson to unveil Wright as sweeper, playing between Terry Butcher and Des Walker, with the full-backs, Pearce and QPR's Parker – replacing Rangers' Gary Stevens on the right – urged to provide the attacking width. Peter Beardsley was sacrificed up front and John Barnes and Chris Waddle would move in from their respective touchlines. The duo had been among those eager for the deployment of a sweeper, with Waddle having become used to the system since his transfer to Marseille and Barnes quickly buying into the idea. 'I talked to Don Howe, who always had a good ear,' Waddle recalled, his argument being that England had individuals every bit as gifted as a team such as West Germany, for whom the formation was a familiar tactic. He remembered Robson entering the training ground and announcing, 'Right, three at the back,' although according to Wright 'the player power bit is a myth'.

Pearce also remembered Waddle having a voice in the tactical discussion but could not recall the precise sequence of events. He knew, however, 'As a 4-4-2 line-up we hadn't really fired. We had been a bit predictable.'

And Butcher is another to have denied suggestions of undue influence by the senior players, saying, 'Any tactical adjustments made during the World Cup were made only by the manager and Don Howe.'

He even remembered the team being sceptical about the wisdom of the new plan after losing against the squad's second string when they tried it out in a practice match.

Robson sent his players out to face the European champions with breath held and fingers crossed. 'I had set up my tactics but a trip, a penalty, another personal error could mean a 0-1 defeat and I would be to blame, just as I had been at fault in West Germany, even though few questioned the line-up before we began. I asked Don and Mike [Kelly] what they thought … they were totally supportive.'

In the end, he need not have worried. Although the left-footed Butcher took time to get accustomed to playing on the right of the back three, England were impressive in a 0-0 contest and came close to winning, with Dutch captain Ruud Gullit admitting, 'We were lucky to draw.' Gascoigne's act of leaving two Holland defenders standing with his own 'Cruyff turn' symbolised a night that hinted at what might be possible. Depending on who one read or listened to, the success of the sweeper system either restored English football's reputation or was proof of the paucity of previous methods. Or both. 'That is the way forward,' said Shilton, the man best placed to observe the effectiveness of the tactics. 'We have to keep the system.'

They didn't. For the final game of the group against Egypt – one that had to be won to be certain of reaching the last 16 – Robson not only reverted to a back four, omitting Butcher, but gave the side an even more old-fashioned English look by playing Wolverhampton Wanderers' Steve Bull alongside Lineker up front. McMahon played in midfield in place of Bryan Robson, whose injured heel had ended his tournament. A headed goal by Wright from a free kick by the increasingly influential Gascoigne was enough for a 1-0 win. The fact that there were few favourable reviews of the performance was of little concern to Robson, who felt, 'We were on route one, on the highway with all the late kick-offs, a good rest before our next game and avoiding the big guns until the semi-finals. It was up to us.'

England now faced Belgium in Bologna on another baking hot day. Howe took half a dozen players for a morning warm-up and had them back inside for an 11.30am team talk. Unsurprisingly, the sweeper returned and Butcher and Walker were outstanding either side of Wright, although it took the oft-replayed volley by substitute David Platt in the final minute of extra time to secure a quarter-final tie against Cameroon. Once again, the delivery for the winning goal was via Gascoigne, but not before Howe and Robson had to implore him to send the free kick he'd won into the penalty area rather than giving in to tiredness and playing it short while the clock ran out. 'Don and I were up on our feet screaming for him to get it into the box where Butcher and Wright had joined Platt and Bull,' said Robson. 'We need not have worried. Even though he couldn't possibly have heard us, he followed our instructions to the letter.'

Robson said that 'the scenes in the dressing room were fantastic … we were exhilarated', although Howe was relieved to see the players heading to their beds at a reasonable hour rather than drinking until all hours. 'The ritual after a victory like that in England is to celebrate late into the night, having a drink,' Robson explained. 'I hate it. It is one of the reasons why I let the England players go straight home after a Wembley international. Don agrees. He always says you punish your body in play and then punish it again in drink. Why do it twice in one day?'

Gascoigne found match-winner Platt as his midfield partner for the quarter-final tie in Naples against a Cameroon side who had begun the tournament by beating holders Argentina. Many of Robson's players had experienced this stage of the competition four years earlier and he was confident that they would handle the occasion. Howe spent the morning of the game taking a few players for a light training session and checking on the fitness of Barnes, who was suffering from a groin injury. Fred Street put the Liverpool man through a series of twists and turns and Howe was able to report to Robson that 'he has done everything'. In the end, Barnes lasted only 45 minutes and would not play again in the tournament.

In fact, nothing was straightforward, with the African side cancelling out Platt's first-half effort and taking the lead with two goals three minutes apart midway through the second half. But two Lineker penalties, the first eight minutes from time and a second just before the midway mark of another extra-time ordeal, saw a relieved England go through. Robson admitted it had been 'bottle' rather than good football that had taken them into a semi-final clash with West Germany in Turin.

The game had showcased the best and worst of Gascoigne, whose rash challenge gave Cameroon an equalising penalty and whose surge forward and perfectly weighted pass put Lineker in the position from which he was hauled down for the winning spot kick. The Spurs man was rapidly becoming one of the most influential players in the tournament – and one of the most photographed and written about. Along with his prodigious talent, his unpredictable behaviour guaranteed the TV cameras and press snappers plenty of good material around the training ground or team hotel. Robson had already labelled him 'daft as a brush' and, on the face of it, he might have appeared a character unlikely to win the approval of a disciplinarian like Howe. Yet Street recalls, 'Yes, Gazza was a practical joker and that could drive some people mad after a while, but Don never had any problems with him in training. He was serious when it came to work and he never stood out as someone who was not pulling his weight.'

The identity of those who would play around Gascoigne in the semi-final was the subject of the longest discussion when, on the eve of the game, Howe joined Robson, Kelly and Sexton, who had been scouting the Germans, to discuss the team for English football's biggest game for 24 years. The chief tactical concern was whether England's new formation, with only Gascoigne and Platt in the centre of midfield, would be overrun by the opposition, whose manager Franz Beckenbauer preferred three in that area. With Barnes injured, Robson was tempted to shore up the middle by replacing him with Trevor Steven. The issue of whether to play with a sweeper had been put to bed. The defensive shape would be unchanged, even if Wright was unfit and Parker had to move into the middle. The following morning, Robson shared his final selection with Howe. The more attacking figure of Beardsley, not

Steven, would replace Barnes, while Wright was adjudged fit. Robson confessed to Howe his inner doubts about whether he had picked the right line-up, but his mate responded, 'It's too late to worry about that now.'

It was too late, also, for any elaborate team talks; not that Robson was around to deliver one. Parker remembered that it was Howe who delivered the last-minute instructions after a shattered Robson found a couch in a doctor's room and took the opportunity for a pre-match nap. Earlier, Robson had needed no other motivational technique than to remind his players of how proud he was of them. Awake, temporarily refreshed and wearing his light grey FA suit, he took his place in the Perspex-backed dugout of the Stadio delle Alpi, a tracksuited Howe, chewing more frantically than ever, sitting on his right.

By the time an hour had been played Shilton was thinking that he couldn't see the Germans scoring unless they got lucky, which they promptly did. Secure in the knowledge that Howe had drilled discipline into them when facing opposition set plays, Shilton saw little danger as the opposition lined up a free kick outside the box and Parker, as instructed, charged towards the man taking a shot, Andreas Brehme. Yet the ball struck Parker and ballooned into air, dropping agonisingly behind the back-peddling Shilton and into the net.

Again Robson and Howe had a decision to make: to keep their shape or to revert to 4-4-2 with a forward player replacing a defender. Butcher was eventually sacrificed as Steven was sent on to play wide on the right, with Waddle moving out to the left. With ten minutes remaining, Parker crossed from the right, Lineker manoeuvred himself some space and sent his shot bouncing past German goalkeeper Bodo Illgner to equalise. England would soon be embarking on a third extra time period in three games. Howe had been often accused of working players too hard in training, but here, perhaps, was evidence that the fitness sessions had been justified and had not left them bereft of energy for the games. According to Robson, 'Don and I learnt from our past experiences, modifying the training and always making sure that something was kept in reserve as a game approached. Playing three sessions of extra-time in succession showed that we were amongst the fittest, if not the fittest, teams in the competition.'

The events of the rest of the night have entered English football legend: Gascoigne's lunge at Thomas Berthold; the yellow card, the quivering lip and Lineker's warning to the bench to 'have a word' with him; Waddle hitting the inside of the post; Pearce and Waddle's failures in the penalty shoot-out; Gazza's tears as England's heartbroken players saluted the fans. 'You feel helpless; you're just like any other fan watching it,' is the memory of Street, who rose from the bench in unison with Robson as Waddle's final kick soared over the bar.

There was no masking the pain on Robson's features as he walked from the field. Howe, who had placed a sympathetic hand on his friend's arm after the decisive penalty, walked a pace or two behind, lips pursed as if to lock in his emotions. He looked less distressed only in comparison to the tortured figure of Robson. There were tears in the dressing room, but little noise apart from that. Howe saw the futility of trying to engage Robson in conversation, leaving the manager to do his talking to the media. Robson called the match 'his most disappointing and most satisfying' as England manager.

Howe was given one of the bronze medals England's squad had been presented with for reaching the semi-finals – even though they subsequently lost the third-place game against Italy. Asked about Gascoigne, he predicted that 'the world is his oyster'; a brand-new world of superstardom that Gazza tackled head-on in fake breasts when the team landed to a hero's welcome at Luton Airport. For the wider game, Italia 90 would come to be recognised as some kind of balm for a national sport still hurting from the tragedies of the 1980s, which had culminated in the FA Cup semi-final at Hillsborough that would eventually leave 97 dead.

Within six years, Gascoigne had been to Italy and back in an ill-fated transfer to Lazio; English football was bathing in the glamour and cash of the new FA Premier League; and football would be coming home for the Euro 96 tournament. And Don Howe would be back on national service.

14

BACK IN THE HOT SEAT

Don is the best coach I have ever worked for and nobody could have done a better job in the situation we have been in.

QPR midfielder Ray Wilkins

DON HOWE'S contribution to the England cause resulted in – for the most part – the continued enhancement of his coaching reputation. In management, however, he had yet to convince the doubters. After his exit from Arsenal and his subsequent success back in a support role at Wimbledon, it appeared that he might have set aside any ambition to put that part of his record straight. But his departure from the Dons in July 1989 would lead, more quickly than he'd imagined, to another opportunity to be his own man.

His appointment as first-team coach at Queens Park Rangers was confirmed before the ink had dried on the newspaper headlines about him leaving Wimbledon. He eagerly accepted the chance to work under his former England player, Trevor Francis, who had returned from Italy to play for Rangers in Scotland and moved south after six months to sign for QPR manager Jim Smith. When Smith moved on to Newcastle United in November 1988, Francis was promoted to his first managerial position, initially continuing as a player as well.

A solid second half of the season achieved a ninth-place finish in the First Division, after which Howe was introduced as successor to Peter Shreeves as coach. Francis announced his intention to remain on the sidelines from now on and then dampened Rangers' fans expectations for the new season by declaring in August, 'The squad is just not good enough and I am not happy. I will be delighted if we finish where we did last year.'

Simon Barker had moved from Blackburn Rovers in a £400,000 transfer a year earlier because 'I was out of contract and I wanted to play at the top level in the First Division', but after Smith's departure he found himself out of favour. 'I spent most of that first season in the reserves so it was a really disappointing time for me. It seemed like Trevor didn't really fancy me as a player.'

Barker had welcomed Howe's arrival on the basis of his record at Arsenal and status within the England set-up, but soon had personal reasons to celebrate the appointment when he became a fixture in the QPR midfield. 'From the time Trevor brought in Don as his assistant my career at QPR never stopped moving forward and moving up,' he recalls. 'Don was great for me. He obviously liked me as a player and seemed to be pushing for me to be involved a lot more. When I got into the first team I blossomed.'

Yet the team's fortunes did not immediately share the same trajectory. After beating Crystal Palace in the opening match, Rangers had achieved maximum points only once more by the time Liverpool visited for their 13th game. What is more, the team was reportedly railing against the harsh nature of Francis's leadership. This had included, infamously, his act of fining midfielder Martin Allen in March for leaving the team before a game in Newcastle to be with his wife when she gave birth. Now Nigel Spackman, the club's Professional Footballers' Association representative, had announced that Francis 'has a lot to learn' about man-management after public criticism of his players. PFA chief executive Gordon Taylor felt compelled to say, 'I am hoping common sense will prevail and the whole matter can be thrashed out within the club during talks between senior players and management.'

Barker, assistant chief executive of PFA at the time of writing, recalls, 'I've had this conversation with Trevor a few times. It was his first managerial experience and he probably looks back and says, "Yes, I could have dealt with situations a lot better," particularly the Martin Allen one, but at the time we were struggling and Trevor came from the era when fathers weren't there for the birth of their sons and daughters. He was learning on the job and you probably learn more from your mistakes than you do from your successes – and he went on to have a very good career as a manager. There are lots of things where we would change the way we did it, but sometimes you have to go through those experiences.'

Barker recalls that, as assistant manager, Howe would have been a buffer between Francis and dissatisfied players. Yet Spackman was dropped regardless, missing the 3-2 victory over a Liverpool team he had left only a few months earlier. He was transferred to Rangers in Glasgow after two further appearances as a substitute.

In the meantime, Ray Wilkins, another man Howe knew well from England, announced he would be moving in the opposite direction when his contract expired at the end of the month. But it would not be to join his former international team-mate. With his side third from bottom in the table, Francis was sacked for what the club called 'differing opinions over his management style', which appeared to amount to the board siding with the players. Howe was placed in charge 'for the foreseeable future', although with managing director Clive Berlin handling contracts and administration, he said, 'I am coach at the moment, which is what I was before – nothing has changed.'

Wilkins, after some second thoughts, recommitted himself to a move to Loftus Road. 'Don Howe is here and I have worked with him before and I know what he expects,' he explained. The former England captain added another established name to a squad that included England veteran Kenny Sansom and up-and-coming or future internationals in David Seaman, Paul Parker and Andy Sinton. Seaman, at QPR since a 1986 transfer from Birmingham City, had been working without a specialist goalkeeping coach and was quick to approach Howe in the hope of acquiring additional support. Howe called his old friend Bob Wilson, who was by then overseeing Arsenal's goalkeepers, and arranged for him to spend a day a week at Rangers, establishing a long-term partnership between Seaman and the man who would become his mentor.

Seaman was also among the Rangers and England players surprised to see how much energy Howe committed to his work in light of his medical history. 'Players have a lot of time for Don because they respect his knowledge and his enthusiasm for the game,' he recalled. 'He was running up and down, really out of breath and panting. We were all worried and told him to take it easy but he just kept running, gasping out, "I'm all right, I'm all right."'

Rangers' star players were quickly joined by the extravagantly skilled South African-born Roy Wegerle, signed from Luton Town for £1 million in early December. 'Don and I were both aware that the QPR board signed me and not him personally,' says Wegerle, 26 at the time and with his sights on playing for the United States when it hosted the 1994 World Cup, having applied for citizenship through his American wife. 'I believe at that stage of his career Don was more interested in the on-field coaching than signing players and dealing with contracts.'

And he adds, 'I was only distantly aware of the fall-out between Trevor Francis and the players, but when I arrived Don had quelled any ill-feeling and was in complete control of the players. We were all very respectful of him and his reputation. Training sessions were physical but varied and enjoyable. I don't think he put the same session together twice in a month. He always kept you thinking.'

As inheritor of the jersey worn by Rodney Marsh and Stan Bowles, Wegerle welcomed the freedom he was given by Howe, a man of organisation who was frequently assumed to be wary of individual talent. 'Don never really told or coached me to play in any particular way,' Wegerle explains. 'He would encourage me to make smart decisions and keep things simple, but also realised I had been signed because of the type of player I was and, hopefully, to be entertaining and to be a reasonable fit for the No.10 shirt, which, as you know, QPR fans are very keen on.'

Wegerle was without doubt what QPR fans considered their type of player. Barker remembers, 'There were good players, as there always were at QPR, where we were brought up on the team of the 1970s, with Stan Bowles and Gerry Francis. We had a very good footballing side.'

Peter Ball, writing in *The Times*, might have needed some convincing of that, though, after watching QPR draw 0-0 at Arsenal in the fourth round of the FA Cup. He said that Howe's 'new side killed the game to gain a draw' and spoke of 'the dead hand of his tactical influence'. Ball concluded, 'His players, eyes shining with the conviction of converts, will assure you that he is not a negative coach. Maybe not. But then, why are his teams so negative? On Saturday, his past and present teams did not muster a shot worthy of the name between them.'

'What would you have done in my position?' said Howe, who was apparently to blame for both teams' failure to score. 'We came to try and get a result, and we battled away.'

Barker, who would happily lump himself in with those 'shining-eyed converts', insists, 'I learnt so much from Don. His reputation was very much as a defensive coach, but my memories of him at QPR was that he used to work on attacking play all the time during coaching sessions. Yes, he was organised, but I would never have put him down as a negative coach.'

Wegerle continues, 'Don wanted a very disciplined defence system and worked diligently with defenders to get it just right. He was a little looser with our attack and gave players like me, Les [Ferdinand], Ray and Andy Sinton a little freedom to express ourselves – although he definitely wanted balls into the box as early as possible and players to be on the end of crosses. Since I wasn't a natural goalscorer like Rush or Lineker I wasn't around for some when they came in and was sometimes afraid to look over at the bench because I could feel Don's glare from 40 yards away.'

Arsenal were eventually beaten 2-0 in a replay, Sansom drilling in a goal against his old club and Wegerle setting up Sinton, before

Rangers took three games to overcome Blackpool and set up a home quarter-final against holders Liverpool. 'We had a little feeling for the Cup that year and we had a good run going,' says Barker. 'We had a great midweek game against Arsenal – a really good atmosphere and we played really well. We thought maybe we had a good chance of going all the way and it was back in the day when the FA Cup really was something special. The Liverpool game was live on BBC at a time when there was very little televised football so it was a big audience.'

The viewers saw Wilkins fire high in to the net to give Rangers the lead, before John Barnes levelled with a long-range free kick after 53 minutes. Howe's players argued that stand-in referee Kevin Lynch, elevated from the role of linesman when Brian Hill went off injured, forced their defensive wall back further than necessary. 'If the proper ref had been there it would not have been the same,' said Howe. 'He pushed us back so far I thought we would end up on the goalline. I have never seen anything like it. He must have pushed us back 15 yards.'[18] The goal changed the momentum of the tie and after Rush fired Liverpool in front it needed Barker to force his way into the box and score a late equaliser. The replay at Anfield, QPR's ninth tie in the tournament, was settled when Peter Beardsley scored the only goal.

'Our run in the Cup was due to us having an excellent starting 11,' says Wegerle. 'When everyone was healthy I was always confident in our abilities, and we proved it against many of the top teams many different times. But smaller clubs often suffered when one or two starting players had injuries.'

Losing six of their final nine League games meant Rangers finished 11th, and it was in one of those defeats that Barker's hopes of an England call-up evaporated. The midfielder, who describes Howe as being able to easily compartmentalise his dual roles for club and country, explains, 'When he was there at the club, that was his day

—

18 Viewing the goal through a modern lens, there appears to be little wrong with the placement of the wall. QPR's rage is probably a reflection of the rarity for a match official to effectively enforce the ten-yard rule in an era before they carried cans of spray foam.

job. But I was having a particularly good time early in 1990 and Don had pulled me aside and said, "Simon, I wanted to let you know you're going to be announced in the England squad at the weekend." I don't know whether he'd recommended me, but I was really excited about it. Then we played Manchester City in a midweek game and I broke my leg. So it never happened and I never got the opportunity again.'

By the time the 1990/91 season began, Seaman had signed for Arsenal and Howe was no longer employed by England, new manager Graham Taylor having at last won the battle to have a full-time assistant manager and given the role to Lawrie McMenemy. After a poor start to the campaign, Howe took the opportunity to make an appointment of his own, giving a job to his old Wimbledon boss Bobby Gould, who had departed the club a year after Howe. Announcing Gould's arrival as QPR coach five games into an eight-match losing streak, Howe explained, 'He won't be my number two. He will work alongside me. He is very good at wheeler-dealing and he knows players.'

Gould, who remembers that 'the roles were reversed and there was no pressure on me' set about putting his knowledge to use. 'The first thing I did was get to work on building a new back four. Don wanted two centre-halves and a left-back.'

Hereford United's Darren Peacock and Grimsby Town's Andy Tillson were signed for £200,000 and £370,000 respectively to shore up the middle, and full-back Rufus Brevett arrived from Doncaster Rovers for £150,000 a few weeks later. But Gould was gone after only two months at Loftus Road. 'The young chairman [Richard Thompson] came to me and suggested that Don should be the coach and me the manager,' he explains. 'I told him I could not do it. I said, "If Don was to come to me and say he wanted to do the coaching and me the management that would be okay, but I do not want you to sack or demote Don." I couldn't do that to him and so I made the mistake of taking the job as manager of West Brom, where the chairman got up and said, "Here is Bobby Gould, but he wasn't my choice!"'

Peacock and Tillson had gone into a side staring relegation in the face after hurtling down the table and they played their part in an impressive transformation. Their joint debuts in a 1-1 draw at Derby County halted a run of eight successive First Division defeats. A month later Rangers embarked on an 11-game unbeaten run that got them to a finishing position of 12th.

Another feature of Rangers' season was the successful strike partnership of centre-forward Les Ferdinand and Wegerle, whose haul of 18 First Division goals was bettered by only two players and included a magnificent solo effort at Leeds United. 'My individual form was due to me settling in with a group of talented players who inspired confidence. I never expected us to lose and it reflected in our performances. Don kept on at me that if I was playing well up front, everyone else would be up for it. I just wish through my career I had been a little more consistent in doing so.'

Among the highlights of the campaign had been a 6-1 Loftus Road thrashing of Luton Town early in the season, on a day when Howe had written presciently in his programme notes, 'I have a strong feeling that once we start scoring, we could get a hatful. I have watched our players in training and know that they have the ability, and someone in the First Division will be on the receiving end.' The most impressive result, however, was a 3-1 win at defending champions Liverpool at the end of March, a game that ended with Howe jumping from the Anfield dugout and directing his players to go and salute the Rangers fans who had been singing behind the goal for the entire afternoon.

Yet by the time Rangers ended the season with a 1-1 home draw against Everton, Loftus Road was alive with rumours that former captain Gerry Francis was to be lured away from his role as manager of Bristol Rovers to take charge of his old club. It was not a prospect that excited Wilkins, who said, 'We will all be disappointed if Don goes.'

A week or so later, Howe was summoned to see Thompson and Berlin. 'All I know is that I will be meeting officials of the club tomorrow,' he told reporters. 'Am I under threat? Nothing surprises me in football anymore.'

Howe was relieved of his duties, even though the QPR club statement read, 'The board have nothing but admiration for Mr Howe and the way he performed in difficult circumstances.' The stories about Gerry Francis were true, and it was framed in the media as a preference for a man 16 years Howe's junior. 'I am very sorry to be leaving,' said Howe. 'I had a very good relationship with the players and did the job as best I could. I can't understand what a younger fellow would be able to do that I couldn't. The chairman is talking about a five-year plan, but I don't know what he means by that. No solid reason was given for my dismissal. I would have been able to accept it more easily if there had.'

Wegerle believes that 'finishing mid-table in my two years there with Don was about right given the size of our squad'. He adds, 'It was a surprise, for me at least, when he was moved on since we were an entertaining team to watch and we were very rarely outplayed – even when we did lose. I was probably the unhappiest member of the team when I heard about him leaving.'

Barker might rival Wegerle for that distinction, saying, 'I was very disappointed because I liked Don so much and he turned my career around. Gerry Francis had a great connection with QPR and done a good job at Bristol Rovers but I think they were justifying it on an age basis, which I thought was disappointing. But that is football. Those within it understand what it is like and that managers don't last very long. I know quite a few of my colleagues were disappointed. In my time at QPR I had ten managers in ten years, including three caretakers, so nothing really surprises you.'

Citing Howe – along with former Blackburn manager Bobby Saxton – as the biggest influence on his playing career, Barker concludes, 'Don wasn't the greatest at man-management. If you were injured he wasn't really interested in you and he wouldn't come in the treatment room. But he was certainly a very good coach and a good organiser of the team. He was very honest and knew the game back to front. He was a good guy and funny without knowing it. He used to teach the strikers to curve their runs to get behind the back four and he used to go on these long arched runs that seemed to take forever. He would never have got on the end of anything. He was being completely serious, but he was being funny without really understanding why. He always had ultimate respect from everybody, but those things made you laugh and smile.'

* * *

Howe's stature within the game was enough for his name to be inserted immediately into conversations about vacant positions. Reportedly, he had a choice of home or away: a return to Wimbledon to work with Ray Harford, or a job at French club Marseille. 'I have not spoken to Marseille,' he said at the end of June. 'But I've spoken to Sam Hammam and will meet with Ray after his holiday.'

He duly signed on for further duty with Wimbledon, but before the 1991/92 season could begin he had departed. Angry at being unable to speak to Sheffield Wednesday and Southampton, Harford – who had previously led Luton Town to unlikely achievement in England's cup competitions – told the club he would leave when his contract expired at the end of the year. Howe resigned one day later, concerned about the impact his presence at the club would have on his perceived integrity. 'I didn't want people to think I'd gone there to step into Ray's shoes as soon as I could,' he said. 'Ray's got problems with the club but I didn't go in there as an intruder. I didn't go there to take over. I went there to work with Ray, not to take his place.'

For the players who remained from the glory days of 1988 it was a particular blow. 'When we won the Cup all the football side was down to Don,' Terry Gibson said. 'We have lost our way a bit over the last couple of years, but with Don back I really fancied our chances to do well.'

Harford ended up leaving Wimbledon in October, becoming assistant to Kenny Dalglish at Blackburn Rovers and eventually helping the club to a Premier League title. When former England centre-forward Peter Withe took charge at Plough Lane there were reports that he wanted Howe back at the club.

In the meantime, Howe had been content to coach part-time at Barnet, where manager Barry Fry had asked him to work with the defence. The team's results that autumn included a run of seven wins in eight games, including six clean sheets, with one fan on a Barnet FC website remembering that 'you could see the organisation and consistency'. Club historian Mick Bodley wrote, 'The team just got better and better, even though Barry would play a back three with two in front and five forwards – with more forwards on the bench; never a centre-half. It was crazy. We had Don Howe as a defensive coach for a while and really tightened up and played with more discipline for three or four games, but when he left Barry said "stuff this rubbish" and went back to his style.'

Early in December 1991, Howe's assistance was requested by another of his former England players, Terry Butcher, who had been player-manager at Coventry City for a year after moving from Rangers. Rob Howe says, 'My dad never did anything for the status. He did it because people wanted him, like Bobby Gould and Terry Butcher. If they wanted him there he was happy to go. And he never went looking for jobs. He thought, "If they want me I will help them and if they don't, that's fine."'

Having more or less hung up his boots in the summer because of injury, Butcher had his team placed sixth in the First Division table after the first few weeks, only to suffer a run of five successive defeats in the autumn. An appointment of previous chairman John Poynton, Butcher was approached by the new man running the club, Peter Robins, and was instructed to release coaches Mick Mills, Butcher's former Ipswich captain, and Brian Eastick. 'Mick took it remarkably well but at the same time he warned me to watch my back,' was how Butcher recalled the moment. 'I was left having to find a quality replacement as my number two. I plumped for my old England trainer Don Howe.'

The arrival of Howe, working without a contract with a view to signing one the following summer, was announced a day after Mills departed. 'I was pleased Don was there,' recalls Stewart Robson, who had left Arsenal early in George Graham's reign and had been signed by Butcher after spending four years at West Ham United. 'When your coach likes you it makes you want to play for him, and I felt that way whenever he was my coach. Coventry became a more disciplined club under him. It was obvious to me Terry wasn't going to last much longer.'

As the Christmas programme approached, Butcher and Howe spoke to every player individually to try to work out why the club's 25-year stay in the top flight was under threat. And this was certainly not the year to surrender that status. The end of the season would see a reorganisation of professional club football in England, with the top division becoming the Premier League, administered by the Football Association and funded largely by a new deal with upstart satellite TV station Sky Sports. The Football League would continue as the second tier of the English game, its teams left scavenging for the financial scraps.

A victory, a draw and a defeat in the next three League games did not change the outlook a great deal and, two days after Coventry needed a late penalty to earn a draw at home in the FA Cup against Second Division Cambridge United, Butcher was fired. Called to the ground on a day off for what he assumed was some kind of planning meeting, Butcher had his two sons with him and left them watching television in his office while he went to see Robins. There were two sheets of paper on the chairman's desk, a press statement announcing Butcher's sacking and the appointment of Howe as his replacement, and a legal document pertaining to Butcher's contract. 'I should have known it was coming,' he recalled. 'They had already tried to persuade me to take a reduction in wages because I was no longer playing. I wouldn't do it because I knew it would make it easier for them to sack me when the time came.'

Publicly, Robins blamed Butcher's sacking on his refusal to agree to a reduction in the £250,000 annual contract he had been given on the basis of him playing as well as managing. Referring to results, he added, 'Had we left it any later it could have been extremely difficult to reverse the trend. We have said on many occasions this is the most important season in our history. We are totally committed to bringing Premier League football to Highfield Road and we have made this decision to make sure we achieve that goal.'

Having given Howe that responsibility, Robins declared that 'Coventry are in safe hands' and announced an 18-month contract for the new manager. In an interesting contrast to his comments at Wimbledon – not that anything can be read into it – Howe said, 'I have enjoyed being back in the First Division since coming to Coventry and I have no qualms about taking over from Terry. But if things had not been the way I wanted, I would have shaken hands, said "cheerio", wished them all the best and walked away.' He did, however, reiterate his surprise and disappointment at Butcher's departure.

Ironically, Howe's first match in charge was against QPR. After drawing 1-1 and then losing at Manchester City, Coventry then kept five consecutive clean sheets. If such a sequence gave joy to Howe supporters, then his critics might equally have pointed out that they scored only one goal in that time, David Smith's winner against Crystal Palace being followed by four goalless draws. It was Coventry's failure to score in 12 of their final 18 games, winning only three of them, that kept them mired in a relegation battle right to the end of the season.

'We didn't do particularly well under Don,' admits Robson, who, despite his admiration for Howe, admits that his greater maturity since playing for him at Arsenal made him a different character for his manager to deal with. He remembers one team meeting to illustrate his point.

'Don had obviously seen a psychologist and he put a chair in the middle of the room and said, "I'm going to ask two questions and it's just a yes or no to each question." I was playing well, and was captain and things were going well for me at that time. "Am I getting the best out of you?" was his first question. He went round all the players and Kenny Sansom[19] and I were the only ones who said "no". His next question was, "Are you getting the best out of yourself?" He said, "You can say what you like – I'm not going to get angry."

19 Sansom had left Howe's QPR side to join Coventry for £100,000 on the previous season's transfer deadline day.

'Then he asked me why I said he wasn't getting the best out of me. I said, "I promised myself when you came here, Don, that I wasn't going to be intimidated by you. You weren't going to stop me doing the things that I am doing now. I am enjoying my football and I'm taking more chances. I'm gambling with the ball a bit more and I'm running games. I knew if I lost the ball once you would have a go, so I wouldn't say you are getting the best out of me. I'm getting the best out of myself."'

Having warmed up, Robson decided to speak up for his team-mates. 'I am surprised that all the players here said "yes" because I know that someone like Peter Atherton is scared. He was playing well before you turned up and now you are questioning him. You said, "I heard Peter Atherton was quick but the way Neil Webb went past him he can't be." You put that in the paper, so how do you think he feels? And now he's not playing as well. And you made Andy Pearce play with a broken toe at Manchester City and the first mistake he makes you go and give him a bollocking. So you're not really getting the best out of him.'

Robson continues, 'Don waited and waited until I made a mistake against Aston Villa at the end of the season. He said, "You, Roy of the Rovers, you told me I couldn't get the best out of you." He had been holding back for weeks. He was a very proud man and he had not come straight back at me. Saying all that, he was an honest man and he wanted to do well. He was disciplined and he was strict in training and those things were great attributes.'

Such qualities, along with a Micky Gynn goal, saw Coventry end a run of six winless matches with a 1-0 home victory over West Ham in their penultimate game. It sent them into the final day of the season needing a draw at Villa Park to avoid relegation and enter the promised land of the Premier League. At half-time, Coventry were heading down; trailing by two goals while Luton Town, who had not won an away game all season, were a goal up at already relegated Notts County. But while Howe's team were unable to change the 2-0 deficit, two second-half goals by Rob Matthews condemned Luton to the demotion they had consistently sidestepped for most of the previous decade.

Howe, who had been assisted by his former England coaching colleague Mike Kelly, headed off for his summer holiday after learning from his chairman that he would have a new, and familiar, working partner for the new season. Bobby Gould was returning to Highfield Road, although this time the question of who worked for who was to be addressed by him and Howe each being given the title of co-manager.

The partnership was never to be resumed, however. After a few weeks off, Howe declared that he'd had enough of the 150-mile round trip from his home in Hertfordshire six times a week. The breaking point had come when he was travelling home from watching a play-off game at Derby. 'I was driving home on the M1 when I got stopped for speeding. The policeman said I'd been doing 120mph. He said I was very lucky because he'd been told only to warn people, not to book them. I drove the rest of the way doing under 70 and when I got back I thought, "This is daft."'

Explaining his resignation, Howe said, 'It was getting me down even before the day had started. After a month's break since the end of the season I decided enough was enough. I am too old and well set where I am to want to move. I want to stay in the game either as manager or coach, but I have promised myself a job nearer home. Now they have Bobby Gould I don't feel like I am leaving them in the lurch.'

Gould recalls, 'It was all because of the commuting. Don's wife, Pauline, had a great relationship with my wife Marge and she phoned me up to talk about it. I said, "Pauline, you and Don have got to do what is right for you, so that you can get the best out of your husband."'

* * *

Chelsea were the next club to attempt to get the best out of Howe, wasting little time after his departure from Coventry to recruit him as first-team coach under manager Ian Porterfield ahead of the 1992/93 campaign, their fourth back in the top flight since being Second Division champions. 'If I had been forced to sit at home doing nothing I would have gone mad,' said Howe, who would be greeted by familiar faces at Stamford Bridge. Three of his Wimbledon FA Cup winners, Dave Beasant, Dennis Wise and Vinnie Jones, were now there, although the latter was soon on his way back to the Dons. 'Chelsea have a lot of exciting players and I am sure they are going to do extremely well this season,' Howe predicted.

Wise was delighted to become reacquainted with the man whose deployment of him at Wembley had shaped the biggest day of his career four years earlier. 'I knew from my days at Wimbledon that he was one of the best coaches around,' he said. 'He was very shrewd tactically and I really welcomed him coming to the club. He brought in a sense of discipline and that is vital. He gave us a hard pre-season and we looked a leaner, sharper unit all round.'

Howe had been given complete control of training by Porterfield, who was in his second full season as the club's manager. According to Graeme Le Saux, a 23-year-old left-winger who had come through the Chelsea system, 'Don came in and helped put in some football structure and got us playing better,' even though his arrival had been a surprise to some.

'It was a bit of a strange job for him in a way, wasn't it?' Le Saux suggests. 'He was there as assistant coach to someone with no real experience. Maybe he thought it would just be a gentle semi-professional type of role, rather than the full cut and thrust of being a head coach – a bit more out of the spotlight, just doing the stuff you love on the training pitch. He couldn't not have football in his life and maybe that was the best solution for him without being too stressful. But Chelsea at that time wasn't a happy place.'

By this stage of his career, Le Saux was out of favour with Porterfield, having displayed his anger at being substituted regularly when he threw his shirt at the manager as he left the field during a game against Southampton a few months earlier. 'I had been in and out the team for a while and I had that flare-up with Ian,' he explains. 'That was the final straw from my point of view. It was just an emotional reaction and I didn't know I'd done it until afterwards. It was just a reaction, a cry for help. I was frustrated and unhappy and I didn't think

I was getting a fair opportunity because other players were getting picked and retaining their places without putting in the work. The culture was all wrong and I think even the players that were part of the problem would admit that now. It wasn't professional. There was a lot of stuff going on behind the scenes.

'Ian was friendly and likeable, but he didn't have the authority you needed. From a younger player's point of view it felt like the senior players were picking the team. Don had to try to sort that out as well, but the whole atmosphere seemed to lift from my perspective when Don came in. He was fantastic in that respect.'

Life in the dressing room was not easy for Le Saux, labelled an 'intellectual' by the media and made to feel like an outsider in the sport. As he put it in the introduction to his autobiography, 'I was ridiculed for reading *The Guardian* rather than staring at the half-naked women on Page 3.'

He explains, 'I didn't have any other professional experiences at that point, no other reference points. Chelsea was disappointing in many ways and it was a tough environment for me.' But even with first-team opportunities remaining sporadic, Howe's presence gave him something positive to focus on. 'I found him a fascinating character, a proper football guy with lots of stories and great experiences that he shared with you. He was obsessed with the game and was the first management person I worked with that made me think and realise that there were students of the game out there with real knowledge. I had a thirst to learn and he was a fantastic source. You would pick up tips from him on the tactical side and the stand-out memory with Don at Chelsea was sitting in one of the Portakabins at Harlington with a video recorder and he kept showing us the European Cup Final between AC Milan and Steaua Bucharest in 1989. Milan battered them but he wasn't showing it to us because of the [4-0] scoreline; he stopped it when Steaua had the ball and you could see three AC Milan players in the shot, pressing and winning the ball back high up the pitch. We talk about Liverpool's high press these days, while he was talking about it in 1992.' And, it should be added, as Arsenal's players did back in the 1970s.

Le Saux continues, 'If you were someone who wanted to listen and learn it was fantastic. He didn't have time to understand me or what I was going through, but I think he saw someone who was enthusiastic and wanted to learn and was very open-minded. Culturally we were probably quite different, but he appreciated me for my football and probably realised that there was a lot of politics at the club and that you had some cynical people in that dressing room. He would occasionally try to talk you round and keep you motivated, and he was good at that.'

Rob Howe offers a story about Chelsea defender Steve Clarke, who went on to become Scotland manager. 'Steve was going through a really bad time and my dad walked around the pitch with him for about an hour, just talking to him asking him why he was not playing well, asking if he was worried about something. Steve told me, "He just took the time out to walk and talk with me about that bad form I was going through. He sorted it out and I came through it." I think that was what my dad did it for – he just wanted to make people better.'

Chelsea approached the second weekend of December in fourth place in the Premier League table behind unlikely pacesetters Norwich City, having lost only five of 18 matches. After they won at Everton via a Robert Fleck goal on a cold day in late November, a proud Howe was handing out brandy in paper cups as the players arrived back in the dressing room, telling them, 'Get those drinks out lads; you have been absolutely fantastic today.'

When they beat Tottenham Hotspur 2-1 for their fourth successive win, *The Times* was prompted to say, 'A young team thrown together in the aftermath of an early-season pile-up of injuries is maturing into a unit that just might mount a challenge for the title.'

Gareth Hall, a 23-year-old Wales defender who felt he was still learning the game after progressing through Chelsea's youth team, recalled, 'He had the biggest impact on us as young players because he was such an excellent coach. He lived and breathed football and he started introducing us to sitting down and watching videos in the evening when we were at the hotel for an away game. He is the best coach I had in my time as a player, without a doubt. His knowledge was superb and he could get his message across as well. Some coaches have the knowledge, but the art is getting it across to the players in a simple form they can understand.'

According to Hall, Howe's training sessions were 'engaging for all' and easy enough to understand that every player took something from them. Howe would remind his players, 'I can't kick the ball for you; I can give you an idea or an option, and then it's up to you.' Hall explained, 'That is where you become a good player or an average player. He put the onus back on the players.'

Chelsea extended their unbeaten run in a 0-0 Friday-night draw at Middlesbrough, putting them into second place. Yet the day brought reports that Howe was back in hospital. Having been suffering from a chest infection, he was admitted for precautionary checks after he developed pains – four years on from his previous heart surgery – and was out of action for a month. 'It was just angina this time,' says son Rob. 'If you have a triple bypass operation your life changes and he was eating healthier, but you can slip back into the old ways and lifestyle. My dad was always fit and used to go running, but he did have an ability to put weight on. That was just like a scare; his body is telling him to be careful.'

Wise remembered, 'I can't tell you how much we missed him. He kept everyone on their toes and refused to let standards slip. He was just what we wanted and needed and his loss was a huge blow to us. When he was working with us we were up there … but after he left we lost our way and that was very disappointing. We felt that as a team and as a unit we were going places, making real progress.'

Stating that 'I'm feeling good now', Howe returned to duties in time to see Chelsea lose their League Cup quarter-final tie against Crystal Palace on 6 January, which made it seven games without a win in all competitions, but he was undoubtedly less of a presence in the second half of the season. When Chelsea lost to Aston Villa on 13 February it meant they had failed to win any of their 11 Premier League games since that December victory over Spurs. 'I don't think it would have been a coincidence,' says Le Saux, who was sold to Blackburn Rovers before the end of the season. 'Don was very influential and he must have been a great help to Ian. It felt as though there was a much better focus when Don was around. The focus was football and getting on with playing rather than all the other stuff that was going on.'

Wise recorded, 'Since I arrived at the club we had had the team of the 1970s shoved down our throats. We wanted so much to achieve something for ourselves on our own to get our own place in the history of Chelsea Football Club. When we lost Don Howe our hopes for the season went with him.'

Having had his team in contention for the title a couple of months earlier, Porterfield was fired and replaced as an interim measure by David Webb. The scorer of Chelsea's winning goal in the 1970 FA Cup Final, who had previously managed Southend United, lost his first match in charge before a seven-game unbeaten run stabilised the club's position and took them to a finishing position of 12th.

When Glenn Hoddle, who had just guided Swindon Town to the top flight, was named as Chelsea's new permanent manager at the end of the season, Howe was offered an opportunity to remain at Stamford Bridge, but only in the role of scout. Seeing it as a 'token' position he chose to leave.

Hall felt that Howe's departure was 'a crying shame' and believes that the team might have gone on to big things had he remained. 'We had some fantastic games with him and it was a joy to come into training,' he concluded. 'Don Howe loved football and I am glad that I came across him during my time in football because he was a proper football man.' It is a view echoing that of Chelsea historian Rick Glanvill, who concluded that 'Don Howe's time at Chelsea was a case of what might have been'.

Before becoming one of the game's most influential coaches, Don Howe earned a reputation as a stylish right-back, earning 23 England caps while playing for West Bromwich Albion (Colorsport)

Don Howe disembarks with team-mates as England return from the 1958 World Cup in Sweden. They had been knocked out by the Soviet Union (TopFoto/PA Images)

Raised as a Wolverhampton Wanderers fan, one of Howe's proudest moments was carrying club legend and England captain Billy Wright from the field after his 100th international against Scotland in 1959. Ronnie Clayton helps him bear his team-mate's weight, with Johnny Haynes, Bryan Douglas, Peter Broadbent, Ron Flowers, Eddie Hopkinson and Graham Shaw also pictured (S&G and Barratts/EMPICS Sport)

Howe (centre) leads the West Brom players in their December 1963 protest against the methods of manager Jimmy Hagan, whose refusal to allow his squad to warm up in tracksuit trousers before training caused a walk-out (Trinity Mirror/Alamy)

Howe (right) doesn't look too impressed as new Arsenal manager Bertie Mee chats with Terry Neill, John Radford, Tommy Baldwin, Frank McLintock and Bob Wilson after his surprise appointment in the summer of 1966. But it was a pivotal moment in Howe's career (PA Images)

Howe finds the press at his door as speculation grows about his future at Arsenal in the summer of 1971 (Pierre Maneyy/Hulton Archive)

Howe makes it to the middle of the front row after accepting his first managerial position at West Bromwich Albion. Back row (left to right): Colin Suggett, Roger Minton, Alan Merrick, George McVitie, Jeff Astle, Tony Brown, Asa Hartford. Middle row: Alistair Robertson, Graham Lovett, Jim Cumbes, John Wile, John Osborne, Lyndon Hughes, Ray Wilson. Front row: Hugh McLean, Hughie Reed, John Kaye, Don Howe, Alan Glover, Len Cantello, Bobby Hope. (Roger Jackson/Central Press/Getty Images)

Manager Terry Neill lifts the arm of coach and 'brother' Howe in front of the Arsenal fans after victory in the 1979 FA Cup Final (Bob Thomas)

Howe was at Ron Greenwood's side as he led England back to the World Cup finals for the first time in 12 years in 1982, although Howe's influence on the team was a much-debated part of their exit from the tournament (Bob Thomas)

In charge at 'The Arsenal'. Don Howe is pictured as manager at the club's official photocall before the 1984/85 season, a campaign that ended in disappointment after the Gunners led the table early on (Trinity Mirror/Alamy)

At club and international level, players knew they were in for a tough session when Howe was the coach. Flanked by manager Bobby Robson, he gets his message across to the England players in 1986 (Bob Thomas)

Wimbledon manager Bobby Gould and defender Terry Phelan celebrate with Howe after their surprise 1-0 victory over Liverpool in the 1988 FA Cup Final, one of Howe's greatest club coaching achievements (David Cannon/Getty)

When the media had their sharpest knives out for Bobby Robson, the England manager was grateful for the support of his great friend and colleague Howe. 'I loved the fella,' said Robson, pictured here at a game in Israel in 1988 (Andrew Cowie/Colorsport)

Howe and Robson watch helplessly as England go out of the 1990 World Cup semi-finals on penalties against West Germany in Turin (Peter Robinson/EMPICS Sport)

Howe helps Terry Venables console Gareth Southgate after his penalty miss condemned England to defeat in the Euro 96 semi-final against Germany (Neal Simpson/EMPICS Sport)

After more than half a century in the profession, Howe, pictured here in 2006, eventually retired to play with his grandchildren and tend the garden – and watch football, of course (Popperphoto)

Arsenal and Bournemouth applaud as the Emirates Stadium pays tribute to Howe after his death in December 2015 (Ian Walton/Getty Images)

15

COMING HOME

The Don, so universally respected within the game, he never gets the England job, he just comes with the job.

***The Times*, February 1996**

IT WAS only three years since Don Howe had found himself a couple of penalty kicks away from the pinnacle of his sport, the World Cup Final. Now, here he was working one day a week in the eighth tier of English football. When asked why he was helping with the coaching at Newbury Town, in the Second Division of the Diadora League – as the Isthmian League was styling itself at the time – his answer was simple: 'Why not?' Maybe nothing illustrated his love of the game more than this unlikely liaison.

Newbury Town was an unremarkable non-League club, previous winners of the Hellenic and Athenian Leagues and apparently happy to trundle along in the lower reaches of the Isthmian League. That was until Martyn Deaner took over at the club and looked to invest some of the money he had made from the oil business.

Martin Hicks, who had played more than 600 games in Reading's defence and had just finished a two-year stint at Birmingham City, was appointed player-manager and was able to surround himself with several experienced Football League professionals. 'We were full-time, which was unusual at that level,' he explains. 'We had seven or eight older ex-pros and Martyn also found people jobs so they would work in the morning and we would train in the afternoon. It was a good situation, but it meant people wanted to beat us and we were expected to win every game, so there was extra pressure. Martyn was a very rich man and his son Andy played for the club, which was part of why he got involved.'

Despite rebounding from defeat in the second game of the 1993/94 season with an unbeaten run of 11 matches in all competitions, Hicks soon discovered one drawback of combining playing and coaching duties. 'I found it was very difficult to keep myself fit and to coach everybody else,' he says. 'When you are coaching, you are not really doing it yourself so after a few weeks I felt I was getting more unfit. I was still trying to play so I spoke to Martyn about it and he suggested getting in someone one day a week to coach, so that I could become a player for that day. I thought it was a great idea. I thought it would be someone from the same level, someone we probably hadn't even heard of.'

Hicks certainly wasn't expecting Deaner to approach him some time later and say, 'I've got Don Howe.'

'Oh yeah? Come on, you are joking,' was his not unexpected response.

'To this day I don't really know how Martyn knew him,' Hicks laughs. Yet Deaner and Howe went back to their respective days living in the Midlands and Newbury's benefactor took a chance that Howe was not content to spend his days pottering around the house and contributing analysis to Channel 4's live coverage of Italian football.

Howe confessed, 'If someone had said to me after the 1990 World Cup that in three years I would be coaching in the Diadora Second Division, I would have poked my tongue out at whoever it was.' Recalling the approach from his ambitious friend, he explained, 'A few days later I decided to give it a go, not knowing anything about non-League football.'

'Honest to God, it was just amazing,' Hicks continues, 'because Don came down as though he was just a shopkeeper from Newbury.

He was just so lovely and ordinary. Many people in the country had an idea of him being a miserable bugger, but that couldn't have been further from the truth. The lads loved him. He was so enthusiastic – often in a funny way because he couldn't run the way he used to. They loved his enthusiasm and his passion for the game.'

Howe would turn up for training on Wednesdays, with Hicks remembering, 'Every time he came it was, "What do you want me to do? What didn't you do well on Saturday? If you didn't defend very well, let's do some defensive work." It all came from me. He never tried to come in and take over. His enthusiasm was brilliant.'

Hicks and his players were thrilled to watch a master at work. 'I was speechless. I had done my badges and you get this idea about what great coaches are like, that they must give passionate talks and lots of information. But he showed me that it's a simple game. His coaching sessions were so simple, but everything had a target. You started with one thing in mind and you followed it through for the next hour or so and you got to where you wanted to be. He started by going back to basics, maybe just having two people passing a ball backwards and forwards. Then you do it with the other foot and then you do something else and it was developing and developing and within 20 minutes you are playing a nine versus nine, trying to get into that game what we were lacking on Saturday. It was very simple and done through logic. It was not, "I'm a great coach, you have got to keep up with me." It was, "Let me see what your capabilities are and we will work on that."'

Howe said at the time, 'I'm pleased to say I am pleasantly surprised not only by the commitment of the players, but the tactical thinking of the coaches.' Although only attending a few games himself, Howe was able to assist in the specifics of match preparation. Hicks explains, 'We might have a big game coming up and had watched these people and were thinking of doing certain things. There was a game where the opposition had a left-back overlapping like he was a winger. I mentioned to Don that he got so many crosses in. I told him what I was thinking about doing and he said, "Yes, that's a good idea, but have you thought about maybe doing this?" He suggested putting our better winger up against their left-back so that he had to defend against him more than getting forward. He was trying to turn the problem round. We had Peter Rhoades-Brown, from Chelsea and Oxford United, so we swapped him over to that wing. It was a simple thing that I hadn't thought about. What a great idea.' And not so far removed from the one involving Dennis Wise and John Barnes that had worked so well at Wembley in 1988.

Newbury were on their way to taking the Diadora Second Division title, winning 32 and losing only three of their 42 matches. They also made it to the quarter-final of the FA Vase before losing 2-0 at Taunton Town, a game that had prompted the visit of a national newspaper. Asked why he was helping out such a humble club, Howe replied, 'I do it because I enjoy it. It's interesting and stimulating. What I do with them in training is no different to what I did at Arsenal or Chelsea. There are some good players at this level and every week I see lads who could make it in the League with a little help.' Yet when invited to give his opinion on Newbury's performance, Howe deferred to Hicks, his boss.

The reason for the interest in Howe's involvement in non-League football was that the day after Newbury took the field for their big game, he would be reporting for England duty once again as the national team began another new era under its latest manager. While Howe was helping Newbury on their upward trajectory, Graham Taylor's stint in charge of England was plummeting towards an undignified ending. Depicted in the tabloids as a turnip and ridiculed for team selection and tactics, Taylor had been condemned to missing out on the 1994 World Cup finals in the United States by defeats in Norway and the Netherlands. In November 1993, after England had conceded inside 20 seconds against hapless San Marino before achieving a meaningless 7-1 win, the former Lincoln City, Watford and Aston Villa manager resigned.

Howe's was the first name mentioned as a possible short-term replacement; someone who could take charge of spring friendlies against

Denmark and Germany while a permanent successor was identified. FA chief executive Graham Kelly confirmed, 'There will be a caretaker and he will not come from a club because we do not want to disrupt any club's season. He will be in place by the New Year. I cannot rule out Don Howe.'

Yet within 24 hours, Howe had done that himself. 'If the FA approached me and asked me to do that my answer would be no,' he said. 'I enjoyed my ten-year stint as England coach, but now they should go for a younger person. I've had my go. Ten years was enough.'

Peter Swales, the Manchester City chairman who was also head of the FA's international committee, was undeterred. 'I've read Don's comments, but we are still hopeful we can get him to take on the commitment.' Kelly, however, said he was unaware of any decision to make such an approach to Howe – to the delight of the *Daily Mirror*. Never slow to revel in apparent FA confusion, the newspaper responded by depicting the nation's favourite fool, comedian Norman Wisdom, as the man running the organisation.

Names such as John Lyall and Dave Sexton were thrown around as possible caretakers, while Howe did suggest he would be happy to offer guidance if a young candidate such as Ray Wilkins was given an opportunity. But his advice to the FA was to forget about an interim appointment altogether and give the role full-time to Terry Venables. 'The England job is all about coaching rather than managing and Terry is a terrific coach,' he said. 'He has worked on the continent with Barcelona and these days the game-plan is so important at international level.'

As the weeks went on, it appeared that the FA were indeed thinking along those lines. Any reticence was caused by off-field events since Venables had led Tottenham Hotspur to the FA Cup in 1991. Installed as chief executive by new owner Alan Sugar not long after their Wembley triumph, Venables had handed over team affairs to Peter Shreeves. But in May 1993 he was dismissed by Sugar after allegations about misdealings connected to his private business interests, eventually losing a High Court battle for reinstatement. BBC's *Panorama* went on to allege he had raised the £1 million to purchase a stake in the club on the strength of the assets of a company from which he had already resigned. And there were claims of a £50,000 'bung' paid to facilitate a transfer.

It was during the fallout – with Venables threatening legal action and the FA investigating possible breaches of their regulations – that the position of England manager became vacant. Seemingly assured that they had identified the right candidate from a football perspective, FA officials were loath to commit themselves while uncertainty remained over the reputation of their chosen man. 'The FA is left with a difficult decision,' Kelly said early in January 1994. 'It is no secret Terry Venables is the favourite for the post and the FA is examining all obstacles that have been thrown across its path as a matter of urgency and fairness.'

The solution all parties appeared to be approaching was a contract that allowed for termination in the event that Venables was proved guilty of anything. Before the month was up, he was in position – with the title of coach rather than manager – and turning his attention to creating a support staff.

Bryan Robson, a former England captain seen as a potential long-term candidate as manager, was named alongside Howe, who was returning to international football only weeks after saying, 'I've had my go.' Robson, still playing for Manchester United, and Howe, still doing a day per week at Newbury, were both part-time appointments. 'I'm delighted to have on board such experienced professionals as Bryan and Don,' Venables said. 'Don has invaluable experience of the international scene and is an outstanding coach.'

Sexton had also been named to take charge of the Under-21s, and Venables would write shortly afterwards, 'When I started to pick my coaching team I had no hesitation in including Dave Sexton and Don Howe. Neither are in the first flush of youth but they're both still so sharp and complete football nuts who have lost none of their enthusiasm for the game.'

It was with Howe that Venables discussed plans for training sessions once the team convened for their first game against Denmark in

March. Venables asked Howe to play the role of an American football-style defensive coordinator, while Robson would concentrate on skill elements with individual players and the manager himself would get the forward players used to his desired attacking formation. 'I effectively doubled the days available to me by getting Don to organise a defensive pattern and work with the back four and the goalkeeper on defence and defensive corners and free-kicks, while I worked with the front six on the new pyramid pattern and the attacking corners and free-kicks. Then we put the two halves together.'

Into the squad for the first time were left-back Graeme Le Saux, an admirer of Howe from his time at Chelsea, and Tottenham winger Darren Anderton. Southampton's Matthew Le Tissier, ignored by the previous England management, was the third uncapped player in a party of 18. Back in the fold after three years was 33-year-old Peter Beardsley. Venables had wasted little time in indicating that his team would be built around skilful players. Speaking of the need for 'imagination', he explained, 'We know that we have got to find quality.'

Anderton, whom Venables had signed for Spurs from Portsmouth in 1992, recalls, 'There was a lot of positivity around the set-up. The way the England team played under Graham Taylor wasn't great and there was a World Cup that summer that we weren't going to. It was a dreadful feeling. But people knew what Terry was about. He had managed at Barcelona and he knew football. People were excited to get the ball down on the deck and pass it again.

'I knew him at Spurs. He liked lots of shape, lots of tactical play and his knowledge of the game was second to none. I was seen as an exciting talent who was thrown in with some other new boys and there was a buzz about what could be. People forgot very quickly what had gone on before. There was a feelgood factor because Terry was in charge and had appointed people who were so well-respected.'

Tony Adams would write, 'I could not think of three better people to be in charge of the England team. It is crucial to have figures who are respected by international players. There you had a team manager, a coach and a players' player.' He recalled that Howe was 'just obsessed with the game', adding, 'He had studied the Dutch closely and analysed the Brazilians. In meetings Don would enthusiastically be getting carried away and saying how we should play like them.'

Given Venables's desire to execute a creative, fluent, modern type of football, Howe might have been seen by some as an odd fit for the new regime. His hat served to add to the old-fashioned image some maintained of him. 'Don was a contradiction in that sense,' says Le Saux. 'He was very old-school in some ways, but equally he was very modern and innovative. He was very interested in the international side of things and studied the game. For me, old-school is someone who just doesn't change their ways. He played a certain way with Wimbledon that would be considered an old-school physical style, but you are working to the identity of that team and the components of that team. At Chelsea, I didn't feel he was stuck in the past as a coach. It was the opposite with him. He made you think and he made you challenge and try to solve problems. And that is modern thinking.'

The players had no doubts about the wisdom of Howe's recruitment. 'Terry just knows what is needed at every level,' Anderton enthuses. 'Tactically, he loved his team to get on the ball and have more possession than the other team, which is more important in international football than anything because if you give it away you don't get it back for five minutes. At Tottenham, Terry worked on the defensive side as well as the attacking side, but it gave him free rein to work with the forward-thinking players knowing he could trust Don to work with the back four, or back five or six with midfield players sitting in front. That came down to trust, and Don had earned that through what he had achieved and what he had been part of. You could sense straight away the trust Terry had in him. Don Howe was just a legend, someone you looked up to and had so much respect for.'

Le Saux believes that the willingness of Venables to turn to a man who had already been part of two previous England regimes 'was one of his great strengths'. He explains, 'The most confident people are the ones who bring people in to challenge them. They know their own weaknesses and Terry was brilliant like that. He didn't have to pretend he was confident or put on a front; he was very much himself and Don would challenge him. And that was just the stuff we saw. I'm sure behind the scenes they had really good discussions about how they should play. They complemented each other and were both excellent coaches and tacticians. They had different perspectives, but once they made a decision they were very united and they had authority. I don't mean they were shouting and screaming, but they had that presence, that credibility with a squad that was full of characters.'

Manchester United right-back Gary Neville was another who observed the benefits of Venables's willingness to listen to other voices, never seeing his invitation to players to contribute to discussions as weakness or indecision. 'Don might come into the dressing room and contradict him,' he would recall. 'Don might win the argument. Maybe it showed Terry's self-confidence and experience that he was able to be talked round without it seeming as though he was being undermined.'

Anderton describes a typical England training session at that time. 'You would have your warm-up and then a bit of fun with the ball – piggy in the middle, that sort of thing. Then Terry always liked to do a bit of shape work, to reiterate what he wants, what he expects. It was a little repetitive, sometimes a little bit boring, but you know exactly what your job is when you go on the pitch. Terry would take the forwards and do a bit of shape that way and Don would take the back four – and maybe a Paul Ince or David Batty to sit in front – and would work it and work it. The defence had born leaders like Tony Adams and Stuart Pearce and Don had their respect as well. It was a really good fit. You would work in groups and then put it all together and work against others as a team. I had been brought up as a wide player and you know you track back to help the full-back; you try not to leave him one-on-one with a flying winger. So you would do a team shape. Very repetitive but something Terry always believed in.'

Faith in Howe's defence increased when England kept clean sheets in their first four games under Venables: 1-0 and 5-0 wins against Denmark and Greece and a goalless draw against Norway before the end of the season, and a 2-0 defeat of the United States to begin

1994/95. 'All I wanted for the first few games,' Venables would explain, 'was to enable them to feel good about themselves again … get a few results, don't give any goals away.' He could see 'their self-belief grow with every game'.

The Umbro Tournament staged in England in the early summer of 1995 saw Neville's arrival in international football. Explaining that he 'learnt so much from Don Howe', Neville's eyes were instantly opened by the way in which the different units of the team practised separately, as opposed to the small-sided games he was used to at United. 'Under Don it was much more about tactical shape and coordinating everyone's movement. As a defence we were drilled with military precision,' he wrote.

Neville's debut in a 2-1 win against Japan at a near-empty Wembley proved to him that 'Don had a strong voice'. Venables was in the process of praising his players for their performance when Howe interrupted. 'You may be happy, but I'm not,' he barked at his boss. 'We conceded a goal from a set piece and that's ridiculous. We worked on that in training.'

England needed a late Anderton equaliser to draw 3-3 with Sweden at Elland Road, before ending the tournament by losing 3-1 to Brazil back at Wembley. Anderton explains, 'Don always had words of wisdom that you took on board. He was very thoughtful, not a ranter and raver, a good communicator. I remember the day after we played Sweden he said, "You do these runs that not many do and I love that. A lot of wide players will just stay out wide, but I like that you want to come inside and get involved. But sometimes that can make the team very narrow. So when the ball goes to your full-back, make a run in to out, towards the wide man so the full-back can clip it over him. With your pace and energy you can get there." That was such a great thing to have in your arsenal. He was always very complimentary, but he would also say little things like that that put ideas in your head. It was a joy to work with him. When you had a little pat on the back from Don you felt great.'

While Venables wanted that kind of flexibility from his forwards – with split strikers, midfield diamonds and Christmas

Tree formations all being tried and tested – so Howe was charged with drilling different defensive systems. Venables craved fluidity at the back; the ability to adapt to opposition tactics without having to change personnel. As the friendlies continued and Euro 96 grew closer, Venables was being drawn increasingly to a back three – but not the three central defenders with full-backs pushing forward that Howe and Bobby Robson had used in the 1990 World Cup. Venables preferred full-backs playing in narrow positions either side of a centre-back, with attacking wide men having the task of coming back to cover the opposition full-backs when they ventured forward. 'You might say that's a lot of work, but the winger is not going to have to go any further than the full-back,' Venables reasoned. If, however, the opponents played with wingers, England would pull someone back from midfield to central defence, allowing the full-backs to go wider and form a traditional back four.

The key to that was finding someone equally at home in midfield or as a centre-back. And then Howe would spend time drilling that individual to angle his stance and force play into the middle of the field, keeping it in front of the back three rather than allowing the opposition to get round the back. That allowed Adams to step forward and attempt a tackle while the full-backs covered him.

Le Saux, who had settled into the role of left-back since his move to Blackburn, recalls, 'Don had to work with us as a back three sometimes, with me as a wing-back or in a defensive back five. Terry was an innovator and he and Don must have sat down with the tactics and gone, "What about this?" or "How will this work?"' Venables remembered his players expressing some nervousness at his defensive desires. 'They were a bit worried about having fewer men at the back,' he said. 'But I explained that the ball wouldn't get into our defensive third so often because we'd stop it in midfield.'

Venables was one of the first coaches in English football to make a habit of using a crane by the training pitch to capture elevated video footage of training sessions. 'Armed with those tapes, Don hammered us until we were as coordinated as synchronised swimmers,' said

Neville. 'They were brilliant sessions, as good as I've seen. I learnt how to anticipate angled passes behind me and to close down my winger.'

Neville recalled Howe encouraging him to become more attacking in his outlook and to deliver more crosses, yet it was the detail of his defensive coaching, including specific foot and head movements, that left its mark most profoundly. One of Howe's methods was to have staff members stationed on the opposite side of the field from where an attack was coming, holding up different coloured bibs. 'You could see the four defenders synchronizing their head movements,' Neville explained. 'We had to shout the colour of the bib. If you failed Don would yell, "You're ball watching."'

Regardless of defensive formation, Howe impressed upon his players the importance of hard work and executing the basics. 'You are just coming at it from a different angle,' Le Saux adds. 'If you play with the back three you are different, but the principles are the same. Once you are set as a defensive unit, you defend in the same way in that system. The intensity of the press is the same and one of Don's founding principles would be high energy, high pace for 90 minutes. He had it in his head that if you worked harder than the opposition and press them high and early you would win the game. Without any data, that is what he was obsessed by and why that AC Milan final was so important to him.[20] The point he made was that superstars work hard. "This is the best team in the world and they work harder than anyone else." I think he knew I was a worker and why he liked the Wimbledon guys like Dennis [Wise] who gave everything. He wanted to know that every player had that desire and that attitude. If you had that, you had a chance with him.'

Le Saux's opportunity to perform in front of a home crowd at the 1996 European Championship finals would be ended when he broke his

---

20 When Howe was asked to take a training session for the England women's team before a European qualifier against Portugal in February 1996, it was his favourite AC Milan tape he produced before taking the players to the field. 'I just wanted them to ask questions about what they were seeing,' he said. 'What shape was the defence? What was the midfield doing? I wanted them to see how a team like Milan presses, not as individuals but as a team, and to look at it as professionals.'

tibia, dislocated an ankle and ruptured a tendon in his right leg during Premier League champions Blackburn's game against Middlesbrough, leaving Stuart Pearce as the undisputed England left-back. 'Graeme would have been left-back, left-half or left-wing,' admitted Venables, who had already informed Pearce that he was no longer the first choice. Fierce competitor that he was, Pearce assured the manager he would work hard and be ready for any opportunity.

While Pearce had experienced the intensity of tournament football before, Howe had been making sure that England's younger players had a sense of the potentially life-changing event that lay in front of them. Anderton recalls, 'We were training about a year before Euro 96 and we came off the pitch up at The Belfry. We had just had three or four days of training. It was me and Steve McManaman and a couple of the young boys.' Howe, who had played in one World Cup finals, been a squad member at another, coached into the latter stages of three more and experienced the nation's excitement when England had last hosted a major competition 30 years earlier, began, 'Do you realise how big this is going to be and the opportunities you have here?' and shared his memories, observations and emotions of tournaments past. 'That was when it began to sink in,' says Anderton. 'As a 23-year-old, when you are playing for England and enjoying life and things are going well at your club, you don't even think about it.'

So profoundly did Howe's words hit their mark, Anderton promptly turned down a transfer to Manchester United. 'After Don said how huge it was about to be, that really preyed on my mind. I could have signed for United after that summer, but I had it in my mind that Euro 96 was going to be so big after he said that. I struggled after I first went to Spurs and I didn't want to go and struggle at United and end up out of the team and not be involved in the Euros. I kept thinking about Don's words.' In fact, they haunted him as he endured a season battling against a groin injury that reduced him to a handful of Premier League matches. 'That year was appalling for me, with all the frustration and the reality that I might not be part of everything.'

Venables had always said that his approach would be to watch as many club games as possible, but that he and his coaches would also base their judgements on what they saw in front of them in training and in an England shirt. 'Terry knows what I am all about,' Anderton told himself as he received extra treatment from England and former Spurs physiotherapist Dave Butler.

Not only did Venables lose Le Saux from his first-choice defence, but Liverpool's Mark Wright, restored to the team to play the lone centre-back role, was also ruled out after damaging knee ligaments in the friendly against Hungary a month before the tournament. Adams would replace Wright in the line-up, while the man earmarked to play as midfielder or defender as the situation dictated was Aston Villa's Gareth Southgate, even though he was winning only his third cap when he came on as substitute for Wright against Hungary at Wembley. Further forward, the toughest decision Venables faced was telling Beardsley that he was not needed in the 22-man squad because Teddy Sheringham would be the second striker, with Middlesbrough's Nick Barmby the natural understudy to the Tottenham man.

England's first competitive match in almost three years arrived in the wake of tabloid tales of players' wild and raucous antics in a nightclub during their pre-tournament Far East tour, followed by several thousand pounds' worth of damage caused on the flight home. The kick-off to the event brought the focus back to football, even if it was a disappointing 1-1 draw against Switzerland, with Alan Shearer's goal cancelled out by a penalty converted by Kubilay Turkyilmaz. 'We should have scrambled through 1-0,' Venables noted. Anderton, who with McManaman filled the wide positions, admits, 'We were dreadful in the first game. Terry could quite easily have changed five, six, seven or eight of us, but he didn't. He kept the same team and that is what Terry is all about. He trusts himself and he trusts his players.'

Instead, Venables described articles calling for the heads of various players as 'vicious, vindictive and personal' and got on with preparing for the next match, against Scotland. 'That week gave us the time we needed to iron everything out,' said Venables. 'Everything we wanted to cover, we covered. I would have liked to do some other things that were perhaps more entertaining, but Don Howe and Bryan Robson did the ball work with them and I used my time with the tactical side of it.'

After a goalless first half against the auld enemy, Southgate moved to the left of the defence and Pearce was replaced by Jamie Redknapp. The new-look midfield took only seven minutes to help Neville set up another Shearer goal. Again, the opposition had the chance to equalise from the penalty spot, but this time David Seaman turned away Gary McAllister's spot kick. Within two minutes, Anderton had played the ball to Paul Gascoigne, who flicked it over Colin Hendry with his left foot and volleyed a memorable goal with his right. When ITV interviewed Venables for a documentary about the tournament more than two decades later, he couldn't help but leap from his seat as he described the goal in tones that still betrayed disbelief.

Venables now plotted to beat the international team he most admired, Holland, even though a point would have been enough to secure a place in the quarter-finals. 'We end up playing a flat back four against Holland, instead of a back three,' Pearce reminded that same documentary crew. 'You've had success with a back three and then he changes it for one game. That is what good managers do and get results with it.'

This particular result was emphatic, the performance breathtaking. 'We just played Holland off the park,' was Venables's simple summary of a perfectly executed game-plan. With the England players interchanging positions in a manner that the Dutch themselves would have been proud of, they stormed to a 4-1 victory, with Shearer and Sheringham scoring two goals each. Howe would have enjoyed the victory even more had Patrick Kluivert not scored a late consolation for Holland. 'You could win a game 4-1, but if the goal conceded was a bad one he'd be livid,' Neville noted.

It had been one of Wembley Stadium's most uplifting occasions. 'The volume of support we received was quite extraordinary,' according to Venables, who was taking great pride in 'knowing we had captured the imagination of the nation'. Meanwhile, the tournament had found a soundtrack in 'Three Lions', the single comedians David Baddiel and Frank Skinner had released with The Lightning Seeds, and its anthemic chant, 'Football's coming home', which reverberated from the Wembley stands to pubs, clubs and living rooms around the country.

It all added up to a level of hype that Neville admitted kept him awake at night. But Anderton recalls that England were fortunate to have the steady hand of Howe to guide them through the mounting excitement. 'He was such a calming influence,' Anderton says. 'There was a lot of euphoria, but Don had seen it and done it and was so calm. Throughout the tournament he would just come and talk to you and he had a nice mellow way about him. He was just the ultimate professional in everything he did.'

England's reward for winning their group was remaining at Wembley for the rest of the tournament, although the quarter-final against Spain ended goalless after extra-time. The introduction by UEFA of a 'golden goal' rule was supposed to reduce the amount of games that made it all the way through the additional half-hour to penalties, but Venables pointed out that 'the new system had an inhibiting effect and made both of us more cagey'. It was England who triumphed in the shoot-out, with Pearce's scream of redemption when he scored his penalty – six years on from Turin – and Seaman's final save providing the enduring images.

Four days later, Howe and England found Germany once more barring their path to a major final. The frustrations of failing to score against Spain quickly disappeared as Shearer headed them into the lead in the third minute, his fifth goal making him the tournament's leading scorer. For Venables, the success of Shearer had been further vindication of his policy of sticking with those he trusted after the player went into Euro 96 without having scored an international goal for 21 months. The manager had even assured him several weeks in advance that he would be England's spearhead in the competition. The hosts' lead lasted only until Stefan Kuntz's equaliser after 15 minutes, but it was they who continued to look more likely to score again as another match headed into extra time.

Encouraged by Venables to forget the golden-goal stalemate against Spain and go all out for the win, England came close to achieving victory in only the third minute when McManaman crossed from the right and a tumbling Anderton saw his shot hit the post. Then the Germans thought they had won, only for the referee to blow for a foul as Kuntz headed in from a corner. Ten minutes into extra time came the agonising moment when Shearer fired across the box and the grey-kitted, blond-haired figure of a sliding Gascoigne failed by a fraction to make match-winning contact.

Penalties again, and this time each team's first five takers found the net. Southgate stepped forward to take England's sixth and put it too close to Andreas Köpke, who turned away the shot with his right arm. Andreas Möller fired high into the net and Germany had ended England's dream once more. Venables and Howe went to console Southgate, who appeared unable to lift his head to meet their gaze after failing with the penalty he had bravely volunteered to take. Howe encouraged Southgate to puff up his chest, to be proud. Grabbing him by the arm and shaking him, you almost expected him to slap Southgate on the face and tell him to snap out of it.

'The feeling and memories of that tournament are just incredible,' Anderton concludes. 'We all talk about it with massive smiles on our faces. What it could have been if we had won it. We were the best team and should have won it.'

So Venables's last act in charge of England was to stand in the middle of the Wembley dressing room telling his players how proud he was of all they had achieved. Aware that many within the FA hierarchy did not want him to continue to the 1998 World Cup and unwilling to fight that particular war alongside continued legal battles, he had made clear his intention to stand down. Even the euphoria and intensity of some incredible Wembley occasions could not force a change of heart.

In his final assessment of his time as England manager, Venables concluded, 'As for the technical and medical staff I think their contributions vindicated my efforts to recruit the best people I could for every job. My two principle coaches, Don Howe and Bryan Robson, were a good partnership and great allies. Don's massive experience and steadiness were supplemented by Bryan's ability to get close to the players.'

With the departure of Venables and the appointment of Glenn Hoddle to replace him, Don Howe's four decades with England, as a player and a coach, were finally over. According to Rob Howe, Hoddle had told his father, 'Don, I'm not sure whether I need you or not.'

'Glenn, that is absolutely fine,' was the reply. 'If you wanted me, I would work for you but you are not sure and I don't want you fitting me in.'

But there was another important figure in Howe's career who most definitely did want him, and one more return journey to make before his time with football was done.

16

DON'T LOOK BACK IN ANGER

Football has been my life and I still have the same feeling I had when I was a youngster.

Don Howe, speaking in 1997

'THE ARSENAL' had never left Don Howe's blood. With his England career in the past and his thirst for management quenched by the gulps and spillages of the previous quarter century, it was natural that Highbury should be the place for him to complete his football life. 'There was something about Arsenal,' says son Rob. 'He just thought they were so much more special than other clubs; they did things better. The way the club was run and the approach to everything was top drawer. He saw it as the way things should be.'

Howe had already made a quiet contribution to Arsenal's success under George Graham, thanks to a new television role he had begun during the 1993/94 season. Channel 4, inspired by the romance of Italia 90 and Paul Gascoigne's subsequent transfer to Lazio in Serie A, had begun airing *Football Italia* in 1992, featuring a live match every Sunday afternoon, along with a popular magazine show, *Gazetta Football Italia*, on Saturdays.

Howe's involvement resulted from a chance meeting with the production team. 'He was waxing lyrical about Serie A,' recalls executive producer Neil Duncanson. 'We knew very quickly that he knew his stuff.' Howe was asked to join the team in support of the lead commentary duo of Peter Brackley and Ray Wilkins. Duncanson continues, 'I remember some dinners with him and he was so passionate, evangelical almost, about football and about Italian football, which in those days was the world's premier league.

'He used to get involved in these labyrinthine conversations with one of our producers, Ray Della Pietra, about the Italian game. They would have these incredibly forensic conversations about tactics and statistics of different teams. You would sit and listen to them for five minutes and then you would go away to do something and come back an hour later and they were still going.'

It was those exchanges with Della Pietra, who was responsible for briefing the commentators on team tactics, that ended up providing Howe with a way to assist Arsenal manager George Graham after his team were drawn against Coppa Italia holders Torino in the European Cup Winners' Cup quarter-finals. 'Don phoned me, asking me to prepare a dossier on Emiliano Mondonico's side,' Della Pietra recalls. 'As well as producing the usual statistical analysis, facts and figures, I added other bits and pieces which made the document a cross between commentary notes and a scouting report. I included stuff like warning the Arsenal players they should be careful not to get too tight to Bennie Carbone in the box, so to avoid running a huge risk of conceding a penalty.'

And after Arsenal beat Torino and Paris St Germain, Howe was back on the phone ahead of the final against another Italian side, holders Parma, in Copenhagen. 'We discussed tactics at length and team selection,' Della Pietra continues. 'It still amazes me that a footballing man of his calibre, stature and experience should want my input and to pick my brain.' Armed with the information Howe had acquired, Arsenal won 1-0, creating a crisis of conscience for Della Pietra. 'I was disloyal to *Calcio*. How could I go behind the back of my one true love? I remember describing Parma's defeat as a dagger in my heart.'

Howe continued his involvement with *Football Italia* for the remainder of the 1990s, always impressing with his detailed preparation and determination to see it as a learning experience. 'If he heard something that he didn't know about he wanted to know every detail,' says Duncanson. 'And I don't think I ever heard him refer backwards to anything – even though he probably had more to reflect on in his career than most. He always looked forward, looking for the new shiny thing they were doing that he'd not seen before.

'On air, he had his own style and no one was going to be copying him. He is the only man I know who could introduce even more vowels to the Italian language than it had already. He would add vowels to teams and make it "Samp-a-doria". But it endeared him to people. You would think some would get pissed off, but everything he said was interesting, thoughtful and original. He gave every match another layer of interest. And he was a lovely guy alongside it.'

* * *

While football had been coming home in the summer of 1996, so Liam Brady had returned to Highbury, the place where it had all begun for him as a 13-year-old. Having ended his playing career in 1990, he'd had spells as manager of Celtic and Brighton and Hove Albion and had even been mentioned as a possible successor to Bruce Rioch as Arsenal manager before accepting the role of head of the Arsenal Academy, overseeing youth development.

Brady had never forgotten the impact Howe made on him as a teenager. 'Don always had a great interest in the young players,' he explains. 'He would attend the trials for the young players and would have a say in who was picked and who wasn't. And I remember a couple of coaching sessions with the young trialists, the players earmarked to join the club. I remember him being challenging. He would get you to try things that he thought you needed in your make-up.' It was that kind of expertise and empathy that Brady desired from the coach of the youth team. 'I wanted to bring Don back but he wasn't too sure he wanted to go back and work with younger players.'

Instead, Howe threw himself into various roles, participating in coaching courses and seminars and acting as technical coordinator for the Football Association. 'It's a terrific job and I enjoy it,' he said. 'It takes me all over the world. I get to work at all levels of youth football – under 16s, 17s and 18s. It's smashing to be able to pass on my experience in such a nice way.'

But it also made him realise what he was missing. 'I don't do as much coaching as I used to,' he said. 'I wish I did. I would like to end my working life doing practical things. Theory is important but I like to test myself and my knowledge by trying to get the best out of players and beat other coaches. I do miss the experience of being in charge of a team because that's the only way to test your ideas out.'

A year after their initial conversation, Brady took a call from Howe. 'He said, "Is that job still available?" – and he came back and worked with me. I had no hesitation.'

Asked if his father would have taken a similar role at any other club, Rob Howe suggests, 'I think he would, but it would have been dependent on who was asking. If it was someone he knew and respected or had worked with previously and the set-up was right. What he was going to do had to be worthwhile doing and obviously at Arsenal it was, with the training facilities and the fact it was Liam Brady.'

The appointment was eye-catching in the context of the role he was to play, but according to former Arsenal physiotherapist Fred Street, who had remained close to both Howe and Brady, it made perfect sense. 'The best coaches for youth teams are people like Don, who have done it all, have a lot of experience and are not after the big job at the club,' he argues. 'Yet usually the youth-team coach is a young man, maybe in his first job, and all he is interested in is being able to put a trophy on his CV so he is better positioned to get a more senior job. Youth team football should not be about winning pots, it should be about bringing kids through the system. Bobby Robson used to say that the highest-paid person on your coaching staff should be the youth-team coach.'

Rob Howe continues, 'The competitive thing is always there and obviously he wanted to win, but I think my dad had a big thing about making people better. That is what he really enjoyed. He said he loved working with the kids at Arsenal because they wanted to learn. If people want to learn and are prepared to listen, he used to love that.'

Brady has no hesitation in highlighting the contribution Howe made over what ended up as a six-year appointment. 'Anyone who had any sort of ambition to become a footballer or the intelligence to work it out realised that Don was a special coach and we were all very lucky to have him around. He would have one-on-one meetings with players and point out to them where they were going wrong and what they were doing right. He just had this respect for people and he never had any favourites. He was never thinking about himself; he was not selfish. It was always about the players and the team and he made players respect what they had to do to be an important member of the team, their duties to the team.'

Rohan Ricketts was one such player who absorbed that message. '[Don] helped mould me into a professional football player,' he said. 'There's so many of us that was touched by this guy.' Among Howe's students were Ashley Cole, destined to become one of England's most celebrated and decorated left-backs; future England forward David Bentley; winger Jermaine Pennant, whose international future appeared destined to advance beyond the multiple games he played for the England Under-21s; and midfielder Steve Sidwell, whose long playing career included spells at Reading, Chelsea and Aston Villa. There was also striker Jay Bothroyd, sold to Coventry City after making the mistake of throwing his shirt at Howe after being substituted, an incident recalled easily by Sidwell. 'Don picked up the shirt and folded it so precisely and neatly,' he explains. 'Like an army colonel preparing his attire. Then he placed it on his seat. You knew Jay was never going to play for Arsenal again.'

That was because Howe placed so much emphasis on ensuring that his players deported themselves in a manner befitting their club. 'He was always telling us to be calm,' Sidwell continues, 'to remember that we represented the Arsenal. When we travelled we had to show impeccable manners at hotels. But he also had a lot of empathy and you would feel comfortable knocking on his door for a chat.'

Sidwell, who had been connected with Arsenal since the age of nine, recalls Howe's arrival. 'Everyone knew about Don. We knew what he was and what he brought to the table, but when he finally put his boots on for training it was an unbelievable, amazing experience. Even talking to him while you were walking to the pitch at the training ground you were learning. It could be small talk about Serie A games he commentated on or talking about Italia 90, but it made you realise how much of a legend he really was. You knew how brilliant this was. He was in his mid-60s but was training us with such enthusiasm.'

Even Bothroyd, when capped by England while playing for Cardiff City ten years after leaving Arsenal, said, 'Don Howe is one of the reasons why I play the way I do today. He schooled me and showed me that even though I am tall, I could be technical as well.'

Ricketts, who was unable to break into Arsenal's first team and included a spell at Tottenham Hotspur in a much-travelled playing career before his own move into coaching, posted an emotional tribute on YouTube after Howe's death, making clear the great affection he retained for a man who had been a stern tutor. Recalling an occasion when he arrived late before a game against Norwich City, Ricketts said, 'The guy strung me up. He said, "You're with the fairies, son. Who do you think you are? You have got to get focused." He started me in the game and walked in at half-time and said, "You. Off." I wasn't doing the business as far as he was concerned.'

Howe's demands on his players were illustrated by his reaction to a surprise defeat. Sidwell explains, 'Don demanded standards. We lost one game in two years and that was at Bristol City, where we lost 5-0. He gave us the biggest bollocking we had ever heard. "You have embarrassed yourselves. You swanned off the coach thinking you can just come in here and beat them, but look how hard they have worked, they really brought you down a peg or two."' Ricketts recalled, 'The next day he had a group of us doing half-laps at Highbury and the other group were running the steps. I was hiding in the stadium at one point because I was vomiting.'

There were light moments too, like the time Howe, in baseball cap, glasses and with a whistle round his neck, demonstrated to a forward how to curve a run. Sidwell remembers, 'Don got the full-back to play the ball and he made this big arching, exaggerated run. As he was getting close to the ball he tripped over and started going down in instalments. We were laughing our heads off. He got up and his cap was facing sideways, his glasses were wonky, and his whistle was the wrong way round his neck. It was like he'd been hit by a monsoon. But he had such a connection with the young players, even though he was old-school.'

Alongside the discipline was a desire to give his players the tools to fulfil their potential. 'The man believed in me,' according to Ricketts, illustrating his point with the memory of the aftermath of a first-team friendly in which he had played for 45 minutes. 'Rohan, how good do you want to be?' Howe challenged. 'You could be really great. You could be like these guys.' Howe pulled out videos of Manchester United trio Paul Scholes, Roy Keane and Nicky Butt. 'He took me in the office to show me the things that they did that were important,' Ricketts continued. 'The nitty-gritty, off-the-ball stuff. He said, "Technically you have got it all." I will never forget that. He really believed in me and he put a lot of responsibility on my shoulders.'

Sidwell adds, 'He had a head start because we were all very talented; a high-calibre of players. But he made sure that the best people brought the others along.'

The result was that Brady and Howe achieved the balance of winning trophies and teaching the game. And there was no greater indication of the first element than success in the FA Youth Cup. In 2000, Arsenal overcame Coventry City 3-1 away and 2-0 at home to win the trophy. A year later, they did it again, a 5-0 home win against Blackburn Rovers cushioning them against a 3-1 defeat in the second leg. 'He kept our feet on the floor,' says Sidwell. 'He knew we were talented and he told us to express ourselves, but under no circumstance let the other team outwork or outrun us. You could see on his face how much it meant to him winning those FA Youth Cups. He had won so much in his career, but that accolade I imagine was still high on his list. They still say at Arsenal that it was the best youth team they ever had, and it was a sign of our amazing respect for Don that all of us lads showed up at his funeral and stood together.'

If Howe felt any disappointment about his achievements in his third spell at Arsenal it might have been that not enough of his youngsters – drawn from Europe, Africa and South America, as well as around Britain – were given an extended opportunity in the first team. When pushed to predict their potential trajectory into senior football, he replied, 'I don't know. I've got no idea. Ask Arsène Wenger.'

Whatever course their careers took, the players had no doubts that Howe had set them on the right path. Sidwell, embarking on his own coaching career by taking charge of young players at Reading, says, 'Don was from the school of hard knocks, but he had empathy as well. He would say that "this is the direction we are going in and I am going to be with you all the way".'

According to Brady, 'Winning the Youth Cup two years on the trot was the benchmark of you as a team. I can remember Don helping all sorts of players, from the likes of Steve Sidwell to someone like Jermaine Pennant, who had great individual skill. Don had him working for the team and he was bought into it. Don had a great influence on Ashley Cole as well.'

Brady's admiration for a man who had been so important in his own playing career only grew as he witnessed the way he threw himself into a role that, to some, might have seemed low-key for a man accustomed to the latter stages of major international tournaments. 'He was out there in all sorts of weather,' he says. 'He was just an enthusiastic man who loved coaching. I think he thrived on it. It kept him young and it was a good move for him. We kept him going until he was almost into his 70s.'

By the summer of 2003, Howe had spent half a century working in professional football. Finally, he decided that it was enough. Son Rob suggests, 'He was starting to get fed up because the kids were on big money at Arsenal and in the end some of them thought they were the bee's knees. He had just started to see a little bit of arrogance that he didn't like. He thought, "I don't need this anymore." He knew the time had come.'

It was time to spend more time with family, including his grandchildren. 'I think the grandchildren were one of the things that he'd enjoyed most about the Arsenal job because he would train the kids in the morning and had some free time after that,' Rob continues. 'My dad was a big kid and he used to play with them for hours, silly games like *Mousie, Mousie* or them pretending to be dogs and him feeding them with grapes. He had the patience to do it for hours and used to love it.'

Yet still Howe's knowledge was called upon, including sessions at coaching courses run by the English, Welsh and Irish Football Associations. Rob recalls, 'Dad used to make videos. He had Betamax and VHS video recorders and I gave him a laptop. He used to record every game and make these little clips – things like working as a back four, or wing play, centre-forward play – and would use them at the FA or with the kids. I used to have to help him with the technical stuff. He would sit there saying which bits he wanted. He made one to show why Manchester United were so successful and scored so many goals. He said it was because they always got four men into the box; two forwards, the opposite side winger and a midfielder arriving.'

Howe was also in demand for the kind of newspaper and magazine columns where tactical insight rather than outspoken opinion was the requirement. And, in ghostwriting his column for the *Arsenal* magazine for two years, Jem Maidment discovered that he was far less interested in reminiscence than highlighting the exciting things he saw in the modern game.

'We would schedule an hour for our call,' Maidment recalls, 'and three hours later we were still going. It was always about the present or the future. He wasn't always going back and saying Pelé was this or that – you had to coax that out of him and prompt him to talk about the past. When he did talk about it he was very animated, but it was clear that he was always more excited about the next big players or the

Arsenal team. I remember him coming alive when he was talking about Cesc Fàbregas. His passion was extraordinary.'

Late in 2007, Howe was asked by the Football Association of Ireland to become part of a headhunting panel for the Republic's new manager in succession to Steve Staunton. Along with former Ireland striker Don Givens and midfielder Ray Houghton, he was responsible for recommending the former Italy manager Giovanni Trapattoni, who held the position for more than five years.

And it was Howe who was still used most frequently as the benchmark for good defence. In 2009, Patrick Barclay wrote in *The Times* about the expertise that he had brought to his sport and which appeared to have gone missing. Recalling the way England's Euro 96 squad acknowledged Howe's contribution, he added, 'He was an extremely influential coach and is now conspicuous by his absence from a game that, for all the beautiful goals, cries out for defensive organisation.'

He might no longer have been working in the sport, but Howe never stopped seeing football through the eyes of a coach. 'If we were watching a game of football,' says Rob, 'the first thing my dad did was pick up any bit of paper and a pencil and write down the formations the teams were using. I might be saying that it is a crap game because there are no goals, but he wouldn't say anything, he would just be making notes.'

It was a trait that endured even after he had begun to show the signs of the illness that would end his life. 'When he had dementia he would still do that,' Rob continues. 'We had to go round and make sure that Sky was on if there was a game on. Generally, we used to make sure he had notepads around him, but if not he would just look for anything and would work out the tactics. He would ask you what the formation was and then correct you and say, "No, they're not playing in that shape." And he would watch every game. It didn't matter what level. He used to take the dog to the park and he would stop and watch the kids playing or the Sunday morning football.'

It was as Howe approached his mid-70s that his family first noticed behavioural patterns that would lead to a diagnosis of dementia. 'There were some strange things,' Rob explains. 'Things were becoming a concern to him, like money. He was comfortably off and had a really good pension but he kept saying that he had no money. It was one of the signs. Eventually it got to the stage where my mum was having to do everything and he started thinking he needed to go back home to the Midlands. He had to go into care at that point.'

Two days before Christmas 2015, it was announced that Howe had died at the age of 80, his condition having become so advanced that he was no longer eating. Tributes from the football community were heartfelt and extensive.

'It was a privilege to have known and been trained by him,' said Gary Lineker, describing him as 'a great coach and lovely man'. Calling him 'the best coach I ever worked with', Malcolm Macdonald added, 'You will hear that over and over again.' He was not wrong. 'Don Howe was my greatest ever coach,' added Bryan Robson. 'He taught me everything I know.' Former Arsenal and England defender Martin Keown said, 'You couldn't ask for a better coach. He made us feel special,' while Vinnie Jones chipped in with, 'We absolutely adored Don Howe.' And so on.

The video eulogy by former Arsenal youth-teamer Ricketts described Howe as 'a father figure', and signed off with, 'I am very grateful for all the lessons you taught me and all the knowledge you gave me. Thanks very much and I love you, Don Howe.'

'Everyone was brilliant,' says son Rob. 'Arsenal and West Brom were great in sorting everything out. Arsenal took over and said they would speak to all the clubs that Dad was at and handled the organisation of the funeral.' The ceremony was held on 15 January 2016 at Bentley Crematorium in Brentwood, Essex. 'It was overwhelming,' Rob continues. 'We went to a crematorium that could only hold a certain number, but so many people wanted to come they were standing outside. Top footballers, coaches and managers were standing outside because they all wanted to come. That was wonderful.'

It was an appropriate tribute to a man who lived for football but remained unimpressed by its trappings, uninterested in its war stories.

'We used to try to have conversations with him after big tournaments,' says Rob. 'He might say, "Yes, we were unlucky," but he never used to criticise any decisions that were made and it was literally a case of, "I am back home and it's all over and you saw what happened." He never used to talk about it.'

A less modest man – someone more concerned about ramming his résumé down people's throats than getting on with the next job – might have found himself more appreciated by a broader section of the football public. It seemed ironic during England's progress to the final of the delayed Euro 2020 tournament that there were times when Gareth Southgate was criticised for returning to 'the dark days of Don Howe' when he picked a more defensive-looking formation; yet the same social media voices were urging the national team to rekindle the spirit of 1990 and 1996. Apparently they had forgotten, or were too young to know, that Howe had been the coach then, too.

Howe, of course, would have let it wash over him; more excited by the flexibility of the manager's tactics than agitated by any lack of recognition for his part in the past achievements being celebrated with each step England took towards their first final since 1966. 'He was so modest,' says Alan Hudson. 'He didn't need a pat on the back; he didn't need anyone to praise him. He was all about getting the job done. Being at his funeral was very touching. I was there with Bryan Robson and he couldn't speak highly enough of Don. When you have players like that talking about him, then you know what a great man he was. He was one of the great people and it's an absolute pleasure to talk about him.'

Son Rob concludes, 'Dad was never in football for the fame or fortune or the praise. He was in it for the football, and testament to that is that he would go to work with Newbury Town or Barnet or the kids at Arsenal. He wasn't a football snob. He would do anything as long as it was football.'

It was an outlook that made him a hero to so many at so many teams. An attitude that led Bobby Robson to say unashamedly, 'I've loved the fella. And I mean loved him.' Even the shadows in which Don Howe lived for so much of his career could not hide that football loved him too.

ACKNOWLEDGEMENTS

IT HAS been no surprise how many people have told me, in the course of researching this book, what a lovely man Don Howe was; how the stern image that came from the training ground and dugout – much like the one of the cover of this book – concealed a fun-loving man who was quick to deliver and laugh at a daft joke and had time for anyone who fancied a natter about football. I was fortunate to interview him for several of my previous books and was grateful for the time and thoughtfulness he put into those conversations; never a hint of trying to wrap things up and getting on with something else.

I am also grateful for the opportunity to have spoken to many people about his life and times while writing this and other books. They include: Viv Anderson, Darren Anderton, Simon Barker, Simon Bassey, Liam Brady, Steve Burtenshaw, David Court, Ray Della Pietra, Neil Duncanson, Terry Gibson, Bobby Gould, Clive Goodyear, George Graham, Martin Hicks, Colin Hill, Glenn Hoddle, Roy Hodgson, Alan Hudson, Chris Hudson, David Jenkins, Stan Jones, Eddie Kelly, Graeme Le Saux, Malcolm Macdonald, Jem Maidment, Joe Mayo, Frank McLintock, Bob McNab, Gordon Nisbet, John Radford, Stewart Robson, Don Rogers, Jon Sammels, Peter Simpson, Peter Storey, Fred Street, Ian Ure, Roy Wegerle, Alan Whittle, John Wile, Graham Williams, Bob Wilson, Tony Woodcock and the late Ronnie Clayton, Tommy Docherty, Dave Sexton, Alan Skirton and George Wright.

Inevitably, there have been those who have politely declined invitations to be interviewed. Every biographer knows that feeling of frustration, but for the most part there has been no hint that anyone has anything less than utmost respect for Don Howe as a coach and affection for him as a man.

Don's sons, Steven, Richard, Robert and David, have supported this project from the outset and, in particular, I am grateful for Rob's time and insight.

As always, others have been of great assistance without being mentioned in the narrative. Apologies to those I may have omitted from this list: Fiona Armstrong Hall, Gavin Blackwell, Darren Fletcher, Will Gavin, Ron Grant, Stuart Mawhinney, Keegan Pierce, Joanne Pierce, Rob Pritchard, Geoff Snape, Andy Walker, Arlo White, David Woolford and The Gabbie Cabbie. Special thanks to Dave Bowler for sharing so much material and information relating to Don Howe's time at West Bromwich Albion.

The good people at Pitch Publishing – notably Paul Camillin, Jane Camillin and Duncan Olner – have been as supportive as ever. Richard Whitehead has provided his usual receptive ear, sound advice and exemplary editing skills, while my agent, David Luxton, continues to offer wise counsel and guidance.

My family are the ones whose indulgence allows me to keep working on projects such as this. Love and thanks, therefore, to daughters Amy, Sarah, Laura and Karis, grandsons Jacob and Oscar, granddaughter Heidi – the latest addition to this growing list – and, most importantly, wife Sara. I know how easily I get lost in research and writing and she knows it better than anyone. It's a sign of her incredible patience and support how rarely she reminds me.

BIBLIOGRAPHY

Adams, Tony, with Ian Ridley, *Addicted* (CollinsWillow, 1998)

Anderson, Viv, *First Among Unequals: The Autobiography* (Fullback Media, 2010)

Armfield, Jimmy, *The Autobiography: Right Back to the Beginning* (Headline, 2004)

Barnes, John, *The Autobiography* (Headline, 1999)

Bassett, Dave and Wally Downes, *The Crazy Gang: The True Inside Story of Football's Greatest Miracle* (Bantam Books, 2016)

Bowler, Dave, *Three Lions on The Shirt: Playing for England* (Orion, 1999)

Brady, Liam, *So Far So Good: A Decade in Football* (Stanley Paul, 1980)

Brooking, Trevor, *My Life in Football* (Simon & Schuster, 2014)

Butcher, Terry, *My Autobiography* (Highdown, 2005)

Charlton, Bobby, *1966: My World Cup Story* (Yellow Jersey Press, 2016)

Coppell, Steve, *Touch and Go* (Willow Books, 1985)

Fenwick, Terry, with Brian Woolnough, *Earning My Spurs* (Mainstream Publishing, 1989)

Finney, Tom, *My Autobiography* (Headline, 2003)

Giller, Norman, *Billy Wright: A Hero for All Seasons* (Robson Books, 2002)

Glanville, Brian, *The Story of the World Cup* (Faber and Faber, multiple editions)

Goldblatt, David, *The Ball is Round: A Global History of Football* (Viking Press, 2006)

Gould, Bobby and David Instone, *24 Carat Gould* (Thomas Publications, 2010)

Greenwood, Ron, *Yours Sincerely* (HarperCollins, 1984)

Harris, Bob, *Bobby Robson: The Ultimate Patriot* (de Coubertin Books, 2020)

Harris, Harry, *Italia 90 Revisited: The Players' Stories* (Empire Sports Publications, 2020)

Hayter, Reg (editor), *The Arsenal Football Book* (Stanley Paul, 1969)

Herbert, Ian, *Quiet Genius: Bob Paisley, British Football's Greatest Manager* (Bloomsbury, 2017)

Hoddle, Glenn, *Spurred to Success* (Macdonald Queen Anne Press, 1987)

Howe, Don and Brian Scovell, *The Handbook of Soccer* (Pelham Books, 1988)

Hunter, Norman, *Biting Talk: My Autobiography* (Hodder & Stoughton, 2003)

Jones, Vinnie, *It's Been Emotional* (Simon & Schuster, 2013)

Keegan, Kevin, *My Autobiography* (Little, Brown, 1997)

Le Saux, Graeme, *Left Field: A Footballer Apart* (HarperSport, 2010)

Macdonald, Malcolm, with Colin Malam, *Super Mac My Autobiography* (Highdown, 2003)

Malam, Colin, *Gary Lineker: Strikingly Different* (Stanley Paul, 1993)

McLintock, Frank, *True Grit* (Headline, 2005)

McOwan, Gavin, *The Essential History of West Bromwich Albion* (Headline, 2002)

Morse, Graham, *Sir Walter Winterbottom: The Father of Modern English Football* (John Blake, 2013)

Neill, Terry, *Revelations of a Football Manager* (Sidgwick and Jackson, 1985)

Neville, Gary, *Red: My Autobiography* (Bantam Press, 2011)

Pearce, Stuart, *Psycho: The Autobiography* (Headline, 2000)

Reid, Peter, *Cheer Up Peter Reid: My Autobiography* (Trinity Mirror Sport Media, 2017)

Robson, Bobby, with Bob Harris, *Against The Odds: An Autobiography* (Cornerstone, 1990)

Robson, Bobby, *Time on the Grass: An Autobiography* (Arthur Baker, 1982)

Robson, Bobby, *World Cup Diary 1982-86: So Near and Yet So Far* (HarperCollins, 1986)

Robson, Bryan, *Robbo: My Autobiography* (Hodder & Stoughton, 2012)

Sansom, Kenny, *To Cap It All* (John Blake, 2008)

Saunders, Donald, *World Cup 1962* (William Heinemann, 1962)

Seaman, David, *Safe Hands: My Autobiography* (Orion, 2000)

Shilton, Peter, *The Autobiography* (Orion Books, 2004)

Spurling, Jon, *All Guns Blazing: Arsenal in the 1980s* (Aureus Publishing, 2001)

Tossell, David, *Alan Ball: The Man in White Boots* (Hodder & Stoughton, 2017)

Tossell, David, *All Crazee Now: English Football and Footballers in the 1970s* (Pitch Publishing, 2020)

Tossell, David, *Bertie Mee: Arsenal's Officer and Gentleman* (Mainstream, 2005)

Tossell, David, *Big Mal: The High Life and Troubled Times of Malcolm Allison* (Mainstream, 2008)

Tossell, David, *Seventy-One Guns: The Year of the First Arsenal Double* (Mainstream, 2002)

Venables, Terry, *The Best Game in the World* (Arrow Books, 1997)

Venables, Terry, *Venables' England: The Making of the Team* (Boxtree, 1996)

Venables, Terry and Neil Hanson, *Venables: The Autobiography* (Michael Joseph, 1994)

Wilson, Bob, *My Autobiography: Behind the Network* (Hodder & Stoughton, 2003)

Wilson, Jonathan, *The Anatomy of England: A History in Ten Matches* (Orion, 2010)

Wise, Dennis, *The Autobiography* (Boxtree, 1999)

Winter, Henry, *Fifty Years of Hurt: The Story of England Football and Why We Never Stop Believing* (Bantam Press, 2016)

Woodcock, Tony, with Peter Ball, *Inside Soccer* (Queen Anne Press, 1985)

INDEX

INDEX

Also available at all good book stores

9781801501286

9781785314902

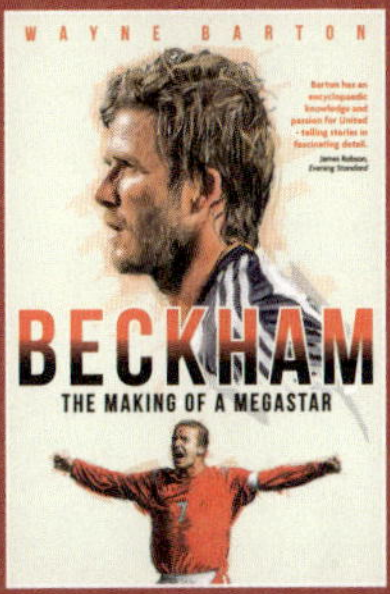

9781785316760

9781785314995

9781801500098

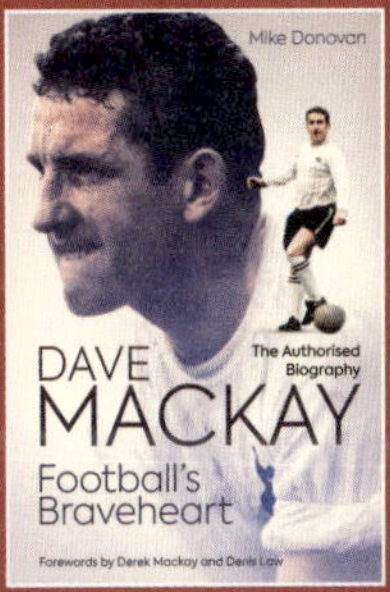

9781785317910

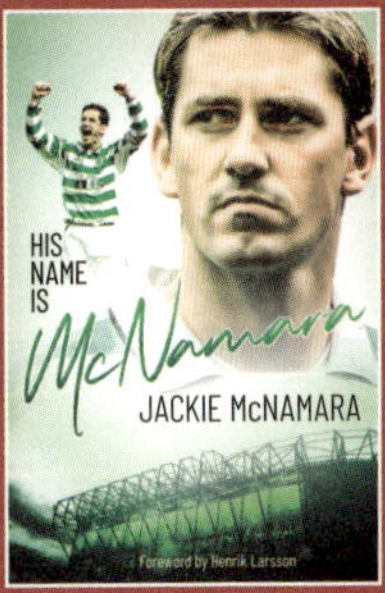

9781785318580

9781785314407

9781785315510

FAIR PLAY